Israel
AN ILLUSTRATED HISTORY

Israel

An Illustrated History

Daniel J. Schroeter

Oxford University Press

New York • Oxford

For Myriam, Sophia, and Naomi

Oxford University Press

Oxford New York
Athens Auckland Bangkok Bogotá Buenos Aires
Calcutta Cape Town Chennai Dar es Salaam Delhi
Florence Hong Kong Istanbul Karachi Kuala Lumpur
Madrid Melbourne Mexico City Mumbai Nairobi Paris
São Paulo Singapore Taipei Tokyo Toronto Warsaw

and associated companies in
Berlin Ibadan

Copyright © 1998 by Daniel J. Schroeter
Published by Oxford University Press, Inc.
198 Madison Avenue, New York, New York 10016

Oxford is a registered trademark of Oxford University Press

Design: Loraine Machlin
Picture research: Lisa Kirchner

Library of Congress Cataloging-in-Publication Data
Schroeter, Daniel J.
    Israel : an illustrated history / Daniel J. Schroeter
      p.   cm. — (Illustrated histories)
    Includes bibliographical references and index.
    1. Israel—History—Juvenile literature. 2. Palestine—History—
  Juvenile literature. 3. Zionism—History—Juvenile literature.
    [1. Israel—History. 2. Palestine—History. 3. Zionism—History.]
    I. Title. II. Series.
    DS126.5.S292   1998
    956.94—dc21   98-15915
                  CIP

ISBN 0-19-510885-X (trade edition)

9 8 7 6 5 4 3 2 1

Printed in Hong Kong
on acid-free paper

On the cover: *Visitors at the Citadel, or Tower
of David*
Frontispiece: *Visitors at the Western Wall*
Title page: *Youngsters dancing on a kibbutz*
Contents page: *Dome of the Rock detail*

Contents

Moses.

Chapter 1

Ancient Israel

The Land of Israel was the birthplace of the Jewish people. Here their spiritual, religious and national identity was formed. Here they achieved independence and created a culture of national and universal significance. Here they wrote and gave the Bible to the world.

Exiled from the Land of Israel, the Jewish people remained faithful to it in all the countries of their dispersion, never ceasing to pray and hope for their return and the restoration of their national freedom.

Impelled by this historic association, Jews strove throughout the centuries to go back to the land of their fathers and regain their statehood. In recent decades they returned in their masses. They reclaimed the wilderness, revived their language, built cities and villages, and established a vigorous and ever-growing community, with its own economic and cultural life. They sought peace, yet were prepared to defend themselves. They brought the blessings of progress to all inhabitants of the country and looked forward to sovereign independence.

—*from Israel's Declaration of Independence*

Moses, the most important Hebrew prophet, led his people out of bondage in Egypt in the 13th century B.C.E. Here, he holds the Tablets of the Ten Commandments, the central moral and religious duties of the Jewish people.

With these words, Prime Minister David Ben-Gurion proclaimed Israel's independence before a rapturous crowd in Tel Aviv. The date was May 14, 1948. Almost 2,000 years earlier the Jewish people had been driven from their homeland, the land of Israel. Now the nation of Israel was reborn.

There is much history in a name, and Israel has had many names over the centuries. The longest-lasting was Palestine, a version of the Greek name Palaistina, which comes from the Hebrew word for the Philistines, a people who lived in the region in ancient times. The Romans called it Syria Palaestina, and the British, who ruled the region in the 20th century, called it Palestine. Upon gaining independence in 1948 the nation came full circle by reclaiming one of its ancient names, Israel.

As Ben-Gurion reminded his listeners on that May day, the Jewish people had been scattered across many lands for hundreds of years. Always, however, they had hoped that one day they would reclaim their ancestral homeland. That hope united Jewish followers of a political movement called Zionism, which began in Europe in the latter half of the 19th century. Zion was a hill in Jerusalem, thought to be a dwelling of the God of Israel. The word "Zion" came to represent Jerusalem and the entire Jewish homeland. Jews exiled to other countries prayed that one day God would restore them to Zion, and the 19th-century Jews who decided to work toward returning to Israel called themselves Zionists. Israel's independence was a triumph for the Zionist movement and its supporters, who established a modern nation in the land where the Jewish people were born.

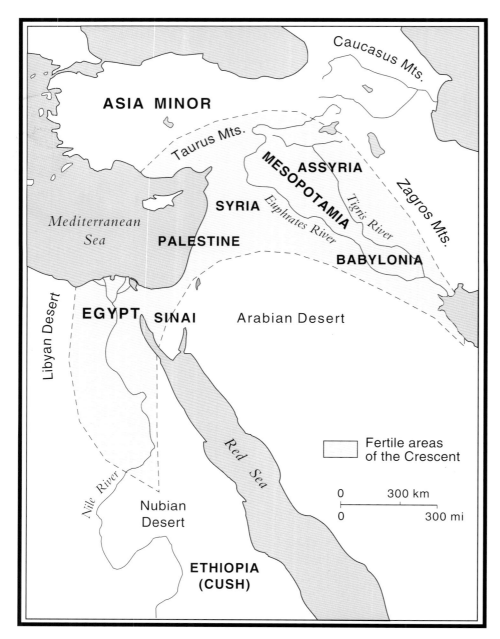

The region known as the "Fertile Crescent" is where the ancient civilizations of the Middle East began. The land of the ancient Israelites lay between Mesopotamia and Egypt.

Today Israel looks back to the ancient origins of its people, its early culture and beliefs, and its association to the land. Of course, Israel is not the only country to search the past for its heritage. Stories of the past shape the identity of every nation. But Israel is unique because the stories of its past are found in the Bible, a book that millions of people throughout the world consider sacred. Biblical stories contribute to mod-

ern Israeli identity. Many Israelis take a deep and lively interest in their country's history, including its earliest history. They feel that they are walking in the footsteps of their ancient ancestors.

Israel is unusual in another important way: most national movements developed because people felt that they belonged to the land in which they lived. Zionism was just the opposite—a national movement for people from many lands. These Jews felt that they belonged not to the countries in which they lived, but to their ancestral homeland in Palestine. To create a nation there, Jews from around the world would have to leave their countries of residence and settle in Palestine. Then they would have to obtain political control over at least part of Palestine. Finally, they would have to establish their independence. To attain this goal, the Zionists had to convince themselves and the rest of the world that the land where Jews had lived and ruled in ancient times rightfully belonged to modern Jews.

Israel entered the history of the ancient Middle East sometime in the 11th century B.C.E., more than 3,000 years ago. At that time two major centers of civilization flourished in the Middle East. One was Mesopotamia, the "land between the two rivers," between the Tigris and Euphrates rivers in what is now Iraq. The other was Egypt on the Nile River in northeast Africa. Both of these valley civilizations depended on extensive farming in the rich soil left by the annual flooding of their rivers. Agricultural production helped support the world's first large cities, such as Ur in Mesopotamia and Memphis in the Nile

Valley. From these cities, rulers built up their power by taxing the people until they controlled empires like Sumeria, which emerged in Mesopotamia about 5,000 years ago. Political power in the cities was based on new religious ideas and institutions. The people of Mesopotamia believed that a city belonged to a god and that the king communicated the god's wishes. Priests controlled the religious ceremonies at temples built for the worship of the city gods. Egyptian government also was based on religious authority. The pharaoh, the ruler of ancient Egypt, claimed to be a god.

The land of the ancient Israelites lay between Mesopotamia and Egypt, and much of its history was shaped by those powers' attempts to control it. Palestine was about 350 miles from north to south and averaged barely 60 miles from east to west. It was not a valley civilization like Mesopotamia or Egypt. Rather, it was a jumble of terrain squeezed between the Mediterranean Sea and an inland desert. Along the coast was a fertile plain that received some rain. But the coastline lacked good harbors and was broken by marshlands, coastal rivers, and mountains, so that commerce was undertaken by caravan rather than by sea. Palestine's inland terrain was rugged and full of contrasts, broken by ranges of hills. Because swift communication was difficult, rulers found it difficult to maintain centralized control over the whole land. Consequently, in the 1,100-year history of the kingdom of Israel, there were few periods when the country was unified under one ruler.

Israel's emergence in history remains a mystery. Who were the first Israelites, and where did they come from? What is the relationship between Israelites and Jews? Historians have no factual answers to these questions. The Bible tells of three stages of Israelite history before the founding of the first kingdom, although there is no direct evidence of these eras outside the Bible. The first era is called the Patriarchal period after the patriarchs, or founding fathers, of the Israelites—Abraham and his immediate descendants. The Bible says that Abraham, a native of Ur in Mesopotamia, migrated to Canaan, as Palestine was then called. God gave Canaan to Abraham and his descendants. Some biblical scholars believe that these events occurred around 1800 B.C.E.

The second period was the time of Exodus, when the Israelites were enslaved in Egypt. The Exodus story is central to Jewish practice and belief. Each year Jews commemorate it with the festival of Passover, which celebrates the passage of the Israelites out of slavery to freedom in Israel. Egyptian records do not mention it, but those scholars who believe that this episode really happened guess that it may have taken place about 1300 B.C.E.

The third era, Judges, according to the Bible lasted for about two centuries. The "judges" were leaders of the tribes of Israel who fought the influence of rival cults.

During this period, Israel became a nation and its law codes took shape. As the tribes of Israel started coming together, they clashed with the seafaring people known as the Philistines. The Bible says that Samuel, who achieved a great following as a holy man and a priest, was one of the judges. But the invasion of the Philistines made the Israelites seek a strong leader, so Samuel reluctantly selected the powerful warrior Saul as Israel's first king.

These stories concerning the birth of ancient Israel became an important part of the Israelites' religious beliefs. But historians must read between the lines of the Bible to guess how this new people and nation emerged. Whenever possible, historians use documents that date from the period they are studying. The problem with using the Bible as a document is that no one really knows who wrote it or when. The Bible recounts events in the history of ancient Israel over hundreds of years. It is impossible to say how much of the text that survives today was faithfully passed down over the centuries and how much was altered or added as time went on. It is also impossible to know whether the original stories were meant as factual history or as inspiring myth. Did Abraham really exist, or does the character of Abraham represent

God's Covenant with Abraham

In the Hebrew Bible, God promises the land of Israel to Abraham (originally named Abram) and his descendants. This promise appears several times in the book of Genesis:

When they had come to the Land of Canaan, Abraham passed through the land to the place at Shechem to the oak of Moreh. At that time the Canaanites were in the land. Then the Lord appeared to Abraham, and said, "To your descendants I will give this land." So he built there an altar to the Lord, who had appeared to him. (12:5-7)

And again:

The Lord made a covenant with Abraham, saying, "To your descendants I give this land, from the river of Egypt to the great river, the river Euphrates" (15:18). Late in Abram's life, God appeared to Abram and made his covenant, saying to him "Behold, my covenant is with you, and you shall be the father of a multitude of nations. No longer shall your name be Abram, but your name shall be Abraham; for I have made you the father of a multitude of nations. I will make you exceedingly fruitful; and I will make nations of you, and kings shall come forth from you. And I will establish my covenant between me and you and your descendants after you throughout their generations for an everlasting covenant, to be God to you and to your descendants after you. And I will give to you, and to your descendants after you, the land of your sojournings, all the land of Canaan, for an everlasting possession; and I will be their God."

In another important part of the covenant, God said, "This is my covenant, which you shall keep, between me and you and your descendants after you: Every male among you shall be circumcised" (17:10). The word "covenant" is *brit* in Hebrew, and to this day the circumcision ceremony for Jewish boys is called *brit*.

The biblical promise to Abraham became a fundamental belief of the Jews in ancient times. For some Jewish and Christian supporters of Israel in modern times, it gave the Jews the right to restore their political sovereignty over their ancient homeland.

In The Angel Prevents the Sacrifice of Isaac *(1655), Rembrandt depicts a scene from the life of Abraham, who was ordered by God to sacrifice his son, Isaac.*

many different leaders who contributed to the emergence of a new people? Were the Israelites really enslaved in Egypt? And did Moses lead them out of bondage after God sent plagues to torment the Egyptians?

Whether or not the Bible stories happened the way they are described, they served an important purpose. From them the Israelites forged a sense of identity. That sense of identity begins with Abraham, their patriarchal founder. In the stories about Abraham, God creates a special connection to the Israelites and to the land of Canaan, later known as Israel. To affirm this connection, God establishes a covenant—an agreement or promise—with the people. They must keep the covenant by circumcising all males, or removing the foreskins of their penises. This was the first of many practices that the Israelites adopted over the centuries to reflect their belief that God set them apart from other peoples.

The story of Exodus reinforces the Israelites' connection to their land and to God, who is named YHWH. After God frees the Israelites from slavery, they camp in front of Mount Sinai. God calls Moses to climb the mountain to receive stone tablets "with the law and the commandment." Moses remains on the mountain for 40 days and the Israelites, feeling hopeless when he does not return as expected, make a golden calf so that they can have a visible god. While they are celebrating before the golden calf, Moses comes down from the mountain. Seeing the people worshipping the calf, he smashes the stone tablets given to him by God, for he knows that the people have broken their covenant. He then asks God to forgive the people, and God reveals his mercy.

Moses receives a new set of tablets containing the Ten Commandments, the moral and religious duties of the Israelites toward God and their neighbors. The first commandment is: "I am the Lord your God, who brought you out of the land of Egypt, out of the house of bondage. You shall have no other gods before me" (Exodus 20:2–3). The people proclaim their faith in YHWH. For Jews the most important part of the Exodus story is that at Sinai YHWH, the one and only God, remade his covenant with the Israelites.

For nearly 40 years the Israelites wander in the desert. During this time they change from a people who had been slaves and who had forgotten their God into a unified people, faithful to the one God. Only after this change occurs and a new, free generation is born in the wilderness are the Israelites prepared to return to the Promised Land. During the migration back to Canaan they forge a new identity, their 12 tribes uniting to form a nation.

The Bible tells us that, unlike the Canaanites, who worshipped many different gods, the Israelites should pray only to YHWH, the God of Israel. Monotheism, the belief in only one god, is another feature that set the Israelites apart from others in the region. The stories of Abraham and Moses explain the monotheism of the people later known as Jews. But monotheism probably developed over hundreds of years, not in a single revelation. Some leaders of the ancient Israelites wanted their people to worship one God, but they did not always insist that the God of Israel was the only God. Not until the 6th century B.C.E. did monotheism really take hold. Then Jews edited and rewrote many traditions of the Torah, the first five books of the Bible, to make them compatible with monotheism.

But when did Israel come into being? Archaeologists have found the earliest known reference to Israel—outside the Bible—in Egypt. Written about 1207 B.C.E., it is part of a victory ode on a monument to Pharaoh Merneptah, marking an Egyptian expedition into Canaan. The inscription reads, "Israel is laid waste, his seed is not." The meaning is unclear, but the phrase does

The remains of the Davidic wall on Ophel Hill in Jerusalem were uncovered during archaeological excavations of ancient Israeli sites. Jesus passed by here on his way to the Temple.

Israel's King David, who ruled in the 10th century B.C.E., was crowned here, in the town of Hebron.

tell us that people known as Israelites existed in Canaan by that date.

Did the Israelites migrate from other regions in the Middle East, taking over the land of Canaan, or were they descendants of the Canaanites? Perhaps some came from outside, but it is likely that many of the Canaanites eventually became Israelites. The legend of the 12 tribes of Israel, separate groups with a common origin, was a way of giving a number of different groups that lived in the same land a shared or common identity. It was similar to the American celebration of Thanksgiving—very few Americans are descended from the original Pilgrims, but all Americans celebrate the story of the Pilgrims as if they are shared ancestors.

Israelite identity was also linked to the Hebrew language. Like much about the early Israelites, the origin of Hebrew is

something of a mystery. It belongs to a large family of ancient Middle Eastern languages that scholars call Semitic (*Shemi* in Hebrew, from Shem, one of the sons of Noah in the Bible). Hebrew is descended from Akkadian, an early Semitic language of the people who came after the Sumerians in Mesopotamia.

Canaan had many different population groups—and many Semitic languages and dialects. Hebrew probably emerged as a language spoken among these groups before Israelite history began. After the establishment of the Israelite state, another Semitic language called Aramaic competed with Hebrew. Aramaic eventually became the common language of most Jews in Israel.

The biblical account of Israel's beginning carries the story of the Israelites forward from the period of Judges. Kings ruled a united Israel from about 1020 to 922 B.C.E. The most important of these kings was David, who ruled after Saul. Renowned as a poet and musician, David reigned for 40 years. He was the model of a good king, and his reign symbolized Israel's Golden Age. Israelites came to believe that just as there was a covenant between Israel and God, so was there a covenant between God and the dynasty, or ruling family, that David established.

The Bible gives us the political history of David's reign. Crowned in the town of Hebron, he ruled over the tribe of Judah. Later he captured Jerusalem from a Canaanite people known as the Jebusites. David worked ruthlessly to increase his power, driving the Philistines from the region, seizing control of all of Israel, and

uniting all the Hebrew tribes under his rule. He even enlarged Israel beyond Canaan's original boundaries by defeating some neighboring states.

David established Jerusalem on Mount Zion as Israel's capital and religious center. There, where YHWH was believed to be present, he built an extensive royal court. From it he sent trained priests and government officials into Israel's new territories to absorb other ethnic groups into the kingdom. David's son Solomon (c. 965–c. 922 B.C.E.), praised in the Bible for his wisdom and his construction projects, built an elaborate palace and temple complex. This temple (later called the First Temple by Jews when a second one was built) was the center of the worship of YHWH. The area around it was the scene of sacrificial rites and of pilgrimages during festivals, especially the three major festivals related to the agricultural seasons. The slaughtering of lambs in the spring was associated with Passover (Pesach), and the time of grain reaping in the early summer was associated with Weeks (Shavuoth), when worshippers made offerings to YHWH. The end of the growing season was associated with Booths or Tabernacles (Succoth), and during this time farmers built booths in their fields to celebrate the harvest. These festivals changed and took on new meaning when Judaism developed in later centuries.

During Solomon's rule the Israelites colonized new territories and the king consolidated his authority. The number of religious, administrative, and military officials increased greatly, bringing central control and unity to diverse regions and peoples. But after Solomon's death the monarchy split into two kingdoms: Judah to the south and Israel to the north. The Bible claims that this division came about in part because many people resented being forced to work on Solomon's building projects.

The first king of the northern kingdom was Jeroboam. He established Tirzah as his capital but made Bethel the center for the worship of YHWH. Omri, who became king in 878 and founded a dynasty, moved the capital to Samaria, which became an important town with a royal palace.

The biblical prophets are very critical of the northern kingdom of Israel. Take, for example, the way they describe King Ahab, who married the daughter of the king of Tyre, which was one of the states of Phoenicia, a coastal region northwest of Israel where Lebanon is located today. Ahab "went and served Baal, and worshipped him. He erected an altar for Baal in the house of Baal which he built in Samaria" (1 Kings 16:32–33). Baal was a popular god throughout this part of the Middle East, and the prophet Elijah condemned Ahab for breaking the covenant with YHWH.

Judah outlasted the northern kingdom of Israel. In 722 B.C.E. the Assyrians, another Middle Eastern power that dominated an-cient Palestine for a time, conquered Israel. This event appears in the Bible to have fulfilled biblical prophecies such as the words of Hosea, who had warned of impending disaster: "Samaria shall bear her guilt, because she has rebelled against her God; they shall fall by the sword, their little ones shall be dashed in pieces, and their pregnant women ripped open. Return, O Israel, to the Lord your God, for you have stumbled because of your iniquity" (Hosea 13:16-14:1). The Assyrians deported the conquered people of the northern kingdom, most of whom were probably resettled into foreign regions and absorbed into the local populations. But the fate of the deported people is unknown, giving rise to legends about the 10 lost tribes and hopes for their eventual return.

The southern kingdom of Judah existed for 150 years after the fall of Israel. Judah was not perfect, however—the prophets also condemned some kings and people of Judah for their sins. According to the Bible, Judah had good kings like Hezekiah (725–697 B.C.E.) who tried to rid the kingdom of non-Israelite religions, and bad kings like Hezekiah's son Menasseh, who reintroduced old religious practices, such as building altars for other gods. Menasseh committed all kinds of abominations: "and he burned his son as an offering, and practiced soothsaying and augury, and dealt with mediums and with wizards. He did much evil in the sight of the Lord, provoking him to anger" (2 Kings 21:6). The good king Josiah (639–609 B.C.E.) once again reformed religion, ridding the country of foreign gods and promoting the centralized religion of YHWH and the Jerusalem Temple. A biblical account says that during Josiah's reign the Israelites discovered a law book while repairing the Temple. This book, later associated with part of the book of Deuteronomy in the Bible, contained details of the covenant between God and the Israelites.

The prophets claimed that Judah would perish because of the sins of people like Menasseh. In historical terms, however, Judah's destruction had more to do with the political struggles among the regional powers. Judah had survived by maneuvering and balancing its relationships with the powerful Egyptians and Assyrians. But Assyria declined in power, and in its place a new force arose in Mesopotamia: the Chaldeans, whose capital was in Babylon. In 587 B.C.E. Nebuchadnezzar, the ruler of the Chaldeans, conquered Judah. His army destroyed Solomon's Temple, rounded up many Judeans, and marched them off to Babylon.

The exile of the Judeans to Babylon marked a turning point in their history. Other ancient peoples, when conquered and driven out of their homelands, lost their identities as they merged with their captors or with other peoples. But the Judeans managed to keep their separate identity, their sense of connection to their distant spiritual homeland, and their faith.

It is also likely that monotheism gained ground during or soon after the exile. Before the exile, those who promoted the temple-based Jerusalem religion claimed that YHWH alone should be the God of Israel. This idea was hard to sell in a region where people were used to worshipping many gods. People felt more secure if they could ask for protection from several gods, and they were comforted by possessing personal idols, or images of gods. Many people had difficulty accepting the idea that they should worship only the God of Israel and make no idols. It was even harder for them to believe that YHWH was not simply the God of Israel, who lived on Mount Zion in Jerusalem, but the one and only universal God. But when the Judeans found themselves in Babylon, without a temple, cut off from the land God had given to them, the idea of a universal god to whom they were still linked probably began to seem more attractive.

The Judeans spent about 50 years in Babylon. Then Cyrus, ruler of the Persian Empire (now Iran), conquered Babylon. Because he wanted the support of all of the many peoples under his rule, Cyrus told the exiles that they could return to Palestine and restore the Temple in Jerusalem. Some returned, while others remained in Babylonia. They completed the Second Temple around 516 B.C.E.

Judah was now a province of the Persian Empire, but its people followed their own laws and religious practices. The Bible provides details about an important Judean official who served in the Persian court, Ezra the scribe. He came to Jerusalem in the latter half of the fifth century to govern according to ancestral law and to reestablish central control of the Temple in Jerusalem. At this time religious leaders put the sacred traditions and writings into their final form as the officially accepted Five Books of Moses, or Torah. Officials also took drastic steps, according to the biblical account, to put an end to the foreign religious practices that many of the people who had remained in Judea had adopted. Ezra, in the biblical account, called all the people of Israel together and ordered men to leave their foreign wives who had corrupted them with their abominable practices. Nehemiah was another noted Judean official in the Persian court. Like Ezra before him, he governed Judah and pursued religious reforms. Apparently many people did not obey Ezra's decree about the foreign wives, and Nehemiah renewed the efforts of his predecessor. In a final speech in the biblical account, Nehemiah tells us:

> I saw the Jews who had married women of Ashdod, Ammon, and Moab; and half of their children could not speak the language of Judah, but the language of each people. And I contended with them and cursed them and beat some of them and pulled out their hair; and I made them take oath in the name of God, saying, "You shall not give your daughters to their sons, or take their daughters for your sons or for yourselves." (Nehemiah 13:23–26)

The terms "Jew" and "Judaism" took on new meaning at this time. "Jew" is derived from Judah, which was "Yehud" in Aramaic, the common spoken language of the period. The Jews (*yehudim* in Hebrew, *yehudin* in Aramaic) were the descendants of the people of Judah, as opposed to the local population that had remained or settled in Israel during the period of exile. But as the religion of the Judeans became more widespread, the term Jew came to refer to people who followed Judaism, the religion of the Second Temple of Jerusalem.

The religious laws of Judaism set Jews apart from other people. The Sabbath rituals, including the commandment to stop all work on the seventh day of the week, became firmly established during this period. The restored Temple became Judaism's most important shrine and pilgrimage center. There priests called Cohenim conducted religious ceremonies, including sacrificing animals to God.

At the same time, the spread of the Torah allowed Jews outside Jerusalem and even outside Israel to follow what they believed was the way of life set out for them by God. They formed synagogues, places of worship outside the Temple. Synagogue worship did not require priests and sacrifice. Judaism had become two things at once. It was a faith linked specifically to Jerusalem and the Temple, and it was also a universal religion that could exist anywhere. This twofold nature guaranteed Judaism's survival over thousands of years as Judaism kept its national and ethnic qualities but also adapted to changing circumstances.

The Greeks put Judaism to a great test of survival. In 332 B.C.E. Alexander the Great, in his sweeping conquest of the Middle East, took over Palestine. Greek culture and language mixed with the cultures of the Middle East to produce a new culture called Hellenism. Everywhere they went the Greeks built Greek-style cities, often next to existing Middle Eastern towns, complete with Greek civic institutions such as councils, elected magistrates, and gymnasiums, which were places not only of exercise but of culture and learning.

After Alexander's death in 323, a number of Hellenistic dynasties divided his empire. Two of the most powerful were the Ptolemies in Egypt and the Seleucids in Syria, north of Palestine. Judea fell under the rule of the Ptolemies in 301. The Ptolemies gave the Jews a large measure of independence, allowing them to govern themselves according to their ancestral laws. Still, Greek culture and customs influenced the Jews, especially rich and sophisticated people who had the most contact with non-Jews. The Tobiad family, for example, were international traders and tax-farmers—that is, they bought from the government the right to collect taxes and were entitled to keep the taxes they collected. The Tobiads lived in palaces and had the courtly manners of Greeks. Other wealthy Jews also adopted Greek customs, but most Jews were simple farmers who considered such customs alien. A gulf grew between the prosperous Jews, who were attracted to Greek culture, and the poor, who were not.

The Seleucids seized control of Judea around 200 B.C.E. At the same time a new force, Rome, was moving out of the central Mediterranean toward the Middle East. The Hellenistic dynasties, fearful of the coming showdown with Rome, struggled to gain as much power as possible. A contest for control began in Jerusalem, with some factions of Jews supporting the Ptolemies, others the Seleucids. Then a series of dra-

Alexander the Great's sweeping conquest of the Middle East produced a new culture, Hellenism, traces of which can still be seen in Israel today.

In this scene from the Maccabean War, the victorious Maccabees vanquished their enemy. In the left foreground is an elephant used in combat by the Seleucid forces.

matic events unfolded that led to rebellion. The Seleucid ruler, Antiochus IV Epiphanes, appointed a high priest, Jason, who turned Jerusalem into a Greek city, renamed Antioch to honor the Greek king. Next, Antiochus IV replaced Jason with another high priest, Menelaus, who was not even from a lineage of high priests recognized by the people. Menelaus, supported by the Tobiads and other pro-Greek reformers,

was probably ready to take even further steps to hellenize Judea. Some of the Jews began to rebel against the Greek reformers, and this caused the Seleucid king to act. In 167 B.C.E., he banned the practice of Judaism in Jerusalem, and sent government agents to the countryside to enforce the decree. Jews were forbidden to observe the Sabbath, perform circumcisions, and follow their other distinctive customs. Antiochus outlawed monotheism and introduced idol worship, converting the Temple into a shrine to the Greek god Zeus. Seleucid authorities enforced the new rules harshly. The very survival of Judaism was at stake.

Some of the pro-Greek Jews accepted the new rules, and quite possibly, Menelaus himself may have encouraged Antiochus to ban Judaism. But other Jews, especially in the countryside, rebelled against the Seleucids and their Hellenistic Jewish supporters. The first rebels were rural people, many of them from northern Judea. Their leader was a priest named Mattathias. When an officer ordered the elderly Mattathias to perform a sacrifice to a foreign god, he refused. Mattathias killed the officer, destroyed the altar, and headed for the hills with his five sons and some followers. After Mattathias's death his third son, Judah the Maccabee, led the resistance along with two other sons, Jonathan and Simon. The Maccabees—some scholars think the name means "hammer"—swept down into villages to gather followers and then retreated into rural and mountainous regions. Theirs was not just a war against the Seleucid armies. It was also a fight to win the allegiance of the Jews.

This bronze coin, dated from around 200 B.C.E., is stamped with a seven-armed candelabrum of the Tabernacle, an important decorative symbol in Judaism.

The Maccabees were successful in their struggle, which ended in a victorious battle against the Seleucid army at a place called Beth Horon, on the way to Jerusalem. Antiochus stopped trying to ban Judaism, but that was not good enough for Judah, who now considered himself the lawful leader of the land. The Maccabees captured the Temple in the year 164, restoring it to Judaism. To this day a festival known as Hanukkah ("dedication") celebrates the recovery of the Temple. Hanukkah lasts for eight days. According to legend, when the Maccabees captured the Temple, they found only enough oil to light the lamp for one day, but miraculously it burned for eight days.

The Maccabean struggle for the freedom and independence of the Jewish homeland inspired modern Zionists, who saw a parallel with their own attempt to create a Jewish nation. The Maccabees saved Judaism from destruction and made Judah independent for the first time in more than 400 years. Simon and Jonathan established a dynasty known as the Hasmoneans. Ironically, in some ways the Hasmoneans resembled the former Hellenistic rulers. They aggressively seized new territories and forced whole ethnic groups, such as the Idumeans, to convert to Judaism, circumcising the men and making the Torah everyone's law. The Hasmoneans considered all of Palestine to be the ancestral homeland of the Jews.

The Hasmoneans ruled for about 100 years. During that time the Romans were busy building a world empire. In 63 B.C.E., when Hasmonean independence no longer suited them, they conquered Judea and made it a vassal, or dependent, kingdom of

the Roman Empire. The Hasmoneans had to pay tribute to the Romans and could no longer appoint their own rulers. The Romans eventually eliminated the dynasty. But they did allow the Jews to practice their religion, to maintain the high priesthood, and to keep the Sanhedrin, the main council in charge of all religious and legal matters.

In 37 B.C.E., the Romans appointed a Jew to rule Palestine: King Herod. Herod was an Idumean, one of a people recently converted to Judaism. His father, Antipater, had gained considerable influence under the Romans. The Romans put Herod in charge of the Galilee in northern Israel. Although Herod was a Jew, he enforced order over other Jews with particular harshness. After he had some Jews executed without authority from the Sanhedrin, however, his position became shaky. He therefore made his way to Rome, where the Roman authorities decided that he was just the man to be king of Palestine.

The Romans believed that Herod, as a foreigner and a recent convert to Judaism,

This relief comes from the Arch of Titus in Rome, erected to commemorate the 70 C.E. Roman victory over the Jews.

The Second Temple

The Second Temple of Jerusalem, based on the First Temple, was completed about 515 B.C.E. The Romans destroyed it in 70 C.E. Jews believed that God resided at the Temple, which was a place of religious rituals run by priests. Members of the Levite tribe were the Temple's guards and gatekeepers. The Mishnah contains descriptions said to have been written by Rabbi Eliezer ben Jacob, who knew the Temple before its destruction:

In three places do the priests keep watch in the sanctuary: in the room of Abtinas, in the room of the flame, and in the room of the hearth. And the Levites [keep watch] in twenty-one places: five at the five gates of the Temple mount; four at the four corners on the inside [of the Temple wall]; five at the five gates of the courtyard; four at the four corners on the outside [the wall of the courtyard]; and one at the office of the offering, and one at the office of the veil, and one behind the Mercy Seat [outside of the western wall of the holy of holies].

The room of Abtinas was probably where incense was made; Abtinas was the name of the family that knew the secret of making incense. The holy of holies commemorated the place where a sacred portable sanctuary called the Ark had been kept in the First Temple. The Ark was lost, but its place was rebuilt in the Second Temple.

A major activity at the Temple was sacrificial worship, which took place daily and at times of pilgrimage during religious festivals. Priests sacrificed various kinds of animals: birds, oxen, goats, and sheep. Says the Mishnah:

Rings were on the north side of the altar, six rows of four [rings]—and some say, "Four rows of six each"—at which they slaughter the Holy Things. The shambles was north of the altar. And on it were eight short pillars, and square blocks of cedarwood were on top of them, and iron hooks were set into them. And three rows were on each one, on which they would suspend [the slaughtered beasts]. They flay them on marble tables between the pillars.

Animal sacrifices had many purposes. Jews offered sacrifices to purify themselves from influences or actions they

This modern model in Jerusalem shows what the Second Temple, since destroyed, looked like in 50 B.C.E.

believed had tainted them, to atone for their sins, to seal vows of oaths, and to give thanks. The destruction of the Temple, however, ended the practice of animal sacrifice in Judaism.

The Temple Mount was the seat of institutions connected to Judaism. These included the council known as the Sanhedrin, which under Roman rule became the main institution of Jewish government and the highest authority of Jewish law. The Sanhedrin supervised the priesthood, set the dates of

festivals, and functioned as a law court.

King Herod ornamented and enlarged the Second Temple, making it one of the largest and most impressive shrines in the world at that time. The historian Josephus described the sanctuary after Herod was finished with it:

He decorated the doors of the entrance and the sections over the opening with a multicolored ornamentation and also with curtains, in accordance with the size of the Temple, and made flowers of gold sur-

rounding columns, atop which stretched a vine, from which golden clusters of grapes were suspended. The grapes symbolized the people of Israel.

The only part of the Temple that remains standing is a stretch of the Western Wall, also known as the Wailing Wall. Many Jews consider this wall sacred. It is the site of intense devotions—and also of conflict with Muslims who regard the Temple Mount above the wall as one of the holy places of their Islamic faith.

would be unpopular with the Jews—and therefore loyal to Rome, which would protect him. They were right. Herod served the Romans well. Like Solomon, Herod ordered many construction projects. He founded a bustling port city named Caesarea on the Mediterranean coast, which grew to be one of the larger cities of the Roman Empire. Its ruins are still visited in Israel today. Herod also built places of refuge, palaces and fortresses high on hilltops, such as Masada overlooking the Dead Sea.

Herod wanted to hellenize Palestine and bring it more fully into the Roman Empire, but he did not outlaw Judaism or introduce the worship of Roman gods. Instead he used his good ties with Rome to guarantee that the religious rights of the Jews would be respected in the empire. He also totally rebuilt Jerusalem and the Temple, turning the city and its great Jewish shrine into one of the marvels of the ancient world.

King Herod became a ruthless tyrant in the last years of his reign, executing both political enemies and family members alike. After Herod's death in 4 B.C.E., the Romans divided up the territory between a number of his surviving sons, who were much less effective rulers. More and more, Palestine came under the direct control of the chief Roman official, the procurator. Many Jews became increasingly unhappy with Roman authorities who were increasing their tax demand and interfering in religious matters.

Not all Jews, however, were united. From the time of the Hasmoneans, a number of groups, with different ideas about Jewish belief and practice, competed for power and influence in the Temple. One such group was the Sadducees, or *Zadokim*

in Hebrew. Their name indicated that they venerated the priestly lineage descended from King Solomon's high priest, Zadok. The Sadducees formed a kind of priestly upper class, who obtained important positions in the Temple establishment. Their chief rivals were the Pharisees. Their name came from *Perushim*, or "separated ones"— separated both from non-Jews and from other factions within Judaism.

The Pharisees differed from the Sadducees in a number of ways. Most important, they based their authority not only on the written Torah but also on their interpretation of the oral Torah, an idea that was to shape the future of Judaism. The Israelites had not only inscribed God's revelations to Moses on Mount Sinai in the written Torah but had also told them to each new generation. The Pharisees interpreted this spoken, or oral, tradition. But the more conservative Sadducees rejected the notion of authority based on an oral Torah. They limited their domain to the written law of Moses, of which they were the official interpreters.

Other Jewish groups also began to question the established order. They anxiously awaited the coming of the messiah (Hebrew *mashiah*, meaning one who is anointed with holy oil). According to tradition, the messiah was a leader who would one day arrive to restore Israel to the golden age that had existed in King David's time. The Essenes, who separated themselves from the rest of Israelite society, were one of the groups waiting for the messiah. We know about this group from the writings of the historian Josephus, who betrayed the Jews and sided with the Romans.

The Torah—the first Five Books of Moses in the Hebrew Bible—is written on a parchment scroll. It is the foundation of all Jewish beliefs and practices.

Archaeologists from the Hebrew University explore a cave near the Dead Sea, similar to the one where the Dead Sea Scrolls were found.

In 1947 a Palestinian shepherd made a remarkable discovery: ancient documents in caves at a place called Qumran, near the Dead Sea. Known as the Dead Sea Scrolls, these documents opened a window to the beliefs and practices of the Jewish messianic groups. They have added enormously to our understanding of both early Judaism and the emergence of Christianity.

Scholars do not know for certain what group kept this library at Qumran, but some of the scrolls' writings are about beliefs and practices that many historians identify with the Essenes or others like them. These beliefs and practices differed from what we know about the established religion in Jerusalem. The scrolls' authors were extremely strict in their observance of

ritual purity, believing that even the Pharisees lived in sin. They considered themselves exiles, waiting for the restoration of an ideal Jerusalem under two messiahs: a king-messiah descended from David, and a priest-messiah descended from Aaron, Moses' brother who led the priesthood.

Many sects emerged from this period of religious change, the most successful being the Christians. The first Christians were Jews who shared many of the messianic ideas of the Essenes. Christians also shared many of the Pharisees' beliefs, including the ideas of resurrection, or the survival of the soul after death, and of punishment after death for sins committed during one's life-time. Both Pharisees and Christians based their authority on the Bible, and both

In 1947, a Palestinian shepherd discovered these ancient documents, called the Dead Sea Scrolls, in caves at Qumran. Like the Torah, the Dead Sea Scrolls are written in Hebrew, an ancient language that has been revived in modern Israel.

promised their followers salvation. But the Christians saw the Pharisees as their main rivals. The Pharisees' scholarly interpretation of scripture, based on the oral Torah, challenged the Christian belief in the meaning of the Bible. Eventually, Christians wrote the New Testament and added it to the Hebrew Bible, which they called the Old Testament.

Over a few centuries, Christians became separated from Jews by two important differences in belief. First, Christians believed that Jesus Christ was the messiah, an idea that Jews rejected. Second, Christians departed from the way of life outlined in the Torah, the basis of Jewish practice. For example, Christians regarded circumcision, the symbol of God's covenant with Israel, as unnecessary because the coming of Jesus had established a new covenant.

While these and other religious movements were competing, political turmoil increased. In 66 C.E. the Jews revolted against Roman rule. The revolt was launched by the Zealots, an extreme faction that split from the Pharisees under the leadership of Eleazar ben Simon. Their messianic movement hoped to liberate the country from evil Roman rule and, with God's help, establish a divine kingdom. Not all Jews supported the Zealots, however, and the rebels split into rival groups. In Jerusalem the extreme rebel faction seized control of the city and wiped out the Roman garrison. Rebellion spread throughout the countryside. The governor in Syria, the seat of Roman power in the region, met fierce resistance and failed to quell the uprising. The emperor Vespasian sent Roman legions under the

command of his son Titus to suppress the rebellion. In 70 C.E., the Romans captured and destroyed Jerusalem.

A few pockets of resistance remained. Rebels had seized the mountaintop fortress and palace of Masada that Herod had built. In this remote outpost they held out until 73 C.E. Josephus left the only account of the siege. He wrote that when the rebels realized that they could hold out no longer, the entire population (except for two women and five children) committed suicide so that they would not be captured and enslaved. Although historians do not know whether this really happened, Masada has become a symbol of modern Israel's fight for freedom and national dignity. Its importance as a national symbol is similar to that of the Statue of Liberty in the United States.

Some Jews did not make war against the Romans. Pharisees like Yohanan Ben Zakkai took a more peaceful, cautious approach to countering Roman power. According to legend, this famous teacher had himself smuggled out of Jerusalem in a coffin in 68 C.E., while the Romans were

This bronze coin was issued in 68 C.E. during the first Jewish revolt against the Romans.

besieging the city. Ben Zakkai became a symbol of the survival of Judaism. The Romans destroyed the Temple in Jerusalem, but Ben Zakkai founded a school in Yavneh, which became the new center of Jewish authority. There priests proclaimed the new moons that determined when Jews would celebrate their holidays, and there the Sanhedrin met.

Sixty years after their first rebellion, the Jews made a second major effort to free the country from Roman rule. For three years Palestine was in revolt. The rebels' leader was Simon Bar Kokhba, whom some called king and messiah. As a sign of political sovereignty, the Jews minted coins bearing Bar Kokhba's name (but not his image, which would have been a sort of idol). Bar Kokhba gained control of Jerusalem and much of Palestine, but the Roman emperor Hadrian violently put down the rebellion, killing thousands of Jews and destroying much of Judea. The Romans took many Jews away as slaves, and other Jews fled Palestine as refugees. This spreading out of the Jews to many lands is called the Diaspora.

Some Jews remained in Palestine, but the Romans banned them from Jerusalem and brought in non-Jews, such as Syrians and Arabs, to settle the land. Nearly 2,000 years later, many Zionists regarded Bar Kokhba as a national hero who fought for Jewish independence. Before Zionism, however, Jews saw the Bar Kokhba revolt as a great tragedy that brought an end to Jewish life in Eretz Yisrael, the land of Israel (as Palestine was called by Jews).

Despite the destruction brought by the revolt, Jews outside of Eretz Yisrael thrived. The Jewish community in Babylon, which was part of the Persian Empire, became the main center of Jewish life and culture. In Israel, the center of Judaism shifted to the Galilee region, with its two main cities of Tiberias and Sepphoris. For the most part, the Romans left the Jews of Galilee alone. Most people in the Galilee were peasant farmers, and the region became nearly self-sufficient. Merchants exported olive oil and other agricultural products. People also practiced crafts such as weaving and glass making.

The new Jewish leaders were not the priests who had been closely attached to the Temple. They were a group of sages, or rabbis, who probably grew out of the Pharisees. The "founding father" of the rabbis was Hillel, who came to Palestine from Babylon and lived until about 10 C.E. He founded a school known as Beit Hillel, the House of Hillel, and was famous for his ethical sayings and lawmaking abilities. Stories about Hillel abound in the Jewish tradition. The most famous story tells of a man who asked Hillel to teach him the whole Torah—while standing on one foot. Hillel replied, "What is hateful to yourself do not do to your neighbor. That is the entire Torah. All the rest is commentary. Now go forth and learn." Hillel's descendants led rabbinical schools for centuries.

Rabbis became the leaders of the Jewish community. They believed that their authority came from Moses, whom they called "our rabbi." God's revelation of the Torah was given to Moses, and the rabbis were responsible for interpreting and teaching it. The written and oral Torahs were closely connected. The written Torah did not change, but the interpretation of it, based on the oral Torah, did. The rabbis' interpretation of the Torah evolved and adapted to the changing circumstances of a Judaism without the Temple.

Judaism acquired a new outlook after the destruction of the Temple. Jews had sinned, but they could redeem themselves by leading virtuous lives, that is, by following the Torah. This way of life, with its many laws, practices, and beliefs, was called the *halakhah* (law). This outlook provided the Jews with a way of facing the future. They would accept Roman rule but follow the Torah.

The rabbis were widely regarded as holy men who had knowledge of the law. But several centuries passed before their legal authority extended over the entire Jewish population and before the rabbinical courts controlled both religious and nonreligious matters. Many local customs remained, and few people were willing to strictly observe all the rules and regulations that the rabbis wished to enforce.

The first rabbi with extensive powers was Judah Ha-Nasi, who lived from about 170 to 220. He was very wealthy, and he emphasized the nobility of his birth and his descent from King David. Rabbi Judah dominated the Sanhedrin and was given the right to levy taxes. But he was most famous for completing the Mishnah, a massive book in Hebrew that contained two centuries' worth of the rabbis' debates and moral and spiritual teachings. The Mishnah deals with all kinds of everyday problems of rituals, practices, and beliefs. It became the principal guide to Judaism in Israel and Babylon.

Another massive work, the Gemara, was compiled from several centuries' worth of rabbis' discussions on issues raised in the Mishnah. Much longer than the Mishnah, the Gemara is filled with stories and debates that try to bring unity to the sayings of the rabbis and relate them to the written Torah. In the second half of the 4th century, Jewish scholars combined the Mishnah and the Gemara into a multivolume work called the Jerusalem Talmud. Jews in Persia completed the second or Babylonian Talmud in the 6th century; it was longer and more influential than the Jerusalem Talmud. The Talmud, especially the Babylonian one, remained the basis of Jewish practice and belief until the modern period. It is still used as a guide by Orthodox Jews.

The growth of Christianity shaped the lives of Jews during this period. At first Roman authorities outlawed Christianity, but in 312 Emperor Constantine legalized it and became a Christian. Over the next century Jews became a minority under Christian rule in Palestine. The Roman Empire itself soon fell apart under attack by Germanic peoples of Europe that began establishing their own kingdoms. Palestine

Glass bottles like these, dating back to the period of the first and second Jewish revolts, may have been used for water and oils.

was in the eastern part of the old Roman Empire, which survived as the Byzantine Empire. The Byzantine Christians called Palestine the Holy Land because it was the birthplace of Jesus and of Christianity. They built lasting Christian monuments in the ancient land of Israel, especially in Jerusalem. After the 5th century, few Jews remained in Israel. Important centers of Jewish life developed elsewhere in the Middle East and later in Spain and other parts of Europe.

A new identity soon enveloped the majority of the people who lived in what had once been ancient Israel. In the 7th century, the new religion of Islam arose in the Arabian Peninsula. Inspired by this new faith, the Arabs burst out of their desert homeland to conquer much of the Middle East and North Africa. Islam became the dominant religion of these regions, and Palestine became part of the wider Arab and Islamic civilization.

Chapter 2

Muslim Palestine

I n 634 Islamic Arab armies swept from Arabia into Palestine and defeated the armies of the Christian Byzantine Empire. The Arabs captured Jerusalem in about 638. For the next 1,300 years, the rulers of Palestine were Arabs or other Muslims, as followers of Islam are called. The only break in Muslim rule was during the period when Christian soldiers from Europe, the Crusaders, controlled parts of the Holy Land.

The Islamic rulers let Christians and Jews remain in Palestine, although their status was lower than that of Muslims. Over the next few centuries, the Arabs' culture and language and the Islamic faith came to dominate Palestine. Some 20th-century Palestinian Arabs trace their origins to the Canaanites, the ancient people who lived in Palestine before the Israelites. But the cultural identity of modern Palestinians is linked to Arabs and the Arabic language. Like Arabs in other Middle Eastern countries, the Palestinians identify not only with the countries where they live but also with the larger Arabic-speaking world that stretches from Morocco in northern Africa to Iraq.

As with the Israelites, historians know little about the origins of the Arabs, who appear in historical documents at about the same time as the Assyrians, in the 9th century B.C.E. These Arabs were wandering, or nomadic, desert tribespeople called bedouin. They probably originated in the northwestern corner of the Arabian Peninsula. As their numbers grew, they migrated north in search of greener pastures for their livestock. Arabs lived in Palestine from the 5th century B.C.E.—the book of Nehemiah in the Bible mentions them. Around the 4th century C.E., Arabs began migrating into southern Arabia. It was also around this time that the term Arab came to refer to all the people of Arabia. They spoke Arabic, a language that belongs to the same Semitic language family as Hebrew.

During the 7th century Arabs adopted Islam, the third great monotheistic religion born in the Middle East (after Judaism and Christianity). The new religion began in a trading town called Mecca in western Arabia where a man named Muhammad lived. According to Muslim belief, God (Allah in Arabic) revealed himself to Muhammad, "God's messenger." Muhammad accepted his role as prophet and warned the Meccans to be prepared to face God on the day of

Bedouin, such as this man praying on horseback, lived in Palestine from about the 5th century B.C.E. These nomadic, desert tribespeople still live in Israel today. This 19th-century Orientalist drawing is somewhat of a romantic depiction.

This illustration from a 16th-century Persian manuscript portrays the angel Gabriel (far left) leading Muhammad, astride a magical horse, to Paradise. Muhammad's journey from Jerusalem is one of the reasons Muslims consider the city to be holy.

from the true path. They believed that Muhammad was the last prophet, sent to make that path clear. A sacred book called the Quran contains God's revelations to Muhammad. The Quran, together with other sayings of Muhammad, became the basis of Islamic law, which is called the shari'a (the way). Like the halakhah in Judaism, the shari'a examines all aspects of life and instructs Muslims to follow the strict rules laid down by God.

While in Medina, Muhammad built a military force capable of defeating his enemies, which included some nearby Jewish tribes. He emerged victorious after several battles in which he slaughtered many enemies who did not come to agreement with him. By 629 he was sending troops to raid Palestine.

In 630 Muhammad returned triumphantly to Mecca, already the site of a small but important shrine containing a black stone known as the Ka'aba. Muslims believe that Abraham built the Ka'aba, which became the holiest site in Islam. By the time of Muhammad's death in 632, the tribes of Arabia, unified under their new faith, were ready to expand well beyond the boundaries of Arabia. In just a few decades they had conquered much of the Middle East, spreading their faith as they went.

The Arabs benefited from the weakness of the empires that ruled the Middle East. In the years before the Arab conquests the Byzantine and Persian empires were at war. The Persians conquered Jerusalem in 614, then the Byzantines regained control in 628, driving back the Persian army. Drained by this conflict, the Persian Empire collapsed before the Arab invaders. Much

judgment, when God determines whether each person's actions on earth have earned eternal punishment or paradise. Many Meccans, however, rejected Muhammad's claim to prophethood, calling him a fake or a madman.

In 622 Muhammad fled to the town of Yathrib, later known as Medina, where some of his supporters invited him to govern. His flight from Mecca to Medina marks the first year of the Islamic calendar.

In Medina Muhammad established an Islamic community to spread his teachings, which drew many beliefs and traditions from Judaism and Christianity. Muslims considered Jews and Christians "People of the Book" because they too had received God's revelations, as recounted in the Bible. To Muslims, Abraham was the first Muslim. Moses and Jesus were considered important prophets. Yet Muslims also believed that Jews and Christians had strayed

The Dome of the Rock (center) is a mosque built in the 7th century on the Temple Mount in Jerusalem. Muslims believe that the rock is where Abraham intended to sacrifice Ismail (or Isaac, in the biblical tradition) and where the Prophet Muhammad traveled to heaven during his Night Journey to Jerusalem.

Byzantine territory in the Middle East also fell to the Arabs, although part of the Byzantine Empire survived until 1453, when the capital, Constantinople, was captured by the Muslim armies of the Turks.

Palestine was one of the Arabs' early conquests. For 1,000 years Arabs had migrated there from Arabia. The Islamic conquest, however, brought a whole new wave of Arabs to Palestine. In addition, because Arab culture soon dominated the region, many of the local non-Arabs adopted Arab culture.

After Muhammad's death the leadership of Islam passed to his successors, the caliphs.

The center of Muslim power moved to Syria when the first Arab dynasty, the Umayyads, established their capital in the Syrian city of Damascus. Jerusalem became Islam's third-holiest city, after Mecca and Medina. According to Muslim tradition, Muhammad had originally faced toward Jerusalem during prayer, before changing to face Mecca. Atop the Temple Mount the Umayyads built a shrine called the Dome of the Rock. Ibn Battuta, a 14th-century Arab

The Noble Sanctuary

In 692 the Umayyad Caliph 'Abd al-Malik built the Dome of the Rock on Jerusalem's Temple Mount, which Muslims called *Haram al-Sharif,* "the Noble Sanctuary." The Dome of the Rock is the earliest Islamic mosque still standing in its largely original form. On the southern end of the *Haram,* the Umayyads built the Aqsa or Farthest Mosque, identified with a verse in the Quran: "Glory to God who took His servant for a night journey from the Sacred Mosque [in Mecca] to the Farthest Mosque." It became the principal place of public prayer for Muslims in Jerusalem.

The early Muslim rulers built their shrine on the Temple Mount to connect the new religion of Islam with Jerusalem and the sites sacred to Christians and Jews. An inscription on the Dome of the Rock reads, "O people of the book, do not go beyond the bounds of your religion and do not say about God except the truth. Indeed, the Messiah Jesus son of Mary was an envoy of God and his word he bestowed on her as well as a Spirit from him. So believe in God and in his Envoys and do not say 'three'; desist, it is better for you. . . . Indeed the religion of God is Islam." The inscription proclaims the superiority of Islam over the "people of the book," the Christians and Jews.

In later years a more specifically Muslim tradition became associated with the Dome of the Rock. Muslims believed that the Angel Gabriel brought Muhammad from Mecca to Jerusalem on a "Night Journey." After arriving in Jerusalem, the Prophet ascended to heaven from the rock on the Temple Mount and prayed with Abraham, Moses, Jesus, and other prophets. Jerusalem became known in Arabic as *al-Quds* ("the Holy"). The *Haram* is visited by Muslims from around the world during their pilgrimages to Mecca.

This interior view of the Dome of the Rock shows the rock from which Muhammad is believed to have risen to paradise. High on the roof of the dome is an Arabic inscription proclaiming the superiority of Islam.

In 1099, western European Christian knights waged a holy war (the Crusades) against the Muslims in Palestine. In this 14th-century French manuscript painting, the Crusaders stand outside a castle, attacking the Muslims within.

from Morocco who covered more than 75,000 miles in his travels around the Islamic world, marveled at the Dome of the Rock:

> . . . a building of extraordinary beauty, solidity, and elegance, and singularity of shape. It stands on an elevation in the center of the mosque and is reached by a flight of marble steps. It has four doors. The space round it is also paved with marble, excellently done, and the interior likewise. Both outside and inside decoration is so magnificent and the workmanship so surpassing as to defy description. The greater part is covered with gold so that the eyes of one who gazes on its beauties are dazzled by its brilliance, now glowing like a mass of light, now flashing like lightning.

By the end of Umayyad rule in 750, other sites in Palestine had also become sacred to Muslims. One was the city of Hebron, believed to be the burial place of the patriarchs Abraham, Isaac, and Jacob and their wives Sarah, Rebecca, and Leah.

Muslims called Hebron *al-khalil,* meaning "friend," which referred to Abraham (Ibrahim in Arabic). Some Muslim traditions say that the Prophet visited Hebron.

An Arab dynasty called the Abbasids arose and ended the Umayyad caliphate. The Abbasids founded the capital of Baghdad in Mesopotamia, now Iraq. They took control of Jerusalem but were generally uninterested in the city. Palestine was far from the center of Abbasid power in Iraq, and the caliphs did little to maintain order there. As a result, Palestine was wracked by political turmoil and violence. The Abbasids continued to rule the Muslim world in name until 1258, but by the mid-9th century they could no longer control their vast territories. Local dynasties became the real rulers. As in ancient times, Egyptian dynasties often controlled Palestine, using it as a buffer against rival powers in Syria or Baghdad. When Egyptian control waned, Palestine suffered from bedouin raids.

The non-Muslim inhabitants of Palestine found Arab rule bearable. Under Islamic law, Jews and Christians were *dhimmis,* people protected by the state. They could practice their religions, although each male adult had to pay an annual tax. *Dhimmis* also had to follow rules designed to demonstrate their inferior status, such as wearing badges or clothes dyed a special color. With the exception of collecting the annual taxes, however, government authorities sometimes neglected to enforce such regulations. For example, *dhimmis* were forbidden to build houses of worship, but this rule proved impractical, and Jews and Christians built synagogues and churches in many parts of the Islamic world. Despite their inferior status, the Jews of Palestine and even some of the Christians preferred Arab to Byzantine rule, which was much harsher. In some places, such as Hebron, Jews had helped the Arabs overthrow the Byzantines.

Palestine's non-Muslim communities were numerous and diverse. Christians of many denominations and ethnic groups made up the largest part of the population of Jerusalem. They included Greeks, Aramaic-speaking Syrians, Armenians, Georgians from the Caucasus mountains to the south of Russia, Latins, and Copts, who practiced a very early Egyptian form of Christianity. These denominations had their own rites and often spoke their own languages. Jews, too, fell into various factions. The Rabbinates accepted the rabbis' authority in interpreting the Torah. The Karaites, who emerged in the 8th and 9th centuries, rejected the Talmud and the oral Torah in favor of their own interpretation of the Torah. Also present were the Samaritans, who had split away from the Jews in the 4th century B.C.E. Samaritan practices were based solely on the written Torah. Muslim authorities accepted all of these groups into the population.

The Crusaders were less tolerant. These western European Christian knights pledged to wage a holy war to recapture Jerusalem from the Muslims. They arrived in Palestine in 1099 to find the Muslims weakened by political divisions and fighting. The Crusaders captured Jerusalem and slaughtered the city's Muslims. William of Tyre, who wrote a history of the Latin kings of Jerusalem, describes the bloodbath in gruesome detail:

Saladin and the Crusaders

Saladin, leader of the Muslim army that defeated the Crusader army in 1187 and captured Jerusalem, became the most celebrated Muslim ruler in medieval history. In this moment of victory, he tears the Holy Cross out of the Christians' hands.

Saladin (in Arabic, *Salah al-Din Yusuf*) led the Muslim army to victory over the Crusaders on July 4, 1187. He defeated the Christian army in the hills at Hattin a few miles west of Tiberius, and a few months later Jerusalem was again in Muslim hands. The horrified Christians launched another Crusade, but they never recaptured Jerusalem. Saladin became the most celebrated Muslim ruler in medieval history. For many modern Arabs he symbolizes liberation from foreign occupation.

Before going to battle with the Crusaders Saladin, who was born in 1137 or 1138, became ruler of Egypt and founded a new dynasty, the Ayyubids. A talented and often ruthless military and political leader, he gained firm control of Egypt and then extended his control over Palestine and Syria. Despite his ruthlessness he won a reputation as a just ruler and a staunch up-

holder of Islamic law. Saladin was much more merciful to the Christian inhabitants of Jerusalem than the Christians had been to the Arabs and Jews when they conquered the city a century earlier. Wrote European historian William of Tyre:

Now I shall tell you of a great act of courtesy that Saladin did for the ladies of Jerusalem. The women and daughters of the knights who had been killed or taken in the battle had fled to Jerusalem. After they had been ransomed and had left the city, they came before Saladin and craved for mercy. When he saw them he enquired who they were and what it was they were asking. They told him that they were the wives and daughters of the knights who had been killed or taken in the battle. He asked them what they wanted. They explained that he had their husbands and fathers in prison and that they had lost their lands, and they

called on him for the sake of God to have mercy on them and give them counsel and aid. When Saladin saw them weeping, he had great pity on them and said that they would be informed as to which of their husbands were alive and he would have them all freed. They made enquiries and found some of them, and they freed all those who were in Saladin's custody. Then he ordered that the ladies and maidens whose fathers and lords had been killed in the battle should be provided for generously from his goods, more to some and less to others according to who they were. He gave them so much that they praised God and man for the kindness and honor Saladin had shown them.

By the time of his death in Damascus, Syria, in 1193 Saladin had built an empire that covered much of the Middle East. Although Saladin's dynasty endured for only about 60 years, Palestine remained under Muslim control until 1917.

In 1453, Turkish soldiers captured Constantinople, the Byzantine capital of the Eastern Christians. The Turks renamed the city Istanbul.

It was impossible to look upon the vast numbers of the slain without horror; everywhere lay fragments of human bodies, and the very ground was covered with the blood of the slain. It was not alone the spectacle of headless bodies and mutilated limbs strewn in all directions that roused horror in all who looked upon them. Still more dreadful was it to gaze upon the victors themselves, dripping with blood from head to foot, an ominous sight that brought terror to all who met them. It is reported that within the Temple enclosure alone about ten thousand infidels perished, in addition to those who lay slain everywhere throughout the city in the streets and squares, the number of whom was estimated as no less.

Most Jews had probably already fled the city, but the Crusaders killed those who remained or sent them off as captives. Then they established the Latin Kingdom of Jerusalem. They adorned the city's Christian shrines and made the Dome of the Rock into a Christian church. They also conquered Hebron, turning a Jewish synagogue there into a church. Christian soldiers killed or exiled many Jews from cities around Palestine.

In 1187 the powerful Kurdish ruler of Egypt named Saladin recaptured Jerusalem and the rest of Palestine, although the Crusaders retook the city of Acre in 1191 and held it until 1291. Saladin restored Jerusalem's Islamic character but allowed Christians to stay. He built a number of Muslim institutions, including schools, mosques for worship, and a hospice, or place of rest for Muslim travelers. Through his efforts Jerusalem became more a part of Islamic civilization than it had been before the Crusades. The Jews who returned welcomed the Muslim restoration.

From 1260 to 1516 Palestine's rulers were the Mamluks, a dynasty based in Cairo, Egypt. The Mamluks had been brought to Egypt from the Eurasian steppe region as children to work as slaves. They were raised to become Muslim soldiers. In 1250 they took control of the government in Egypt, and soon made Palestine part of their empire. Although Palestine had little political importance for the Mamluks, their rule brought a period of peace and prosperity to the region. Mamluk trade flourished in the 14th century, for Egypt was at the crossroads of the great spice route that linked the Italian merchant republics with India by way of the Red Sea. Egypt also produced silk, cotton, and textiles. Palestine benefited from the bustling caravan trade in these goods.

But Palestine's fortunes declined along with the Mamluk dynasty. In the early 14th century a Turkish dynasty called the Ottomans began building an empire. The Turks

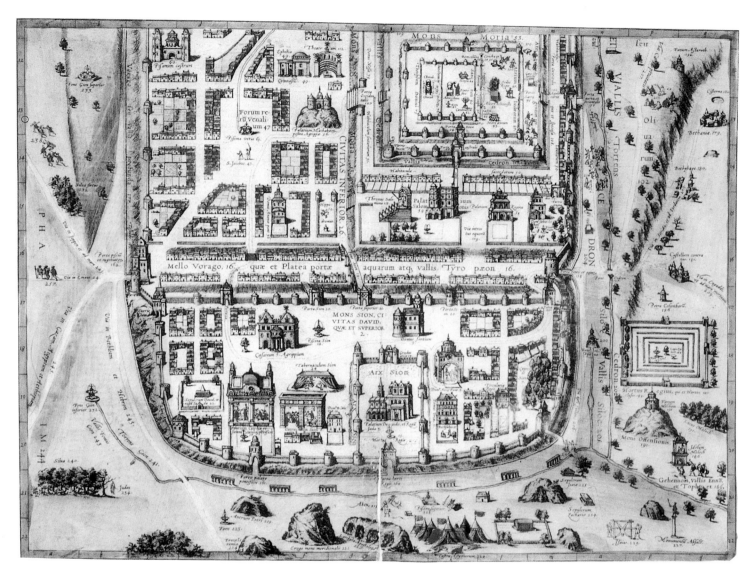

had originated in Central Asia, and gradually moved west into the Islamic lands. They became Muslims and adopted the Arabic script. In 1516 the Ottoman Turks led by Sultan Selim I captured Palestine. They wrested Asia Minor from the Byzantines and went on to conquer much of the Middle East.

Under Sultan Suleyman (reigned 1520–66), known as "the Magnificent" to Europeans and "the Lawgiver" to the Turks, the Ottoman Empire became one of the largest in history, threatening all of western Europe. The Turks besieged Vienna, captured Rhodes and Belgrade, and took control of much of the North African coast. The Ottomans also brought new developments to Palestine. Jerusalem enjoyed renewed prosperity. The Ottomans rebuilt the Islamic monuments and

built walls around the entire city. These ramparts still encircle the Old City of Jerusalem today.

The Turks sent governors and administrators to rule Palestine but did not settle there in large numbers. Most of the population remained Muslim Arab, with a significant minority of Arabic-speaking Christians. And during this period many Jews came to Palestine. In 1492, Spain drove its Jewish population out of the country. The Sephardim, or Jews of Spain, made up what was probably the largest Jewish community in the world at the time. Now they were refugees. Where could they go? Many parts of Christian Europe banned Jews, but the Ottoman Turks, heirs to a multiethnic civilization, saw great advantages in welcoming the Sephardim. The Spanish Jews had skills that would help

At the center of this map are Mt. Zion and the City of David. Because the Ottoman Turks who ruled Palestine welcomed immigrants from many cultures in the 15th and 16th centuries, some Jews exiled from other countries sought refuge in the city of Jerusalem.

*Sephardic Jews were ex-
pelled from Spain in 1492
by Queen Isabella and
King Ferdinand. Many
Sephardim then found ref-
uge in different parts of the
Ottoman Empire.*

the Ottoman state, including the ability to manufacture weapons, experience in commerce, and medical knowledge. Thus the Sephardim found new homes in various parts of the Ottoman Empire, including Rhodes, Cyprus, Egypt, and Istanbul, the Ottoman capital city that had been called Constantinople under Christian rule.

A new wave of Jews arrived in Palestine during this period. The Ottoman government, known as the Sublime Porte, encouraged them to settle there. The main Jewish communities were in Jerusalem, Tiberius, and Safed. During Suleyman's reign Jerusalem's Jewish population increased by about 50 percent. In recognition of the Jews' growing importance in the city, Suleyman allowed them to have a place of prayer at the still-standing Western Wall of the destroyed Second Temple. The Western Wall acquired its fame as a place of worship and pilgrimage among Jews at this time.

Tiberius had become an important Jewish town in ancient times after the Romans banished the Jews from Jerusalem. It had languished over the years, but in the 16th century it gained a new lease on life, thanks to two prominent Jewish financiers in the Ottoman court: Don Joseph Nasi (d. 1579), and his aunt, Doña Gracia Mendes (1510-69). Doña Gracia was born a Christian in Portugal. Her Jewish parents had been forced to convert to Christianity, as had Portugal's entire Jewish population. Doña Gracia left Portugal in 1537 after her husband's death. She became an international businesswoman, and was involved in banking and the gem trade in many European cities. On the surface she was a Christian, but secretly she remained a Jew. Because it was easier to practice Judaism in Turkey than in most other parts of Europe, she moved to Istanbul. The Ottoman sultan used Doña Gracia and her nephew as diplomats and gave them commercial advantages, such as sole control of the wine trade in parts of the Ottoman Empire. Around 1558 the sultan leased Tiberius to Doña Gracia. She and Don Joseph made it one of the most thriving Jewish communities in Ottoman Palestine.

But the most impressive Jewish community in the 16th century was the town of Safed, perched high in the Galilean hills. David dei Rossi, an Italian Jewish traveler, reported to his brother in 1535:

> He who saw Safed ten years ago, and observes it now, has the impression of a miracle. For more Jews are arriving here continually, and the tailoring trade grows daily. I have been told that more than 15,000 suits have been manufactured in Safed during this year, besides fancy suits. Every man and every woman who works woolen fabric earns an abundant living.

The sultan wanted to develop the newly captured island of Cyprus and in 1576 ordered that 1,000 wealthy Jews resettle there. Expecting to be forced to go to Cyprus, the Jews of Safed stopped working, causing major losses to the empire's treasury. "If it is decided to deport [the Jews] to Cyprus," wrote the sultan, summarizing the arguments of Jewish representatives, "the Public Revenue will lose the above-mentioned amount of money [more than 10,000 gold pieces], and the town of Safed will be on the verge of ruin." The sultan cancelled his order.

Safed was important not only for its textile industry but also as a Jewish spiritual center. Jews from many countries came to Safed to study under some of the leading scholars of the period. Jews and mystics were particularly drawn to Safed at this time. They would frequently walk to the tombs of ancient rabbis in the Galilee, fast, and meet for special prayer sessions. The leading thinker of the mystics, Isaac Luria, taught that the Jews' exile had a purpose: divine sparks were scattered throughout the world, and the Jews, by following God's commandments and leading a mystical life, could collect the sparks and restore the wholeness of the universe. Doing so would ensure redemption and bring forth the messianic era. Because many Jews yearned for redemption, the Jewish mystical movement enjoyed great influence.

Jews in the Ottoman Empire spoke many different languages and came from many different lands. The Sephardic Jews brought a new, Spanish-influenced culture to Palestine and other Ottoman lands. But even before the arrival of the Sephardim, the Jews of the Ottoman Empire included the Greek-speaking "Romaniyot" of the original Byzantine Empire, Ashkenazi Jews from Europe (the term came from Ashkenaz, or Germany), and Arabic-speaking Jews. Later Jews from Livorno, Italy, settled throughout the Ottoman Empire, and people from the large Moroccan Jewish community in northwestern Africa came to Palestine. In the 18th century, Jews came to Jerusalem from Yemen in the Arabian Peninsula, Morocco, and eastern and western Europe. Although a small minority, the Jews in Ottoman Palestine came from many different cultures. Jews from around the world had come there long before the rise of Zionism.

The prosperity Palestine had enjoyed in the early years of Ottoman rule waned in the 17th and 18th centuries. Palestine be-

Sultan Suleyman the Magnificent ruled the Ottoman Empire from 1520 to 1566. In recognition of the Jews' growing importance to Jerusalem, Suleyman allowed them to establish places of worship, such as the Western Wall.

came a neglected backwater during this time, ruled by governors in Syria who often exploited the province's resources and over-taxed its people.

The Ottomans neglected Palestine because their own power was fading. After the reign of Suleyman the Magnificent, and especially in the 18th and 19th centuries, the empire began losing territory to the European powers. The Ottomans found it increasingly difficult to control even those provinces that were still officially part of their empire. Some Ottoman provinces were practically independent of the Porte. In Egypt, for example, an elite group of Mamluk soldiers ruled, although they were supposed to be subjects of the sultan. In 1798, a French military expedition led by Napoleon Bonaparte invaded Egypt and began to push into Palestine. Only an attack by the British navy stopped the French. Napoleon's invasion shocked the Ottomans. It demonstrated how weak they had become and made them realize that they had to reform their empire. It also seriously weakened the Mamluks.

The Ottomans sent troops to Egypt, and in 1801 the French left the country. Among the Ottoman troops was an Albanian soldier named Muhammad 'Ali, who seized control of the government. Muhammad 'Ali embarked on an ambitious program of economic and military reforms. His son, Ibrahim, took Palestine from the Ottomans in 1832. Egyptian rule brought greater security to Palestine and encouraged the growth of international trade. Palestine became part of a world economy. Its peasants began to grow cash crops—cotton, grains, sesame, olive oil, and oranges—for export to Europe. But Egyptian rule was also harsh. The Egyptians demanded taxes and drafted peasants into the army.

Protests against forced army service led to a revolt in 1834. Riots broke out around Hebron. Rebellion then spread throughout the countryside and to Jerusalem and other cities. All major elements of the Arab population—farmers, Bedouin, and town dwellers—joined the revolt. It was the first time that so many Palestinian Arabs had fought to resist changes from the outside.

In 1839 the Ottoman Empire, with the help of the European powers, succeeded in reclaiming Egypt and Palestine. Sultan Abdülmejid (reigned 1839–61) reorganized the empire in response to the loss of territory and the Europeans' increased interference. His reforms, known as the Tanzimat (reordering), were intended to improve the Ottoman state's finances and military performance. The sultan also issued decrees, based in part on the ideals of the 1789 French Revolution, that gave all Ottoman subjects equal rights, regardless of their religion. These decrees ended the Islamic practice of defining non-Muslims as *dhimmi*s. The Ottoman government gave non-Muslim communities the right to conduct their own affairs. The Porte hoped that these measures would ensure the subjects' loyalty. But while the sultan promoted equal rights for all, the Ottoman government recognized and even reinforced divisions among the main religious and ethnic groups. This contradiction made it hard for most people to feel any sense of patriotism toward the Ottoman Empire.

The Ottoman reforms changed land-ownership regulations in Palestine. An 1858 law required that all land be registered with the government. Individual peasants could now claim pieces of state-owned land and land that villages held as common property. Peasants were very suspicious of this new measure, fearing that the government planned to exploit them even further through taxation or the military draft. As a result many refused to register their land, or they turned it over to powerful and wealthy city men whom they hoped would protect them from the government. These city notables also bought unregistered land at government auctions. They became absentee landlords who collected rent but lived far from the land they owned. The peasants who worked the fields became their rent-paying tenants. Absentee landlords were often quite willing to sell their land, even to foreigners, to make a profit. This was how the Zionists bought much of their land in Palestine before the First World War (1914–18).

As the power of the Ottoman Empire declined, more foreign travelers and merchants visited the Middle East, and some of them settled in Palestine. The Sublime Porte hoped to stop this trend through direct control. In 1874 Ottoman officials in Jerusalem received orders to report to Istanbul instead of to the provincial governor in Syria. This failed to slow the tide of foreigners but did increase order and security in Palestine. Bedouin raids became a thing of the past, as did exploitation by local governors.

In 1800 between 5,000 and 6,000 Jews lived in Palestine, out of a total population of 250,000 to 300,000. Many of these Jews were simple craftspeople, such as shoemakers, tailors, weavers, carpenters, or blacksmiths. Others were religious scholars or students from many different countries, for the most part supported by Jewish communities abroad. For centuries the principal religious schools in Palestine had been sending representatives to far-flung Jewish communities to raise money for the Palestinian Jews.

Palestine's Jewish population increased in the 19th century for a number of reasons. The Ottoman reforms improved security, making the country a safer place to live. Foreign nations opened offices called consulates that offered protection to ethnic and religious minorities. This served the political ambitions of these nations—by presenting themselves as protectors of minorities, they justified their interest in Palestine. The foreign consulates, especially that of Great Britain, protected many Jews in Palestine from trouble with Ottoman law and Turkish officials; in addition, some Algerian Jews entered Palestine with French protection after the North African country of Algeria became a French colony in 1830. Religion also contributed to the growth of the Jewish population in Palestine. Russian Jews moved there believing that in the Jewish year 5600 (1839–40), the messiah would come.

At the time of the first wave of Zionist immigration in 1882, Palestine's Jewish population had grown to about 24,000 out of a total population of about 470,000. Soon Zionist settlers began arriving. They were different from the other Jews who had settled in Palestine during the centuries of Muslim rule, and they would change Palestine's social landscape forever.

Chapter 3

The Birth of the Jewish National Ideal

n 1882, a group of young, idealistic Jews set off from Russia to settle in Palestine. They belonged to a group called BILU, from the first letters of the Hebrew words of a line in the Bible: "O House of Jacob, come let us walk in the light of the Lord" (Isaiah 2:5). They were following a simple idea—but one that seemed nearly impossible to bring to reality. The Biluists wanted to return to the soil of their ancient ancestors in the land of Israel and support themselves through the fruits of their own labor. They planned to live communally, pooling their resources and sharing everything equally.

These hopeful settlers joined Rishon LeZion ("first to Zion"), a newly formed Zionist settlement in Palestine. One of them, Chaim Chissin, wrote in his diary:

> The happiness in the hearts of this handful of people was such as seldom falls to a Jew. They had returned to the arms of their mother, to a parental home full of welcome. The quiet, unrebellious days of long ago were theirs once more, the time of wandering and bitterness had passed. They were to live an honest life, a life of toil, tilling the soil of the ancient land of

their fathers. Stirred by such noble feelings, the settlers lived together like brothers, they ate and drank together, and shared their joys and sorrows. No one spared himself in the attempt to promote the welfare of the settlement.

Other settlements were soon established. This first wave of Zionist immigration became known as the First Aliyah ("ascent"). The arrival of these immigrants marked the beginning of an organized Zionist movement.

The young Zionist pioneers left Russia practically penniless, with no farming experience and little knowledge of conditions in Palestine. Most were students from Kharkhov, a Ukrainian town in the Russian Empire. Called Hovevei Zion, or Lovers of Zion, they were devoted to the cause of establishing a national homeland for Jews in Palestine. Their headquarters were in the town of Odessa on the Black Sea.

At this time the Russian Empire had more Jews than any other part of the world, 75 percent of world Jewry. Jews had settled in large numbers in Eastern Europe during the 16th and 17th centuries as Poland expanded—Jewish traders and craftspeople

Pioneers of the First Aliyah ("first ascent") came to Palestine in the 19th century from Russia. Extremely poor and entirely unfamiliar with their new home, these pioneers faced a difficult existence.

These pioneers from the First Aliyah founded a settlement in Palestine around 1890. They were part of the BILU movement, founded in Russia in 1882 in reaction to the pogroms in their homeland the previous year.

were exceptionally useful in areas where most people were peasants. The Jews lived in cities with the Poles and in small towns and villages, known as *shtetls,* which often had a majority Jewish population. Wherever they lived, Jews maintained their religion and culture. Among themselves they spoke a language called Yiddish, which resembled German.

Although the Jews were useful to Poland's rulers, the Christian population had deep prejudices against them. Many blamed Jews for the death of Jesus Christ and disliked them for their different ways. The practices that Jews had developed in ancient times to strengthen their identity by setting themselves apart from others had become a source of fear and suspicion to their neighbors.

In the 18th and 19th centuries Russia, Austria, and Prussia divided up Poland. The division placed the vast majority of Jews

inside the new boundaries of the Russian Empire, which meant that Russia inherited a large population of Jews that it did not want. The czars adopted extreme and often cruel measures to try and solve the problem of these unwanted Jews. The Jews had to live within the Pale of Settlement, a zone of the empire that lay between Lithuania in the north and the Black Sea in the south. Laws limited the entry of Jews into certain professions. Jews were barred from public office and from Russian schools. In an attempt to weaken the Jewish identity, Czar Nicholas I (reigned 1825–55) drafted Jewish children into his armies. They had to serve for 25 years, and many were pressured to convert to Christianity. The draft tore Jewish communities apart because it forced community leaders to decide between those who would go and those who would not go into the army.

Jewish children on a street in Zabludow, Poland, a shtetl, in 1916. From about 1600 to the time of the Holocaust, more Jews lived in Poland and Russia than in any other part of the world.

Nicholas died in 1855. His successor, Alexander II, relaxed the terrible drafting policy and began allowing Jews to attend Russian schools and universities. Well-educated Jews could live outside the Pale. They entered more professions and even held public office. The position of Jews in Russia seemed to be improving. Although Jews still used Yiddish in their daily lives, more of them were now learning Russian. While Jews still had few legal rights, some believed they would become equal citizens if they continued to blend into Russian culture. They hoped to live like their brethren in Western Europe, where in most countries Jews were citizens with the same rights as non-Jews.

For most Russian Jews, however, blending into an openly hostile population seemed impossible as they went about their day-to-day lives. They continued to follow Jewish beliefs and practices and had as little contact as possible with Russians. Life in Jewish communities, whether in the small, rural *shtetls* or the growing, bustling cities of the Pale, was largely self-contained. Jews attended their own religious schools from an early age. Judaism guided the rhythm of their lives with daily rituals and prayers, the weekly observance of the Sabbath, and the annual festivals. The world of the Russian peasant or town dweller was alien and hostile.

A substantial number of Russian Jews were Hasidic, members of a movement that started in the late 18th century when the Hasidim ("pious people") rebelled against the domination of the rabbis. The rabbis spent their lives in Talmudic scholarship, poring over texts in religious academies

called yeshivas, but failed to meet the spiritual needs of many common people. Hasidism claimed that excited, joyous prayer was more important than Talmudic study. Many Hasidic beliefs grew out of mysticism and popular Jewish folklore. Such things as superstitions, magic, amulets and charms, and evil or "clinging" spirits called *dibbukim* became part of Hasidism. Some Jews sought the path to the good life through a mystical experience, or personal connection with God, guided by a *tsaddik*, a Hasidic righteous man. *Tsaddikim* founded many Hasidic dynasties. Their devoted male followers formed a world unto themselves, separate from other Jews. Frequently they left even their wives behind.

Most Russian Jews, whether Hasidic or not, followed Jewish laws, opposed change, and were hostile to modern education. But a growing minority of Jews envied the freedoms of Western European Jews and hoped that they too could become citizens of the modern world. They considered traditional Jews, particularly the Hasidim, narrow-minded and backward. These *maskilim* ("enlightened people") formed a movement called the Haskalah, or Jewish Enlightenment. Some of them claimed that before Jews could enter the modern world, they needed to restore their pride in themselves as a nation like other nations. They

wanted to revive Hebrew, which had not been spoken as an everyday language since ancient times, as their national language. As Western European Jews had done in the late 18th century, the *maskilim* began writing in Hebrew about religious subjects, and published Hebrew newspapers, novels, and poetry.

The experience of Peretz Smolenskin (1842–85) shows how the Jewish Enlightenment changed some lives. Born in the Pale of Settlement to a very devout Jewish family, Smolenskin attended a yeshiva. But he began reading Russian literature and secular subjects, for which he was punished. He ran away from the yeshiva, and after wandering in the Pale of Settlement for a few years, arrived in Odessa at the age of 20. Odessa was one of the most open and liberal cities in the Russian Empire, a center of the Jewish Enlightenment. There Smolenskin taught Hebrew and launched a literary career.

Five years later he moved to Vienna, Austria, where he edited a Hebrew monthly newspaper called *Hashahar* (Dawn). He also wrote articles and books, chiefly for his fellow Russian *maskilim*. Smolenskin believed in a modern Jewish identity, one based not only on religious observance: "If many begin to disobey the laws of religion, how is the sense of Jewish unity to be

Waves of mob violence against the Jews, called pogroms, devastated many Russian Jewish communities in cities and shtetls. Many Jews were killed and lost their homes. This painting shows refugees in the aftermath of a pogrom.

maintained?" he asked. *"Yes, we are a people. We have been a people from our beginnings until today. We have never ceased being a people, even after our kingdom was destroyed and we were exiled from our land, and whatever may yet come over us will not eradicate our national character.... We are a spiritual nation—this is the correct doctrine which we must proclaim."*

In the 1880s the growing sense that Jews needed a national identity became linked to a new idea: Zionism, or the quest for a national homeland in Palestine. Jews had moved to Palestine throughout the ages. Their purpose was religious—to see and live in the biblical land. But by 1880 some Jews had a different idea. They thought about going to Palestine not for religious purposes but to plant national roots. This idea was quite different from the traditional

belief that Jews would return to the Land of Israel when the messiah came. The Jewish nationalists wanted to take matters into their own hands, not wait for the messiah. But those who spoke of Zion, or Palestine, as the national home of the Jews had only vague notions of what this would mean.

A great surge of Zionism sprang up after pogroms, or waves of anti-Jewish violence, swept through the Russian Empire in 1881. Throughout history there had been many who hated or feared Jews, and Jews often fell victim to violence during times of hardship, distress, or change. The assassination of the Russian czar Alexander II sparked the pogroms of 1881. His death caused great unrest in Russia, and people blamed Jews for their troubles. Rioters killed hundreds of Jews and destroyed or plundered much Jewish property.

In 1882, Leon Pinsker, a Russian Jewish physician, argued passionately for the foundation of a Jewish homeland. According to Pinsker, Jews would always be second-rate citizens anywhere but in their own nation.

Some Russian Jews already believed that Jews should revive their national culture, although few of them thought this revival should take place in Palestine. The pogroms marked the turning point for many of these Jewish nationalists. After such terror and violence, those who had hesitated to embrace the idea of a Jewish homeland began to look away from the Russian Empire, and toward Palestine. Jews had experienced even more destructive violence before. Why did the events of 1881 lead to Zionism when earlier persecutions had not?

Zionism was not simply a reaction to the racist hatred of Jews, or anti-Semitism. It appeared at the same time that other Eastern European peoples, such as the Slavs, were turning to their histories, cultures, and languages to assert their national pride. Rarely did these ethnic groups regard the Jews as members of their nations, and in turn the Jews felt little in common with them. But nationalism was in the air, and as other Eastern Europeans reached toward national identity a growing number of Jews felt that they too should have a land and a nation of their own.

The pogroms inspired a sense of urgency in Jewish nationalists. Peretz Smolenskin, for example, changed his thinking in 1881 and said that Jews should go live in Palestine. He hoped that there, in the ancient land of Israel, they would create a new society where they could work in the full range of professions.

The first person to write a plan supporting this idea was a Russian Jewish physician named Leon Pinsker (1821–91). In 1882 Pinsker published a short book titled *Auto-Emancipation*. Its message might appear tame by today's standards, but it was revolutionary for Russian Jewry at the time. Earlier Pinsker had supported the cause of assimilation, or blending into Russian culture. He had even helped found a Russian-language newspaper for Jews. But in *Auto-Emancipation* he decisively broke with his past goal of emancipation, or the granting of equal legal rights to Russian Jews as had occurred in Western Europe. He felt that non-Jews would never really accept Jews as equals in Russia, where Jews were considered foreigners without a home; wherever they lived, they faced anti-Semitism. Jews needed to develop as a nation in their own homeland, Pinsker said. This was the meaning of "auto-emancipation." Jews did not need to *be freed*—they needed to free themselves.

Pinsker thought that Jews should buy a homeland, although he did not think that it had to be in Israel. He went to the West to bring his ideas to the wealthy notables of Jewish communities. None took him seriously. Most totally rejected the idea. In Russia, however, he became a leader of the Hovevei Zion, whose members were the first Zionist settlers in Palestine. The First Aliyah of 1882-1903 brought some 20,000 to 30,000 Russian and Romanian Jewish settlers to Palestine.

The fact that Palestine was part of the Islamic Ottoman Empire, already inhabited by Arabs and a Jewish minority who were not Zionists, did not deter these determined settlers. They knew little or nothing about the native population of Palestine. Many of them thought that the land was almost empty. The key to success, they felt, was returning to the soil and becoming farmers, like their ancestors. Self-sufficient and communal, they would create a Jewish society based on social justice, without exploiting anybody. Hebrew would be their language. These first Zionist settlers hoped to see a massive wave of Jewish immigration take place, although they had no clear political plan. They pictured themselves as the vanguard for the Jewish population as a whole, establishing a foothold in the land of Israel.

The hopes of some Zionists quickly fell. Ottoman officials held many of them when they arrived at the port of Jaffa, refusing to let them leave their ships. BILU pioneer Chaim Chissin wrote of his arrival in Jaffa Bay:

> Before the ship had come to a stop, it was besieged on all sides by a swarm of small craft, thick as locusts. The boatmen scurried around the deck looking for passengers, but insisted on a *teskere* [permit] from any Jew who wanted to hire them. Ever since the time when Jews were first denied the right to settle in Palestine, they have only been allowed to enter Jaffa with an official *teskere*. Even with this, it is not easy to obtain entry. All boatmen have been strictly forbidden to bring any Jew ashore with the *teskere,* and if they disobey the ordinance, they are fined.

The Ottomans were used to seeing Jewish pilgrims arrive and sometimes spend years in Palestine, but they did not feel that subjects of the Russian Empire had an unlimited right to settle in Ottoman territory. They certainly did not sympathize with the Zionist cause—why would they want to see a Jewish homeland appear in the center of their empire? Settlers who man-

aged to get over the first hurdle and enter Palestine often encountered dozens of obstacles when they tried to buy farmland.

The first Zionist farmers were utterly unprepared for the challenges that awaited them. They had no agricultural experience and little outside support. Their goal of supporting themselves by growing wheat, barley, and vegetables was doomed to failure. They endured many hardships, including utter physical exhaustion and a constant battle with malaria, a disease spread by mosquitoes. Chaim Chissin wrote in his diary in 1883:

> Our harvest is most unsuccessful, and we have no one to blame but ourselves. Whenever the Arabs told us that it was already too late to sow barley, or that the land was unsuited for it, we never hesitated to tell the "barbarians," with considerable self-assurance, "Oh, that doesn't matter. We'll plow deep, we'll turn the soil inside out, we'll harrow it clean, and then you'll see what a crop we'll have!" We provided ourselves with big plows, sunk them deep into the soil, and cruelly whipped our horses which were cruelly exhausted. Our self-confidence had no limits. We looked down on the Arabs, assuming that it was not they who should teach us, but we who would show these "barbarians" what a European could accomplish on this neglected land with the use of perfect tools and rational methods of cultivation. The only trouble was that we ourselves knew about European methods of cultivation only from hearsay, and our agriculturist, too, knew little because each country has its own peculiarities.

Their initial failure forced the Jewish settlers to accept the advice of Arab peasant

farmers, who knew when to plant and how to work the soil. But while some Arabs were willing to lend a hand, most were suspicious and at times openly hostile toward these strangers who had moved into their land. The majority of the Jewish settlers probably believed that they were not encroaching on anyone's land, and felt entitled to a share of the local water, which was often scarce. In addition, they began farming on land that the Arabs used for grazing their livestock. When the Zionists settled on such land, usually after buying it from owners who lived far away, they tried to keep the Arabs off the pastures. This created new trouble. Earlier changes in land ownership had rarely prevented the local Arabs from using the pastures. Although no written law demanded it, the custom was that pastures were the common ground of entire Arab villages. When Arab shepherds brought their flocks to graze on pastures that the Zionists felt they now owned, skirmishes broke out.

The first major clash between Arab peasants and Jewish settlers took place in 1886 at a settlement called Petah Tikvah. Some peasants, angry because the land they lived on had been sold to the Jews, attacked the settlers. They killed one settler and injured several others before Ottoman troops broke up the fight and arrested some of the Arabs. As the number of settlers increased, so did the number of fights. Always at the root of the conflict was control of land and water. Both the Arabs and the Zionists felt their positions were perfectly justified.

Another problem for the settlers was lack of support from the world Jewish community. The Hovevei Zion office in

Odessa had only limited funds with which to support the settlements in Palestine, and the hoped-for mass emigration to Palestine by Jews from around the world did not happen. Most Jews remained unconvinced by Zionism. In Western Europe and the United States in particular, the vast majority of Jews still believed that their futures lay in the countries where they lived. Many had already assimilated into their local cultures. And many Jews of Eastern Europe, where assimilation was more difficult and persecution more constant, found America more appealing than Palestine. Immigrants to America endured many hardships, but great opportunities awaited them in the long run. Only a small percentage of the Jews who left Russia during this period went to Palestine.

Even for Jews who wanted to return to the soil, Palestine was not the only destination. The Baron Maurice de Hirsch, a rich Jewish businessman from France, was also a philanthropist, that is, someone who gives money to good causes. He formed the Jewish Colonization Association and bought large tracts of land in Argentina. About 1,000 Jews settled in the well-supported Hirsch colonies. Russian Jews established "utopian" (a vision of an ideal place) agricultural communities in the United States.

The First Aliyah Zionists who went to Palestine shared some of these other settlers' goals but moved into a much more difficult and hostile environment. For the Zionist venture to succeed, the settlers in Palestine had to face reality and change some of their original plans and ideals. Some found this too hard and returned to Russia.

The image of the tireless, self-sacrificing pioneer of the First Aliyah became the foundation of Zionism in Israel. Reality, however, differed from that image. When many settlements were on the verge of total collapse, another rich philanthropist, Baron Edmond de Rothschild, took them over. Rothschild was a member of the largest Jewish banking family in Europe. Although not a supporter of Zionism, he felt that Jews should morally improve themselves by becoming farmers. To help solve the problem of Jewish poverty, and to aid the struggling Russian Jews in Palestine, Rothschild invested in the settlements to assure their survival.

Rothschild was not the first person to support Jewish settlements in Palestine. A number of Christian movements had founded agricultural settlements to make the soil of Palestine productive. Some of these also encouraged Jewish farmers because they believed that Jews working the

Petah Tikvah, an early Zionist settlement in Palestine, reveals an image of success. Tree-lined streets and simple houses with fenced yards suggest a life of quiet, peaceful domesticity for the Zionist pioneers.

Rothschild in Palestine

In the late 18th and early 19th centuries, the Rothschild family of Frankfurt built the most famous Jewish banking empire in Europe, with branches in London, Paris, Naples, and Vienna. Baron Edmond de Rothschild (1845–1934) was one of four sons of James Jacob Rothschild, who founded the Paris branch.

Baron Edmond de Rothschild became deeply interested in helping the new Zionist settlers in Palestine. Although he never embraced the aims of the Hovevei Zion or encouraged mass immigration, philanthropy for Jewish settlement in Palestine became one of the major preoccupations of his life. It occupied him to such an extent that he often left the major business concerns of the bank to other members of his family. He contributed a huge amount of money to the Yishuv, as the Jewish communities in Palestine were collectively called. In 1882 some Zionist settlers appealed to Rothschild for support. Despite his dislike of Zionism, he felt a moral and religious commitment to the idea of a Jewish presence in Israel.

At first he gave only a modest sum to the settlers of Rishon LeZion, but soon he became the single most important contributor to the settlements and institutions of the Zionist settlements in Palestine, giving them significantly more than the Hovevei Zion societies were able to raise. Rothschild bought great tracts of land, built houses, and gave money to the often-inexperienced settlers. But he did not simply hand out money and then leave the struggling farmers to their own devices. He looked upon the settlements as his personal possessions and often toured the country, carefully observing every detail on the settlements he controlled.

The settlers' dependence on a distant philanthropist caused some friction among them, and they often resented the heavy-handed ways of Rothschild's overseers. They realized, however, that Rothschild's support was vital to the survival of Jewish agricultural settlement in Palestine. The Russian immigrants possessed neither the financial resources nor the technical skills to make the new settlements succeed.

Rothschild attained legendary status even before his death. Jews looked up to him as "The Father of the Settlement." In 1954, 20 years after his death, his bones were brought from Paris to Israel and buried on a hill named Ramat Hanadiv (Hill of the Benefactor), looking down on the coastal plain near Caesaria where many of the settlements he had supported were located. Modern Israel owes its origins as much to Rothschild as to the Zionist settlers.

Baron Edmond de Rothschild was an important benefactor of the Zionist settlers in Palestine. An extremely wealthy banker, Rothschild bought land, built houses, and donated money to the pioneers.

The Palestinian settlers acknowledged their great debt to Rothschild with this monument located in the town of Petah Tikvah. Without Rothschild's financial support, many of the settlements would have failed.

land would usher in the Second Coming of Christ. Other Jewish philanthropists also sponsored ventures in Palestine. In 1855 Jews had settled on land outside the walls of Jerusalem—land bought by Sir Moses Montefiore, the leader of the Jewish community in England. Their neighborhood, Mishkenot Sha'anim ("tranquil dwellings"), is still marked by a windmill built by the first settlers. In 1870 a French Jewish philanthropic organization called the Alliance Israélite Universelle founded the Mikveh Israel agricultural school near Jaffa, on land purchased from the Ottoman sultan. The Alliance was not a Zionist organization, but it shared the Zionist belief that a return to agriculture would morally improve Jews.

Rothschild, who stepped in to save the Zionist settlements, held the same optimistic idea about Jewish farmers, but had little patience with the inexperienced settlers' ideal of self-sufficiency. He was especially impatient with the BILU's experiments in communal living. Many of the original Hovevei Zion settlers who stayed in Palestine ended up as workers on Rothschild's settlements, earning wages rather than living on the fruits of their own labor.

Rothschild created a centralized administration of agricultural experts, engineers, and other technical staff to control the colonies. Some of these experts came from the Mikveh Israel school, but many more were Christians with experience in French colonial possessions such as Algeria. Rothschild turned to cash crops to make greater profits. Most important were the vineyards he planted, which launched modern Israel's tradition of winemaking. In the long run, however, oranges proved to be a more profitable cash crop. Rothschild also ordered about 250,000 eucalyptus trees to be planted to drain the swamps where mosquitoes bred, thus reducing malaria.

The settlements in Palestine survived thanks to Rothschild's centrally organized, wage-paying plantation system. Even the plantations were not entirely Jewish, however. Because Jewish workers were in short supply, plantation managers also hired Arab workers. Rothschild had hoped to create economically independent Jewish farmers, but by the end of the century the settlements still needed a great deal of support from abroad. For the struggling Jewish rural settlers, Rothschild, known simply as "the Baron," was the grand patron, taking care of all their needs. In 1890 the wife of a Russian settler wrote to her sister-in-law in the Russian Empire:

> We live here in the shadow of the Baron, who feels the pain of his sons, may God be merciful on him, and we know no want. If a woman bears twins, then the Baron provides 4 SR a month for hiring a second wet-nurse and will also send her a second bed— but I pray that God will save me from this excessive blessing. Indeed, I don't have enough time to write of all the good and merciful deeds done by the Baron for us. May God reward him and his administrators as they have rewarded us.

Despite harsh conditions, the Jewish population in Palestine was increasing, not only in the rural settlements but also in the cities. Although Zionism emphasized the pioneering ideal of rural agriculture, Israel was to become a mainly urban society. Some Zionists who arrived in Palestine headed directly to the cities; others went to the cities after failing to make ends meet on the rural settlements. A number of famous and influential Zionists settled in Palestine's cities during the First Aliyah. One of them was Eliezer Ben Yehuda (1857–1922), a Lithuanian Jew who moved to Jerusalem in 1881. His life's work was to revive spoken Hebrew as the national language of the Jews. He compiled the first modern dictionary of the Hebrew language.

The growth of the Jewish population in Palestine was not exactly the same thing as Zionism. Many Jewish settlers were not Zionists, and some were even hostile to Zionist ideas. Throughout the 19th century, Jews came to Palestine from many places for many reasons. Especially important were Jews from North Africa, who formed a community called the *ma'arivim* ("westerners," because they came from the western part of the Islamic world). Non-Zionist Jews from Eastern Europe—both Hasidim and their religious opponents—also settled in Jerusalem, sometimes to escape persecution. This trend increased during the 1870s. In 1874 non-Zionist traditional Jews established Me'ah She'arim, a neighborhood in Jerusalem outside the walls of the Old City. Yemenite Jews, escaping famine and oppression in the southern part of the Arabian Peninsula, began settling in Palestine in the 1880s. Moving to Palestine was relatively easy for them because they were Ottoman subjects. The various Jewish communities in Palestine received support from the *halukah,* charitable donations made by Jews in other nations.

The zealous Zionists of the First Aliyah who chose to "return to the soil" regarded the non-Zionist Jews of the older towns with contempt, as parasites living off the *halukah*. Chaim Chissin's diary reflects the Zionist sense of separateness from the Jews of Jerusalem: "In striving to bring culture to this uncivilized country, we fail to understand that we must also take into consideration the views of the people for whose sake we are doing the work. We need not accept their view unquestioningly, but we must make some concessions to them. We have nothing to do with Jerusalem, with the strange mode of life of its inhabitants nor with the light and shadow aspects of their lives."

When Israelis look back at the early history of Zionism, they take pride in the struggle of the pioneers on the first rural settlements of the First Aliyah. With tremendous sacrifice and hardship, these early settlers greatly affected the future of Zionism. At the same time, these hardworking and committed pioneers had little long-term political vision of how to achieve their goals. If the purpose of some was to create a Jewish homeland based on the ideal of returning to the soil, there were few signs in the 1880s and 1890s that they would succeed. Their goal, in any event, was not shared by the hand that fed them: the Baron.

If Zionism were to succeed, it would have to be supported by Jewish communities in the West. It also needed some backing from Western governments. Without strong international support, how could the Jews establish a homeland in a territory that was occupied and controlled by a government hostile to their interests?

In 1874 non-Zionist traditional Jews established Me'ah She'arim, this neighborhood in Jerusalem outside the walls of the Old City.

The 1880s saw much territorial expansion by the Western European powers, especially Great Britain and France, who built global empires. Europeans conquered and divided up much of Africa against the Africans' wishes. In the 1880s, two parts of the Ottoman Empire came under foreign control: France occupied Tunisia in 1881, and the British occupation of Egypt began the following year. France and Britain called these territories protectorates. In theory they were not colonies. Rather, the foreign government was there to help the natives along the path of reform. In reality, however, foreign military occupation had little to do with helping the native inhabitants. The "scramble for Africa" in the late 19th century had more to do with the power politics of Europe. Each nation tried to outdo the others in gaining new territories,

fearful of the others' intentions. Economic interests also led the Europeans to take control of territory so that they could better exploit its natural resources.

Most of the Middle East, including Palestine, remained under Ottoman control until the First World War (1914–18). But foreign governments interfered in Ottoman affairs in many ways. One major challenge for the Ottoman administration was the growing number of foreigners living in Palestine, including the Zionist settlers. "When a European comes here," wrote Chaim Chissin, "he ignores the local administration and recognizes only his own consul who defends him on every occasion. The government, bound by its agreements, can do nothing with the Europeans, and so they get away, unpunished, with all sorts of tricks. Foreigners enjoy more rights here than the native population."

The Ottoman Empire also had dire economic woes. Unable to pay the rising costs of government and the military, the empire went bankrupt. Western European banks loaned the Ottomans large sums of money, and an association of European powers took control of the Ottoman debt.

Zionism was born during this age of European imperialism, or empire building. Eastern Europe gave Zionism the majority of its settlers, but the Zionists had to look to Western Europe to achieve their political aims. The Ottomans would block Zionist hopes of establishing a sovereign Jewish state in Palestine—but perhaps, through the influence of the Western European powers, the Jews could obtain Palestine for themselves. Still, the Zionists were working against tremendous odds. They would need outstanding leaders to succeed.

Chapter 4

Theodor Herzl and the Zionist Movement

Theodor Herzl looks over the Rhine River in Basel, Switzerland during the Sixth Zionist Congress in 1903. He died the following year. Herzl argued that Jews could be considered equal to other people only if they had their own state.

Zionism reached a new level of recognition in the world through the leadership and determination of one man: Theodor Herzl (1860–1904). His goal was nothing less than the establishment of a state. Herzl understood that this goal could be achieved only through political means and with the support of the Western imperialist powers. His extraordinary effort, his skill in communicating with the public, and his vision of the future made Zionism into a movement that could eventually win statehood.

At first glance, Herzl seems an unlikely candidate for the savior of Zionism. He came from an assimilated Hungarian Jewish family in Vienna that knew little about traditional Judaism. At a young age he had a very successful career as a journalist and playwright, writing in German. He was also an articulate and captivating speaker.

In the 1890s Herzl was working in France as a foreign correspondent for a Viennese newspaper. He witnessed the 1894 trial of Alfred Dreyfus, a Jewish artillery captain accused of selling military secrets to the Germans. Dreyfus was convicted and sentenced to life imprisonment on Devil's Island.

Many people proclaimed his innocence and charged his accusers with anti-Semitism. The "Dreyfus Affair" divided France between Dreyfus's supporters and those who thought him guilty, and Jews around the world took a passionate interest in the case. France freed Dreyfus in 1899 and later declared that he had not committed the crime for which he had been convicted. But for some Jews in France and elsewhere, that Dreyfus had been falsely accused was proof that anti-Semitism remained strong even in countries where Jews had begun to feel at home.

For centuries the Jews of Western Europe had suffered persecution. Often they had to live in certain neighborhoods, called ghettos. Cities and even countries frequently expelled their entire Jewish populations. Monarchs, princes, and nobles might grant Jews the right to live in their domains for a limited period of time—if they thought the Jews would be useful. Because of the many restrictions on the occupations Jews could follow, they were heavily concentrated in the few professions open to them: commerce, money-lending, peddling, and jewelry-making. Some of these professions, such as money-lending, were condemned by the Roman Catholic Church and despised by Christians. Jewish farming had disappeared long ago, and Jews could not own land in most countries.

As in Eastern Europe, Jews lived according to their traditional law *(halakhah)* in self-governing communities. They settled disputes and conducted business among themselves through their own institutions, such as rabbinical courts made up of rabbinical judges *(dayyanim).*

Jewish communities changed dramatically after the French Revolution of 1789. The revolution created a new type of European nation, one in which all people were citizens with equal rights and responsibilities. After much debate by the revolutionaries over whether to include Jews in their brave new world, in 1791 Jews in France received full rights. French armies under Napoleon Bonaparte spread revolutionary principles throughout Europe, emancipating the Jews of other nations. Ghetto walls crumbled when French armies arrived in Italy. French forces occupied various German states and granted Jews civil rights there. Some of these rights disappeared when Napoleon's empire came to an end, but there was no complete return to the ghetto days of the past. Although the pace of emancipation varied from country to country, by Herzl's time Jews had legal rights as citizens throughout Western Europe.

Emancipation had far-reaching effects. One was a weakening of the ties that held Jewish communities together. Although the community still exercised some control over religious matters, Jews were now free to make a choice: they could belong to the community, or they could separate themselves from Jewish life and Judaism. Emancipation forced Jews to examine the nature of their communities and of Judaism itself. Was it possible to remain Jewish and still participate in the life of the wider society? And if one remained Jewish, how could Judaism be made acceptable to gentile, or non-Jewish, society? These were burning questions for the Jewish communities of Western Europe in the 19th century.

Gentiles who opposed emancipation argued that Jews could never become true and loyal citizens because they had their own laws. They asked: If Jews consider themselves in exile—waiting for the messiah to come and return them to the Holy Land—how can they ever be loyal to the countries where they now live? Some people also felt that Jews could never blend into mainstream society because they were morally corrupt, with a natural tendency toward occupations related to money. The Jews, people said, were swindlers and cheats, and their religion taught them that it was acceptable to swindle gentiles. The opponents of emancipation demanded to know how Jews, prone to such evil practices, could ever qualify for citizenship.

As a result, gaining legal rights was only the first step for the Jews. They also had to prove themselves *worthy* of citizenship. Many of them believed that they had to create a new form of Judaism that would be more acceptable in the modern world. The ancient laws that separated Jews from gentiles—such as keeping kosher (following Jewish dietary rules) or praying entirely in the Hebrew language—would have to go.

These ideas gave rise to the Reform movement in Judaism. Members of this movement began to call their synagogues temples. They declared that for them Judaism would be only a religious faith, much like other religions, and not an entire, separate way of life. They would now think of themselves as French, German, American, and English people who were also "Israelites," or "of the Hebrew persuasion."

Not all Jews embraced the Reform movement. But even those who continued to follow traditional religious law had to rethink what it meant to be Jewish and, at the same time, citizens of the countries where they lived. For one thing, the power of the rabbinical leaders would never be the same. Jews were now subject to all the laws of the state and could no longer govern themselves within their communities. Even Jews who strictly observed traditional Jewish law—the Orthodox, as they came to be known—looked for ways to show their loyalty as citizens of their nations.

By Herzl's time, Jews in Western Europe had gone a long way toward integration. Intermarriage between Jews and gentiles was on the rise. So was conversion to Christianity. Most Jews were assimilated into the cultures of Western Europe, and many felt comfortable in non-Jewish company. They spoke the same languages as other citizens and served in their nations' armies. They joined the prospering middle classes, entering such professions as medicine, law, journalism, and business. Many Jews felt that they had gained some acceptance in society and could look back with satisfaction at their achievements.

Alfred Dreyfus, a French Jewish artillery captain, was found guilty of selling military secrets to the Germans in 1894. He was later found innocent. Many Jews at the time believed that Dreyfus's case proved that prejudice against Jews remained strong in France.

Some uneasiness must have lingered at the backs of their minds, however, for although Jews had achieved a large measure of integration, prejudice against them lay not far beneath the surface. A new type of anti-Jewish movement appeared. Modern anti-Semitism descended from all the hateful myths and attitudes about Jews that had developed during the Middle Ages. But it had a new and dangerous twist: racism. Racism is a way of thinking that classifies people according to their race. The simple recognition that different races exist is not by itself racist. The racists who emerged against the Jews, however, went further. They believed that each race had its own *inborn* characteristics and that some races were therefore superior to others. To racists, Jews had bad characteristics and were inferior.

This preposterous theory—which claimed to be scientific—presented a new danger for Jews trying to assimilate into wider society. And for gentiles who accepted it, there was no chance of true equality for Jews. Even Jews who were assimilated and had abandoned their religious practices could never escape their negative racial heritage. According to racists, not even by converting to Christianity could the Jews change their basic racial characteristics.

Closely linked to racist theory was the rise of anti-Semitism as a political movement in the 1880s. It appealed to people fearful of the many changes taking place in Europe. Anti-Semites felt that Jews, whom many people still disliked, were at the forefront of social and economic change in Western Europe. Because many Jews were highly successful in a competitive world, they became scapegoats for other people's discontent. Anti-Semites claimed that Jews secretly ran businesses and governments and were planning to control the world. The anti-Semites published books and newspapers and elected representatives to European parliaments. A French anti-Semitic trade union movement blamed Jews for all of society's economic woes. This was the political climate that gave rise to the Dreyfus Affair.

The journalist Theodor Herzl witnessed the Dreyfus Affair and must have been deeply moved by what he saw. He wrote in 1899 that the Dreyfus Affair—which symbolized the failure of emancipation and

Ahad Ha-Am: "One of the People"

Although he did not play a large role in Zionism's political development, Ahad Ha-Am (1856–1927) was the movement's conscience and one of its most influential thinkers. He was born Asher Zvi Ginsberg in the Russian Ukraine to a strictly Orthodox family who educated him in the Talmud and the Hasidic traditions.

Under the pen name Ahad Ha-Am, "one of the people," Ginsberg published his first article, "This Is Not the Way," in the Hebrew journal *Ha-Melitz* when he was 33. The article warned that major settlement in Palestine was not feasible. What was needed was the revival of a national culture, which could only come about gradually.

Many Zionists criticized his cautious approach to settlement in Palestine, but his followers founded an elite society, B'nai Moshe (Children of Moses), to give voice to the cultural ideals of Jewish national revival. Ahad Ha-Am went to the First Zionist Congress. It was the only one he attended. He scornfully wrote: "[T]he deliverance of Israel will come at the hands of 'prophets,' not at the hands of 'diplomats.'" He believed that what Herzl envisaged was a "state of Jews" rather than a "Jewish state." By this Ahad Ha-Am meant that Herzl's state would be a political entity without any uniquely Jewish spiritual or cultural content. Although Ahad Ha-Am's thinking hardly shaped

the course of events the way Herzl's did, his ideas looked ahead to problems that Zionism had to face. He realized that most Jews would not go to Palestine. Settlement in Palestine could not therefore solve the problem of the Jewish masses in Europe. A spiritual revival was needed first. The settlement in Palestine would serve as the national spiritual center.

Ahad Ha-Am was the first person to state clearly that the Palestinian Arabs would not just disappear and that future conflict was likely. He criticized the Zionists' unsympathetic attitude toward the Arabs and feared that the settlers would exploit the Arab peasants. In short, he foresaw many of the

problems that Israel is dealing with today.

Ahad Ha-Am edited the Hebrew monthly *Ha-Shiloah,* but grew discouraged by his dependence on the Jewish national movement. In 1902 he took a job with a tea company, which later transferred him to London. In 1921 Ahad Ha-Am settled in Palestine—in Tel Aviv, which was rapidly becoming the Zionists' main cultural center. It was the first Hebrew-speaking city run by Jews since antiquity, and Ahad Ha-Am was a leading figure there. Town leaders often sought his advice. Still, he felt that he was not contributing enough to public life. His last years in Tel Aviv were unhappy, and he often

Asher Zvi Ginsberg, known by his pen name Ahad Ha-Am, was a major Zionist thinker who believed in the need for the revival of a national culture for the Jews before anything else.

longed for the life he had lived in London. When Ahad Ha-Am died in 1927, however, thousands of Jews attended the funeral of this revered Zionist thinker.

---

assimilation—had made him a Zionist. But in 1896, when Herzl brought his case for Zionism to the public, the Dreyfus case had not yet become a major public affair. His diaries of the period do not mention Dreyfus as an influence in his conversion to Zionism, but they do describe "the emptiness and futility of trying to 'combat' anti-Semitism."

Herzl probably became a Zionist not because of any single event but through a gradual process of realization. By 1895 he had firmly resolved that nothing short of the establishment of a Jewish state would ever resolve the "Jewish question." But he knew that Jews needed a plan of action to make this happen. In 1896 Herzl published his plan in a short book, not much longer than a pamphlet, called *Der Judenstat* (The Jewish State).

The book begins with the claim that modern anti-Semitism had little to do with the hatred of Jews during medieval times. Rather it was the result of emancipation. Herzl believed that Jews had developed as a bourgeoisie (a money-making middle class) in their ghettos before economic and social changes pushed gentile society in the same direction. Once the Jews were free of the ghettos they had a head start in economic competition with others, and their economic success aroused envy and dislike. Assimilation had failed. Everywhere Jews were regarded as strangers. Jews could escape this trap and exist on equal footing with others only if they had their own state.

Der Judenstat offered concrete plans for establishing this state, for the emigration of Jews to it, and for the type of government

they ought to establish. Palestine was Herzl's first choice for the location of the Jewish state, but he also considered Argentina. He optimistically believed that the governments of nations where anti-Semitism existed would be eager to solve the "Jewish problem" by supporting his plan.

Herzl realized that it would take money for Zionism to reach its goal. He turned to the major Jewish bankers, philanthropists, and notables: Maurice de Hirsch and Edmond de Rothschild in France and Sir Samuel Montagu, Claude Montefiore, and Frederic Mocatta in England. But he failed to gain their support. Some of them were downright hostile. They did not want to help a movement that claimed that Jews had no future in the nations where they lived. Many Jewish leaders felt that despite anti-Semitism Jews should not give up their

DER

JUDENSTAAT.

VERSUCH

EINER

MODERNEN LÖSUNG DER JUDENFRAGE

VON

THEODOR HERZL

DOCTOR DER RECHTE.

❦

LEIPZIG und WIEN 1896.
M. BREITENSTEIN'S VERLAGS-BUCHHANDLUNG
WIEN, IX., WÄHRINGERSTRASSE 5.

hard-won rights as citizens. Baron Rothschild feared that support for a Jewish state would give anti-Semites ammunition to use against Jews—and this would interfere with the work he was already doing in Palestine.

Although Herzl was frustrated by his failed meetings with Jewish notables, he did not give up. He was a skillful journalist and publicist who knew how to press his ideas and bring them to the world's attention. Herzl's thick black beard and handsome, dignified, and manly looks made a great impression on almost everyone who met him or heard him speak. So powerful was his charisma that when he went to Eastern Europe people greeted him with cries that the messiah had come.

Lacking the help of Jewish notables, Herzl decided to turn Zionism into a mass movement. His efforts led to the First Zionist Congress, which met in Basel, Switzerland, in 1897. Writing about the congress, Herzl boasted: "If I were to sum up the Congress in a word—which I shall take care not to publish—it would be this: At Basel I founded the Jewish State."

Delegates came to the congress from all over Eastern and Western Europe. Herzl planned the meeting meticulously, even ordering all delegates to wear white-tie formal attire to the opening session. Formal dress would not only make an impression on the outside world, it would give the delegates a sense of the importance of what they were doing. He also set the length of each speech in advance.

The congress was alive with excitement. Delegates delivered impassioned speeches. Especially riveting was one of Herzl's close

associates, a physician named Max Nordau who was already known throughout Europe for his critical writings on society. Nordau expanded some of the main arguments of Herzl's *Der Judenstat*. The nations of Europe had emancipated the Jews, he explained, because of 18th-century ideas about the rights of individuals, not because they believed that the Jews had been wronged. Many people still felt strongly against Jews, and emancipation could never work because of such racism. Zionism was the answer. It would help restore Jewish communal identity, the authentic Jewish

Theodor Herzl (center) opens the First Zionist Congress in Basel, Switzerland, in 1897. In order to impress the outside world, Herzl ordered all delegates to wear formal attire.

Kaiser Wilhelm II (center, with sash across chest) rides in a spectacular parade through Jerusalem in 1898. Theodor Herzl met briefly with the kaiser in hopes of winning his support for the Zionist cause.

life and inner harmony that had existed in the ghettos.

This historic meeting, the first in a series, set the basic goals of the Zionist movement and its guiding principles. The movement's primary goal was to establish a Jewish national homeland in Palestine through colonization by Jewish workers. In order to unite all Jews and strengthen national consciousness, the congress formed political institutions, acting much like a national assembly. It founded the Zionist Organization, later called the World Zionist Organization, with Herzl as president. The Zionist Organization launched a membership campaign that asked all Zionists to pay a small fee. The drive was called the shekel campaign after the currency of ancient Israel. In 1900 the Fourth Zionist Congress founded the Jewish National Fund to buy land and encourage settlement in Palestine.

As early as the First Congress, Zionists knew that they could not do it alone. They needed help from the governments of Western Europe. Now that Zionism was clearly visible on the European political landscape, Herzl turned his efforts to winning support from a number of political leaders. The European countries were building vast overseas empires, and part of Herzl's plan was to use the growth of European power in the Middle East to the advantage of Zionism.

Some of Herzl's diplomatic overtures were far-fetched and daring. Before the First Zionist Congress he traveled to the Ottoman capital of Istanbul (still called Constantinople in Europe). Herzl was unable to meet with Sultan Abdulhamid II, but he did send him a proposal. Through officials connected with the court, he related that Jews would take on the Ottoman debt in exchange for territory in Palestine. At this time the Ottoman Empire owed an enormous sum to the nations of Europe. Had the sultan accepted Herzl's offer, Herzl would almost certainly have been unable to follow through. It was perhaps fortunate that the sultan turned him down. But the sultan did ask Herzl to use his skills as a journalist to improve the image of Turkey, the home country of the Ottoman Empire. The European press had been criticizing Turkey for the harsh treatment of its Armenian minority. The sultan also requested a loan of 2 million British pounds in exchange for his goodwill. Herzl left Istanbul without any commitment from the sultan to help the Zionist cause. Still, he was not totally disappointed. Simply meeting with Ottoman officials had been quite an achievement.

Herzl was not easily defeated. He expected that the European powers would soon be dividing up the weak Ottoman Empire among themselves, so he began negotiating with the Germans. Germany was a latecomer among the European empire builders. For a long time it had been divided into many small states, which became a unified nation only in 1871. Now the ambitious and bombastic German ruler, Kaiser Wilhelm II, wanted to make Germany a major world power that could compete with the other European powers in the Middle East. Throughout the 1890s Germany developed many connections with Turkey.

Even before the Basel congress, Herzl had hoped to meet the kaiser. "If I understand him right," he wrote, "I'll win him to our cause, that is, if I succeed in reaching him." Herzl believed that the key to understanding the kaiser's personality and his militaristic tendencies was the psychological impact of the kaiser's deformed and unusable left hand, which he always tried to hide from view:

> This abnormality is important for a portrait of him. To me, it brings him nearer as a human being. It indicates that under his many regimental uniforms he is a helpless creature. When I saw the spectacle of the man's power, the brilliance of his court, the warlike magnificence of his legions on parade, I kept my mind on his crippled arm, in order not to be overawed should I ever speak with him face to face.

Herzl's opportunity to meet Wilhelm II came in 1898. Amidst much publicity, the kaiser visited the Holy Land to demonstrate German power in the Middle East. Herzl met with the kaiser in Istanbul. He reported in his diary: "The Kaiser said . . . 'Tell me in a word what I am to ask the Sultan.' 'A Chartered Company—under German protection.' 'Good, a Chartered Company,' and he gave me his hand, which is powerful enough for two, squeezed mine vigorously, and strode out ahead through the center door."

Herzl set out for Palestine with the intention of meeting again with Wilhelm. This was Herzl's first visit to Palestine, and much of what he saw he did not like. About "much praised Rishon LeZion," he wrote, "For a poor village it is fairly well-off. But if anyone has imagined it as much more than a poor little settlement, he is doomed to disappointment. Thick dust on the roads, scant verdure." Then, arriving in Jerusalem after dark, he was greatly impressed: "In spite of my weariness, Jerusalem and its grand moonlit contours made a deep impression on me. The silhouette of the fortress of Zion, the citadel of David— magnificent!" But his initial excitement soon soured: "When I remember thee in days to come, O Jerusalem, it will not be with delight. The musty deposits of two thousand years of inhumanity, intolerance, and foulness lie in your reeking alleys." Even the Wailing Wall, the remaining Western Wall of the Temple sacred to the Jews, disgusted him: "Any deep emotion is rendered impossible by the hideous, scrambling beggary that pervaded the place." Not totally despairing, Herzl wrote, "I am firmly convinced that a splendid New Jerusalem can be built outside the old city walls. The old Jerusalem would still remain Lourdes and Mecca and Yerushalayim. A very lovely beautiful town could arise at its side."

Herzl, at the head of a Zionist delegation, finally succeeded in meeting formally with Wilhelm in the imperial tent: "The Kaiser awaited us there, in gray colonial uniform, veiled helmet on his head, brown gloves, and holding—oddly enough—a riding crop in his right hand." Nothing came of the meeting, and no mention was made of the chartered company that Herzl had proposed in Istanbul. The Germans knew well that the Ottomans were hostile to Zionism, and Wilhelm, it appeared, had no intention of doing anything to threaten Germany's close relations with Turkey.

Having failed to influence the Ottomans through the Germans, Herzl again resorted to direct negotiations with Sultan Abdulhamid. In 1901 he won an audience with the sultan, although he had to promise

Future Supreme Court justice Louis Brandeis was a leader of the American Jewish community and a passionate Zionist. He believed that Jews could be Zionists and still be patriotic to the United States.

in advance not to discuss Zionism. What, then, did the two men discuss for more than two hours? Herzl repeated his earlier message that the Jews could be of great service to the sultan. He hoped that a time would come when the sultan would offer something in return that would be friendly to the Jews. Herzl never saw the sultan again, although he had some correspondence with the Ottoman government. Again, he had failed to achieve any concrete results.

While Herzl's diplomatic ventures were unrealistic and unsuccessful, they did have great public significance. They drew the world's attention to the Zionist movement and showed Jews playing a role in the arena of international politics for a Jewish cause.

Not all Zionists agreed with Herzl's focus on politics and diplomacy. This was especially true among Eastern European Zionists. Western Zionists, many of whom were already assimilated into wider society, were primarily concerned with anti-Semitism. But Eastern European Zionists generally were much more closely tied to traditional Jewish culture. Some feared that Herzl's vision of a Jewish state meant that there would be no great Jewish cultural revival. Herzl envisioned a liberal, open Jewish state, based on the same kind of political principles as those of Western nations. Its citizens would speak many languages. But the Eastern European Zionists included "culturalists" who wanted a spiritual and moral rebirth of the ancient traditions, including the use of the Hebrew language.

The early 20th century brought a split in Zionism between the "culturalists,"

who wanted to restore the ancient land of Israel and the "territorialists," who believed that their first task was to establish a Jewish homeland, no matter where in the world it might be. The Zionists felt great urgency after a terrible pogrom in 1903 at Kishinev in Bessarabia, part of the Russian Empire. Some 45 Jews died, hundreds were wounded, and many lost property. The police made no attempt to stop the rioting or to protect the Jews. Western European Jews rallied to support their brethren in Russia.

Herzl sought an immediate solution and began negotiating with the British colonial secretary, Joseph Chamberlain. Herzl pointed out that it would be useful to Great Britain to have Jews as a loyal element of the population in the British colonies. The two men discussed the possibility of granting the Zionists territory in a number of regions under British control. Chamberlain proposed Uganda in East Africa. At first Herzl rejected this suggestion, but eventually they settled on British East Africa; in fact, the proposed territory was part of the modern nation of Kenya, though it was referred to as Uganda. The British agreed to consider making this territory a Jewish homeland. Herzl told the Zionists that Uganda would be a stepping stone toward the eventual establishment of a Jewish national homeland in Palestine. Most important for Herzl, the Uganda venture would strengthen the relationship between Zionism and the European powers. Herzl believed that the chance to win support from the British, who ruled the largest worldwide empire at the time, was an opportunity the Zionists could not refuse.

Herzl put the British proposal before the Sixth Zionist Congress in 1903—and it practically tore the Zionist movement apart. The congress narrowly voted to send a commission to East Africa, but the commission would have no power to commit the Zionist movement to that territory. The vote led to a major split. Many Zionists adamantly opposed the idea of settlement in Uganda. Some broke down in tears; others stormed out of the meeting. The British withdrew their offer. From that time the Zionists rejected any idea of territory outside Palestine.

Herzl died at age 44, not long after the Uganda controversy. The intense quarrel over Uganda may have weakened his already poor health. Although he died at a time when Zionists were deeply divided, it was largely his energy, his theatrical sense of how to promote the movement, and his captivating speaking ability that had fused the different tendencies of Zionism into a single movement with goals that were now known by both Jews and non-Jews.

At the time of Herzl's death, Zionists were only a small part of the world's Jewish population, but the movement was growing in both Eastern and Western Europe. Even in the United States, where so many Russian Jews had moved to escape persecution, Zionism was gaining acceptance. Louis Brandeis, a leader of the American Jewish community and a future Supreme Court justice, believed that Jews could be Zionists and still be patriotic to the United States, an idea that most American Jews eventually accepted. "Indeed," Brandeis said, "loyalty to America demands rather that each Ameri-

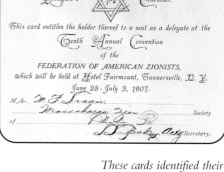

These cards identified their holders as delegates to the Convention of the Federation of American Zionists. Although the movement's goal was a Jewish national homeland, most American Zionists believed that they could remain at home and be loyal to both a Jewish state and the United States.

can Jew become a Zionist. For only through the ennobling effect of its strivings can we develop the best that is in us and give to this country the full benefit of our great inheritance."

Herzl had envisioned a Zionist organization similar to European liberal democracies, with different political parties. And by the early 20th century the movement included three main groups. The first group consisted of General Zionists, who were mainly middle class and liberal, and so closest to Herzl's own background and ideas. The second group consisted of Orthodox Zionists. Most Orthodox Jews opposed Zionism because they considered it a nonreligious movement that went against the traditional belief that Jews would return to Zion only when the messiah came, but some were willing to cooperate with the nonreligious Zionists to secure a national homeland. Their vision of the Jewish state, however, differed from that of the secular or nonreligious Zionists: It would be a state based on the Torah. The third group, the Socialist Zionists, became dominant in Eastern Europe and in Palestine. They had the strongest influence on Jewish settlement in Palestine. The Second Aliyah, which began in 1904, is largely their story.

Chapter 5

Jewish Pioneers and Arab Peasants

In 1890 a woman in the Zionist settlement of Zikhron Yaakov in Palestine wrote a letter about her daily life:

Every day I bring home a basket of eggs laid by my own hens; in the morning we drink good, fat milk from my cows; we have chicken every day for our noon meal, while [in Russia] we would only have such luxuries on holidays. For supper, we drink tea and eat bread with delicious butter. We have never been as quiet and tranquil, without worries, as we are today, and I have never imagined a life which is better than the life we have today. The air is clean and healthy. Everyone out walking passes by our house, all of the things brought into the *moshava* for sale pass by our house, so I buy everything cheaply without having to weary my feet going to the market to buy what I need. I've already learned to speak Arabic quickly, because everything is brought to my home and all of the sellers are Arabs.

Despite many hardships, life had improved for the pioneers of the First Aliyah. The land was more productive, people had more to eat, and many of the settlers were there to stay. The letter describes peaceful relations between Arabs and Jews, with no hint of the conflict that was soon to erupt.

Beneath these peaceful day-to-day relations lay the roots of future trouble. Skirmishes still occurred, although not often enough to alarm most people. More vexing to the Jewish settlers was the Ottoman government's opposition to increased Jewish settlement. The Zionists got around obstacles and bureaucratic red tape by bribing Ottoman officials and buying land from absentee landlords. The Jews' land holdings in Palestine were growing systematically. The Zionist purchases, however, threatened to drive the *fellahin,* or Arab peasants, off the land on which they had lived and grazed their flocks for generations. The peasants began to attack the settlements in a desperate struggle to keep their land and homes.

At first these clashes seemed to be isolated incidents, not part of a larger political struggle. Before long, however, Arabs began to view them differently. Muhammad Rashid Rida, a Syrian Arab and one of the leading Muslim intellectuals of his day, was one of the first to raise an alarm about the dispossession of the Arab population. He wrote in an Arabic

First Aliyah pioneers, photographed in 1910, work in the vineyards of Rishon LeZion, one of the first settlements founded with the aid of Baron Edmond de Rothschild. These vineyards launched modern Israel's tradition of winemaking.

Sword dancers, accompanied by drums and flute, perform at this pre–World War I Arab wedding celebration.

Prominent intellectuals began calling for the reform of Islamic government, and even for religious reform. Rida had started by calling for the reform of Islam through a return to the teachings of Muhammad and the first Muslims. He emphasized the importance of Islam's Arab element and hinted that non-Arab Muslims such as the Turks had corrupted the original teachings of Islam. He eventually become a staunch supporter of Arab nationalism.

Among Arab nationalists the general idea of reforming Islam gave way to a more specifically Arab program of Muslim reform. But what exactly was an Arab? A Muslim (which means "one who submits") was easy to define: a follower of Islam. The meaning of "Arab," however, was changing. Today the term "Arab world" refers to all the countries with a majority of Arabic speakers. That concept took shape in the late 19th century.

The notion of the Arab world was not a purely Muslim creation. At the same time that a few Muslims were talking about an Arab Islam, Arabic-speaking Christians and a few Arabic-speaking Jews spoke of a wider, nonreligious Arabic cultural heritage. In the 1870s Christians in Beirut started an Arabic-language literary revival and published Arabic newspapers. They were among the first to emphasize the idea of Arabness and an Arab homeland in secular terms. In 1905 Najib Azuri, a Syrian Christian who was an official of the Ottoman Empire in Jerusalem, published a statement calling for all Arab lands to be withdrawn from the Ottoman Empire. This may have been the first major vision of an Arab nation independent of the Turks.

newspaper in 1898: "Are you happy to see the newspapers of every country reporting that the poor of the weakest peoples [the Jews], whom the governments of all nations are expelling, master so much knowledge and understanding of civilization methods that they are able to possess and colonize your country, and turn its masters into laborers and its wealthy into poor?"

Rida took part in an Arab nationalist movement that started about the same time Zionism began in Europe. Arab nationalism grew out of the Arabs' realization of how easily Europe was taking control of the Middle East. Arab thinkers asked: Why is the Islamic world becoming weaker while Western Europe is growing stronger? What can the Islamic world do to prevent European domination?

These workers harvest grapes for the wine cellars of the Rishon LeZion settlement in the early 1900s.

Christian intellectuals also criticized Sultan Abdulhamid's support of pan-Islamism, the concept of political unity based on Islam.

As stirring as Azuri's ideas were, few people shared the idea of Arab independence. Most still believed that the unity of the Ottoman Empire was Islam's best defense against the European powers. Leading Arab notables in Palestine held high positions in the Ottoman administration, and therefore had a strong interest in the continuation of the empire. There was no Arab nationalist movement in Palestine to oppose Jewish immigration, which soon took a great leap forward.

In Zionist history, the years from 1904 to 1914 are known as the Second Aliyah. Some 35,000 to 40,000 settlers arrived in Palestine during this period. Among them were many who became leaders of the state of Israel after 1948, including Israel's first prime minister, David Ben-Gurion. The Second Aliyah established "labor Zionism" as the dominant ideology in Palestine. Labor Zionists believed in the power of labor, especially agricultural labor, to build a new Jewish nation.

Labor Zionism had an enormous influence on the development of the state of Israel. It gave Zionist leaders principles that directed their activities and the institutions they established. Its goal was nothing less than a revolutionary new society and the emergence of a new kind of Jew in Palestine.

But the reality of Palestine during the Second Aliyah was far from the ideals of the labor leaders. The goal of turning Jews into farmers was influential, but the majority of settlers moved to the cities rather than to the agricultural settlements. What happened in Palestine often had more to do with practical considerations than with revolutionary ideals. Most of the rural lands worked by the Hovevei Zion settlers had come under Baron Rothschild's control in the 1880s, and for years afterward the plantation with wage laborers was the dominant form of agricultural settlement. When a new wave of Russian immigrants arrived in 1890-91, they founded the settlements of Rehovot and Hadera in the central coastal plains and Metulla in the northern Galilee. Most of their funding came from French philanthropists, who also owned the land. In 1900, the Jewish Colonization Association (JCA)—the non-Zionist organization that Baron Hirsch had founded—took over the administration of Rothschild's colonies. Hirsch had died in 1896, but the JCA continued to exist. It wanted to create a productive class of Jewish farmers who could eventually survive without aid. The JCA shifted away from cash crops grown for export to field crops grown for the settlers' use. To cut costs, JCA administrators often hired experienced Arab laborers, who were willing to work for lower wages than were the Jews. Still, the JCA was the biggest employer of Jewish farmworkers in Palestine before the First World War.

By 1914 the JCA owned 54 percent of rural Jewish holdings in Palestine—colonies controlled by JCA administrators. This arrangement did not appeal to the idealistic immigrants of the Second Aliyah. They also opposed the use of Arab laborers, for they believed that only "Hebrew labor" would transform the Jewish settlements into a nation in Palestine.

The ideas of this ideological vanguard of Zionist settlers grew out of developments in the Russian Jewish community. In 1897, the same year that the World Zionist Organization came into existence in Western Europe, Russian Jews founded the Poalei Zion (Workers of Zion) in Minsk. Members of the Poalei Zion were socialists, part of a movement inspired by the German thinker Karl Marx. Socialists wanted the future to bring a fairer society in which employers would not exploit the proletariat, or wage-earning class. Some Jewish socialists sought to improve conditions for workers in Russia. The Poalei Zion turned to Zionism.

These socialist Zionists did not believe that a new, revolutionary society could be based on capitalism, an economic system

In my little group was A. D. Gordon, but I did not know him and had not even heard his name. I only saw an old man who was drawn toward young people, and who labored cheerfully with them, unbowed in body or spirit by his years. And when, on that first day, I felt myself collapsing under the unwonted labor, and under the fierce heat of the Kinereth sun (it was Tamuz then—August) he cheered me and laughed and repeated (how many have heard him say it!): "Look at me, I am an old man, and I don't lose heart. And you are young and you despair on the first day. Look! Let me show you how to carry a basket full of stones without getting tired."

they considered unjust. To socialists, capitalism was a system in which one class, the bourgeoisie, owned everything made by the wage-earning workers. Socialism intended to end this exploitative system and the misery it created. The Poalei Zion believed that Jews in Palestine would ultimately control what Marx had termed the "means of production." This meant that everything produced on farms or in factories would belong collectively to the entire Jewish community.

The socialist Poalei Zion party was established in Jaffa in 1905. That same year another party, Hapoel Hatzair (the Young Worker), appeared in Petah Tikva. It was non-Marxist but shared the ideal of the "conquest of labor." Its inspiration was Aaron David Gordon, a Russian Zionist of the Second Aliyah who became a legend in his own lifetime. Gordon came to Palestine with his family in 1904 at the age of 48. Although not physically strong, he insisted on toiling on the land until his death in 1922. "What we need are zealots of Labor," he wrote in one of his essays. His spiritual devotion to the idea of Jewish labor ("the religion of labor," as he called it) inspired many young followers. Among them was Rebecca Danith, one of the first woman road workers. She wrote:

More than anyone else of his time, Gordon symbolized physical labor as the road to national rebirth. "Only by making Labor, for its own sake, our national ideal shall we be able to cure ourselves of the plague that has affected us for many generations and mend the rent between ourselves and Nature," he wrote in an essay published in 1911.

Both the Poalei Zion and the Hapoel Hatzair envisioned the triumph of labor, although even the Marxist Poalei Zion thought that the Jewish working class would first emerge in settlements developed under capitalism. But a small vanguard of young idealists wanted to bypass the stage of capitalist support and go straight to collective agriculture, in which no one would own private land and all would work together for the common good.

The first collective settlement of the Second Aliyah was founded at a JCA farm at Sejara in 1907. It came about through the efforts of Manya Wilbushewitz Shohat, one of the few women to play an influential political role in the Second Aliyah. The

Manya Shohat: A Revolutionary Zionist Pioneer

Manya Wilbushewitz (1879–1961) was born near the western Russian city of Grodno. Her father was a wealthy estate owner and a highly religious man. But her mother had received a secular, or nonreligious, education and wanted to educate her 10 children the same way. The children all left the estate and became involved in a variety of political causes. At age 15, Manya ran away from home and went to Minsk to work in her brother's factory. There she organized her first political action, a strike in which 500 workers protested against the overly long workday. She became an active socialist and formed an urban collective in Minsk.

Wilbushewitz's political activities got her into a good deal of trouble with the Russian authorities. The secret police jailed and interrogated her. After leaving prison she joined a terrorist group in a failed plot to assassinate the Russian minister who had worked up the masses against the Jews during the horrible Kishinev pogrom of 1903.

In 1904 she traveled for three months as a member of the Group of Vengeance, a terrorist organization that wanted to avenge Jews who had been killed. On one of her missions, she killed a man suspected of being an informer for the secret police. She escaped arrest and left for Palestine in late 1906.

Not long afterward she went to the United States to raise money both for the collectives and for Jewish self-defense in Russia; she found that American Jews were willing to give money to the Jews in Russia, but not to Zionist collectives. But when she returned to Palestine she was as committed as ever to the idea of establishing collectives. "I had one ideal now," she wrote, "the realization of agricultural collectivism." She explained:

During my absence the idea had taken somewhat deeper root in Palestine. In the colonies of Lower Galilee the Jewish workers lived wretched disorganized lives. They were housed in stables. Some of them had already lost all faith in the burning ideal of "the Conquest of Labor"—the upbuilding of the country by the working class. They could not become individualist farmers, planters, exploiters of others; their Socialist principles forbade it. And they could not continue their competition with Arab labor, for no European can subsist on five piastres a day. I, for my part, had never believed in the Conquest of Labor through the adaptation to the Arab standard of life.

Wilbushewitz finally won the support of Poalei Zion and persuaded the JCA to let her establish an agricultural collective at Sejara. All the members would pool their wages to establish a fund that would buy shelter, clothing, and food for all. The collective consisted of 6 women and 12 men. Committed to the goal of equality for women, Wilbushewitz insisted that women be made full members and perform physical labor like the men. The women wore the same clothing as the men, carried arms, and worked in the fields.

A member of Poalei Zion named Yisrael Shohat saw the opportunity to use the collective as a site for training a Jewish self-defense group. At Sejara he and like-minded comrades established the Jewish guard, Hashomer. Shohat and Wilbushewitz married in 1908.

The collective was a financial success, but the JCA, unhappy about having a woman as a leader, decided against continuing it. However, the short-lived collective of Manya Shohat paved the way for the future development of the kibbutz. She lived for much of her life on Kibbutz Kfar Giladi. Her activities included helping to bring illegal Jewish immigrants to Palestine and, after independence, working tirelessly among new immigrants in transit camps. Because she thought that Arab workers would eventually join with Jewish workers in the labor movement, she was one of the few Zionists who actively searched for a way to coexist with the Arabs. After independence she criticized David Ben-Gurion for Israel's continued discriminatory policy toward its Arabs, who lived under martial law.

Manya Shohat, active socialist and political leader, was committed to the ideal of total equality for men and women. Shohat founded the first collective farm at Sejara, the forerunner to the kibbutz.

Since 1901, people have collected donations for the Jewish National Fund in these blue boxes. Established by the Zionist Congress, the fund is active in purchasing and developing land in Israel.

collective lasted only a year and a half, but it pointed the way to the future. It was the forerunner of the collective farm known as the kibbutz.

Settlers who favored collective farming were determined to establish a basis for their future national life. This clearly would not come about through Jewish philanthropists, who opposed the settlers' nationalist goals and firmly believed in privately owned property. Practical considerations also guided settlers toward collective farms. Non-collective farms based on wage labor hired Arabs, in spite of the commitment to Jewish labor, because Arabs were more experienced, worked for lower wages, and already had homes in their villages. Jewish settlers had no homes and few resources, so farm administrators had to house them. For administrators of privately owned farms, it made economic sense to hire Arabs. But for newly arrived settlers, it made sense to pool resources to form communal or collective settlements.

The Jews tried to avoid hiring Arab workers by employing Jews from Yemen, a country in the southern Arabian Peninsula. Hundreds of Yemenite Jews had come to Palestine in the First Aliyah, driven from their homes by economic hardship and drawn to the Holy Land by deep religious ties. Most settled in the cities, especially Jerusalem, where they joined the growing ranks of religious immigrants. When a new group of Yemenites arrived in 1909, the Jews decided that they could replace Arab labor. The idea probably came from Aaron Eisenberg, the general director of the Planters' Society, which at that time was the largest private colonization company em-

ploying wage laborers. Eisenberg believed that the Yemenite Jews were "natural workers" and would be willing to work for the same wages as the Arabs. Furthermore, they would be content with cheap, modest houses and small plots of land in villages near the agricultural settlements, much like the Arabs. A special Zionist emissary, Shmuel Yavnieli, went to Yemen in 1910 to encourage new immigrants.

During the First and Second Aliyahs perhaps a tenth of Yemen's Jewish community immigrated to Palestine—a larger proportion than from any other country. Yemenites became one of the most important elements of the Jewish population. But the effort to use them as unskilled workers to replace Arabs was an abysmal failure. The Yemenites were unhappy about receiving lower wages than European Jews, who looked down on them and compared them to Arabs. In addition, Arabs proved to be more efficient workers than the Yemenites, who suffered high rates of disease and death.

The Zionists encountered many obstacles, but gradually succeeded in increasing their land holdings. Recognizing this, the World Zionist Organization opened an office in Jaffa in 1908 and decided to get involved in colonization. The director of the Jaffa office, Arthur Ruppin, saw the challenge that the Zionists faced. Of Palestine's population of 700,000, only 80,000 were Jews—and they owned only 1.5 percent of the land. Ruppin formed the Palestine Land Development Company to increase Zionist settlement on land purchased by the Jewish National Fund (JNF).

Ruppin's office sponsored a collective settlement (kvutzah) in 1909 at Um Djuni on the Sea of Galilee. Techiah Liberson, a pioneer woman from Russia, wrote about the new settlement:

> With the beginning of the new year the two of us joined the little kvutzah or commune which began to work on its own initiative and responsibility in Um Djuni. And there at last I began to feel that I have become a full-fledged worker. The year's work in Um Djuni ended with a profit, and yet for a variety of reasons the group fell to pieces. A second group came up to the same ground. I was away then, being down for several months with yellow fever. When I recovered I joined the new group—and out of this group grew the present settlement of Deganiah.

Deganiah became the first kibbutz in Palestine. At first it was not totally communal—members still owned private property and received a monthly wage. A few years later, however, more radical kibbutzim totally abolished private property. Much later still, David Ben-Gurion wrote in his memoirs: "One can say without exaggeration that the kibbutzim constitute a social experiment from which peoples everywhere can take inspiration and ideas. And they are the one true example in today's world of a democratic form of socialism, combining the most advanced economic practices with a respect for individuality and the inalienable rights of every human being, that has never been attained elsewhere."

But Ruppin was no socialist. He insisted that "the Kvutzah did not come into existence as a deliberate social experiment." There were practical considerations. The Zionist Organization had nowhere near the amount of funds available to the Rothschild settlements or the JCA. Nor did Ruppin believe that individual settlers had the agricultural training to work independently. Driven by these concerns, the nonsocialist Ruppin found common cause with the socialist Zionist labor movement.

While Zionists were working to add to their land holdings, they were also sowing bitterness among the Arabs. Political events in the Ottoman Empire gave that bitterness a voice. In 1908 a revolution in Turkey toppled Sultan Abdulhamid and brought a group known as the Young Turks to power. Government was in the hands of the Committee of Union and Progress, led by a group of army officers. The revolution brought freedom of speech and an elected parliament. An active Arabic-language press, freed from censorship, began complaining about the Arab peasants' loss of land to the Zionists.

Events at a place called Afula particularly angered the Arabs. In 1910 Elias Sarsuq, a wealthy Christian businessman and landowner from Beirut, Lebanon, sold the fertile agricultural lands of Afula to the JNF. Sarsuq owned much land in Palestine. The Arab peasants who lived and worked on it gave him a tenth of their produce and paid him rent for the use of the land. The peasants were tied to Sarsuq in another way: he often lent them money and charged high rates of interest on the loans. But although they were poor and exploited, the peasants could at least stay on the land and in their villages.

The Jews, however, bought land to occupy and cultivate themselves, and this is

Life on the Kibbutz

The kibbutz, or collective farm, evolved from the early years of the first kibbutz, Deganiah. Most kibbutzim shared a number of characteristics. Almost all property was owned collectively by all the members. Even individuals' clothes were part of the collective property. People turned in their dirty clothes and received different clean ones. Of course, this often meant that they received clothes that did not fit, and so eventually this practice was changed so that people kept their own clothing.

Members of the kibbutz had no need for money. The kibbutz provided their food, housing, and everything else. They did receive small spending allowances so that they could occasionally travel or vacation outside the kibbutz.

Members took turns in most of the jobs. In the earlier years, women and men were likely to spend equal time working in the fields, the most prestigious job. However, as the kibbutzim developed, women became concentrated more in childcare and housekeeping.

Nevertheless, the kibbutz radically transformed family life. In the early years, many kibbutzim discouraged romantic love between couples. Some even tried to do away with private rooms for couples. Marriage and the family did not disappear, as some people had hoped they would, but kibbutzim typically made the upbringing of children part of the collective responsibility. Children

Young members of a kibbutz, or collective farm, work on a cotton field in Upper Galilee.

had separate sleeping quarters and were taken care of by different members of the kibbutz, almost always women. In recent decades, however, many kibbutzim have decided that children should live with their parents.

To many, the kibbutz was the best expression of Zionism. It brought to reality the ideas of the "conquest of labor" and the return of Jews to the soil. Orthodox Jews founded some kibbutzim, but most kibbutzim were nonreligious and some were quite antireligious. Kibbutz members observed the Sabbath as a day of rest but did not celebrate it with religious ceremonies. They recognized other holidays on the Jewish religious calendar—typically Rosh Hashanah, Hanukkah, and Passover—but celebrated them in a way that had little to do with traditional Judaism. Some kibbutzim stripped all religious content from the holidays and instead hon-

ored their national or agricultural aspects. Many kibbutzim observed Passover, for example, as a spring festival and a celebration of freedom, rather than as a spiritual commemoration of the exodus of the Jews from Egypt. Many kibbutzim did not observe Yom Kippur, the Day of Atonement and the holiest day of the Jewish calendar, because they considered it an entirely religious holiday.

At its largest, the kibbutz population made up only about 3 percent of the country's population, and was spread across more than 250 kibbutzim. But the influence of the kibbutz on Jewish national culture in Palestine and on Israel was out of proportion to its size. Members of kibbutzim have been prominent as national leaders. The kibbutzim have attracted the attention of Jews and non-Jews and welcomed volunteers from countries around the world.

what they planned for Afula. Supported by Arthur Ruppin's office, Jewish settlement began immediately. The local district governor, Shukri al-'Asali, refused to cooperate, even though his superiors ordered him to hand over the land to its new Jewish owners. At this point, armed members of a newly formed Jewish defense corps called Hashomer went to occupy the land. Al-'Asali sent troops to drive them away. The Turkish governor in Beirut had to step in to allow the Jewish settlers onto the lands. Clashes continued, and an Arab was killed in May 1911.

This incident was a forerunner of more serious conflicts. The Arabic press published many articles about it—the beginning of an Arab political campaign against Zionism. During this period the Jews increased their defensive activities. Hashomer spread to many of the agricultural colonies, uniting the idea of the conquest of labor with a new fighting spirit. Many members of Hashomer rode horses, carried bullet belts and rifles, and dressed like Arab nomads, or Bedouin, who symbolized freedom and courage. The Jews of Israel later came to consider Hashomer the beginning of their national military tradition.

For the Eastern European Jews of the Second Aliyah, working the land and defending themselves were vitally important aspects of a national rebirth. But most Jews in Palestine lived in the cities and were not farmers. In the late 19th century Jewish neighborhoods sprang up in western Jerusa-

lem. The city's development received a boost from the Jaffa-to-Jerusalem railroad line, which opened in 1892. At the beginning of the 19th century, Jerusalem was a small city with a population under 10,000. Jews made up about a quarter of the population. During the last decades of the 19th century and until the First World War, the population of the city increased. No one knows the precise number of Jews in the city, but by 1914 Jews may well have made up about half of the total population of a city that numbered between 60,000 and 70,000. Immigrants from Yemen and North Africa contributed to some of this growth. Religious immigrants from Eastern Europe also had spiritual attachments that drew them to ancient Jerusalem rather than to the newer settlements. Many of the new arrivals in Palestine were not Zionists, and they preferred to live among the more traditional Jews. But Jews were not solely responsible for Jerusalem's growth; a substantial number of new Christian and Muslim inhabitants had also arrived.

On the eve of the First World War, more than half of Palestine's 85,000 Jews lived in Jerusalem. The Jewish populations of other towns where Jews had historically lived—Safed, Tiberius, and Hebron—were also on the rise. Perhaps half of Palestine's Jews, maybe more, did not associate themselves with the new settlements (the "New Yishuv") and the Zionist movement. Instead they were linked to the more traditional "Old Yishuv."

But the future lay with the New Yishuv and with towns that had not historically had Jewish populations. The new colonies had some 12,000 inhabitants by 1914. Haifa numbered 3,000 Jews among its population of 20,000. Most impressive, however, was the growth of Jaffa, the principal port of Palestine. It grew from a backwater of 2,750 people at the beginning of the 19th century to about 10,000 people in 1880. Zionist immigrants tended to settle in Jaffa and the cluster of new colonies in the area that are now towns in greater Tel Aviv. The Zionists intended to make Jerusalem the Jewish capital, but Jaffa was their cultural and economic center. In his memoirs, Arthur Ruppin explained why the Zionist Organization had located its Palestine office in Jaffa:

> At the time this seemed an almost inevitable choice. Jaffa already contained the head office of the Anglo-Palestine Company, the agency for the Odessa Committee of the Hovevei Zion and the land development corporation Geulah.... Also in favor of Jaffa was the fact that it was centrally situated among the largest agricultural settlements.... But even more important, the greater part of the new *yishuv* had settled in Jaffa; Haifa had a much smaller number of recent settlers, and in Jerusalem the newcomers went unnoticed among the large majority of the old *yishuv*.

Jaffa did not have enough housing for the Russian immigrants who arrived in the first decade of the 20th century. And so in 1909 a new city, Tel Aviv, was established. It eventually became the largest Jewish city in Palestine. Tel Aviv was carefully planned. Arthur Ruppin devised various bylaws that regulated public life, and residents had to follow them. These bylaws set out neighborhood goals and residents' responsibilities. They even specified that "each property must have a garden three meters wide facing the street, and a fence."

Tel Aviv served as a model for Jewish town planning in Palestine. More than anywhere else in Palestine, it became the center for the development of Jewish national values and a Hebrew-speaking culture. Tel Aviv was destined to become the hub of modern Israel at it approached statehood.

By 1914 some of the cultural foundations were in place for a modern Jewish nation. A thriving press reached a wide readership: Jaffa and Tel Aviv had 29 Jewish newspapers. Hebrew culture was making great strides. Jews founded many Hebrew-language schools, and many people —perhaps 40 percent of the population— spoke Hebrew. Not all Zionist settlers, however, accepted Hebrew as a national language. Some considered German the most important modern language, and many saw no practical advantage in adopting Hebrew. German was the official language of instruction at the Technion, a technical institute founded in Haifa in 1913. This caused such controversy that those who supported Hebrew fought to establish it as the language of education in schools. There was no question about which language

would be used at the Hebrew University of Jerusalem, which opened in 1925. Eventually, the majority of Zionists agreed that Hebrew should be the language of the Jewish nation, even though many found it difficult to learn. Arthur Ruppin, for example, claimed that he shunned public appearances because of his poor Hebrew.

The developments that encouraged the Zionist movement caused increasing alarm among the Arabs. In 1914, however, the First World War suspended Zionist immigration. The war brought great hardship to many of the Jews who remained in Palestine; thousands sought refuge in other countries. The possibility of a Jewish nation seemed to fade. Few among the Jews of Palestine could have guessed that the war itself would give Zionist hopes the biggest boost they had yet received. As for the Arabs, the war would leave them feeling betrayed and bitter.

Members of the Second Aliyah lay the cornerstone of Tel Aviv in 1909. Within five years, this sandy space had grown into a thriving city of more than 2,000 people, complete with newspapers, schools, and homes with gardens.

Foreign Office,
November 2nd, 1917.

Dear Lord Rothschild,

I have much pleasure in conveying to you, on behalf of His Majesty's Government, the following declaration of sympathy with Jewish Zionist aspirations which has been submitted to, and approved by, the Cabinet.

"His Majesty's Government view with favour the establishment in Palestine of a national home for the Jewish people, and will use their best endeavours to facilitate the achievement of this object, it being clearly understood that nothing shall be done which may prejudice the civil and religious rights of existing non-Jewish communities in Palestine, or the rights and political status enjoyed by Jews in any other country"

I should be grateful if you would bring this declaration to the knowledge of the Zionist Federation.

Y. in,

Arthur James Balfour

Chapter 6

The Creation of Modern Palestine

In the early 20th century the European nations called the Ottoman Empire the "Sick Man of Europe" because it seemed at the point of total collapse. It had lost most of its European territory, although its capital, Istanbul, was located on both the European and Asian sides of a waterway called the Straits of Bosporus. The Ottoman Empire had survived this long only because of the rivalry among the major European powers; no country would allow its rivals to seize the Ottoman territory.

This balance of power among the European countries lasted until World War I, when the Turks sided with Germany against Russia, France, and Britain. Because of the German-Turkish alliance, the First World War was fought not only on the battlefields of Europe but also in the Middle East. After the war broke out in 1914, the British, French, and Russians began planning how to divide the remaining Ottoman territories among themselves.

Just as in ancient times, in the early 20th century Palestine was at the crossroads of competing political interests. Other European powers grew increasingly concerned about Germany's expanding presence and

influence in the Middle East—for example, the Ottomans allowed the Germans to build a railroad from Istanbul through Baghdad to Basra on the Persian Gulf. The British were especially alarmed because Middle Eastern oil was a vital source of energy for Great Britain, so they wanted control of oilfields in the Persian Gulf. They had other strategic concerns as well. Since 1881 they had occupied Egypt, which contained the Suez Canal—the waterway from the Mediterranean Sea to the Indian Ocean. The British wished to protect this route to India, their most valuable colony. Palestine's strategic significance became alarmingly clear to the British when Turkish troops from Palestine managed to cross the formidable Sinai Peninsula to threaten the British in Egypt. The French also had concerns in the Middle East. They had longstanding ties with Lebanon, and saw themselves as the defenders of the Maronite church, Lebanon's largest Christian group.

During World War I the British began to think about how they could take control of Palestine. They decided to support the Arabs in a revolt against the Turks. The British believed that if they appeared to be helping

T. E. Lawrence, better known as "Lawrence of Arabia," was a British officer and adventurer who acted as an advisor to the Arabs in their revolt against the Turks during World War I. Although the revolt had little consequence on the military outcome of the war, Lawrence became a legend in his own country.

Arabs win independence, the Arabs would join them in their fight against Germany and Turkey. But Britain worried about supporting a popular Arab movement that might turn against its interests. So instead of seeking an alliance with members of the Arab nationalist movement, the British supported an Arab revolt led by the symbolically important guardian of the holy places in Mecca, the Sharif Husayn. Husayn was a Hashemite, a member of a family that claimed descent from the prophet Muhammad (the title *sharif* referred to a descendant of the prophet). The British suggested that Husayn could become the head of a new Arab caliphate (as the government of the Arab empires in the Middle Ages was called). Negotiations began in letters between the British high commissioner in Egypt, Sir Henry McMahon, and Sharif Husayn.

On October 24, 1915, McMahon sent Husayn a letter promising Arab independence. But the exact boundaries of the Arab territory promised in the letter later became a subject of bitter dispute. The letter to Husayn stated that "portions of Syria lying to the west of the districts of Damascus, Homs, Hama and Aleppo cannot be said to be purely Arab, and should be excluded from the limits demanded." These four districts were cities in Syria; the region to the west being Lebanon. The British probably meant that the future Arab state would not include Lebanon, which had a large Christian population. Because Lebanon was historically an area of French interests, the British may have been keeping their French allies in mind. In 1922, however, the British claimed that McMahon's pledge had

excluded "the whole of Palestine west of Jordan," although the Arabs never accepted this exclusion.

The deal between McMahon and Husayn meant that Britain supported the Arab revolt led by the sharif's Arabian family, especially his son Faysal. One of the key advisors to the Arabs was the legendary British officer T. E. Lawrence, known as "Lawrence of Arabia." He wrote about the revolt in his book, *Seven Pillars of Wisdom,* but he often exaggerated his own role and the importance of the Arab military operations he led. The truth is that apart from capturing the Red Sea port of Aqaba from the Ottomans, the Arab revolt had little military effect on the war. The idea of Arab soldiers fighting for independence, however, had great symbolic importance.

A British government official named Mark Sykes and a French official named Charles Georges-Picot negotiated an agreement to divide up the Ottoman territories. Although the Sykes-Picot agreement of 1916 promised to "recognize and protect an independent Arab State or a Confederation of Arab States," the British and French really planned to rule the Middle East themselves. The agreement spelled out each power's "sphere of influence," that is, the region it would control directly or indirectly. Eager to protect their oil interests, the British insisted that their sphere of influence include most of Iraq, parts of Iran, and the Mediterranean ports of Haifa and Acre. This would allow the British to build a railroad from Haifa to Baghdad. The French sphere included Lebanon, Syria, and parts of Turkey and Iraq. Palestine was supposed to be ruled by an international administration.

While France and Great Britain were making their secret plans for the Ottoman territories, the British introduced another complication. On November 2, 1917, Lord Arthur James Balfour, the British foreign secretary, wrote to the Jewish leader Lord Lionel Walter Rothschild, of the British branch of the family, pledging Britain's support for the Zionist movement. The letter contained what is called the Balfour Declaration: "His Majesty's Government view with favour the establishment in Palestine of a national home for the Jewish People, and will use their best endeavors to facilitate the achievement of this object, it being clearly understood that nothing shall be done which may prejudice the civil and religious rights of existing non-Jewish communities in Palestine, or the rights and political status enjoyed by Jews in any other country." This declaration caused much excitement among the Zionists. At last the greatest European power was officially supporting the idea of a Jewish homeland.

After the war, many people came to believe that the Balfour Declaration was Britain's way of rewarding a Zionist leader named Chaim Weizmann, who was a chemist at the University of Manchester. Weizmann had found a new way to produce acetone, a solvent needed to manufacture an important explosive used in the British war effort. David Lloyd George, Britain's prime minister during the war, helped create this view of the Balfour Declaration in his *War Memoirs,* published in 1933–36. "Dr. Weizmann," wrote Lloyd George, "with his discovery not only helped us to win the War, but made a permanent mark upon the map of the world." In turn, Weizmann wrote in his own autobiography that Lloyd George "makes it appear that the Balfour Declaration was a reward given me by the Government . . . for my services to England. I almost wish that it had been as simple as that, and that I had never known the heartbreaks, the drudgery and the uncertainties which preceded the Declaration. But history does not deal in Aladdin's lamps."

Weizmann was correct. The Balfour Declaration was something much more complicated than a simple reward for his work. But Weizmann, more than any other Zionist, influenced the negotiations that led to the declaration. It is possible that Balfour would not have made the declaration without Weizmann's persistent and determined campaign.

Chaim Weizmann, the most important diplomat and statesman of the Zionist movement, was born in 1874 in the small town of Motol in the Russian Pale. After scientific training in Germany and Switzerland, he arrived in England in 1904. Deeply devoted to the Zionist cause, he became president of the English Zionist Federation in 1917. After the war he became president of the World Zionist Organization. He campaigned tirelessly for the formation of the state of Israel and was the most important Zionist leader outside of Palestine.

Always well accepted and admired by the British government, Weizmann was a brilliant spokesman for the Jews. He was a talented and persuasive speaker who was able to command both respect and sympathy. He was also a shrewd political thinker

British foreign secretary Arthur Balfour (center) poses with Chaim Weizmann (third from right) and others in 1925. Weizmann, a scientist and a Zionist leader, campaigned tirelessly for British support of Zionism.

who saw during World War I how Zionist aims and British strategies could be joined in the Balfour Declaration. The declaration fulfilled several of Britain's needs. First of all, the British were really very unhappy about sharing control of Palestine with the French as they had agreed to do in the Sykes-Picot agreement. They wanted the entire area from Mesopotamia to the Mediterranean—including Palestine—to be in British hands. But the British could use the Balfour Declaration to get out of their power-sharing agreement with the French. They would present their support for the Jews as an enlightened and idealistic act, making it very difficult for the French to oppose them.

The Balfour Declaration might also strengthen support for Britain's war aims. Russia was in the middle of its communist revolution, and the British were afraid that this ally would drop out of the war. British leaders reasoned that if they supported the Zionists, Russian Jews among the revolutionary leaders would wish to remain their allies. The British also believed that American Jews would influence President Wilson

to increase his support for the allies. Unfortunately for the British, they had overestimated Jewish political and economic power in both Russia and the United States. The Balfour Declaration had little or no effect on Russian or American war policy.

Another factor that led Great Britain to make the Balfour Declaration was the fear that Germany would announce its own Turkish-German protectorate over Jewish Palestine. After all, the headquarters of the Zionist movement were in Berlin until the outbreak of the war, and German Zionists were fighting patriotically in the German army. So, with the aim of winning international Jewish support for Britain and its allies, the British publicly issued the Balfour Declaration. They did not publicize it in Palestine, however, because there the Arab population would certainly regard it as a betrayal and might even take up arms against British soldiers.

Some Jewish leaders in England were opposed to the declaration. "This small minority," wrote Weizmann in his autobiography, "struggled bitterly to deprive the vast majority of the benefits of a unique act of the world conscience; and it succeeded, if not in balking the act of justice, at least in vitiating some of its application." The wording of the declaration itself was affected by Jewish opponents to Zionism, especially Edwin Montague, a Jew who was Britain's secretary of state for India. For example, instead of Palestine as *the* national homeland, the declaration mentioned the establishment "in Palestine of *a* national home." This subtle change meant that Palestine should not be considered the *only* national home of the Jews. And if Palestine became a "national home," what would this mean for Jews who were content as citizens of Great Britain and other countries? The part of the declaration that talks about the rights of non-Jewish communities in Palestine and the rights of Jews in other countries was insisted on by British Jews who were concerned about their own position in England.

The Balfour Declaration did not define boundaries or explain what a "national home" was. Yet despite its vagueness it boosted the Zionist cause. At the end of the war, when the British occupied Palestine, the Zionists were able to demand that they keep the promise they had made in the Balfour Declaration.

World War I brought great hardships to the Jews in Palestine, which remained under Turkish rule until the end of 1917. More than 40,000 of these Jews were Russian citizens, which meant they belonged to a country at war with Turkey. Some of them thought that they might have a future in the modern Ottoman Empire, especially after the Young Turk Revolution in 1908. One of them was David Ben-Gurion, who studied law in Istanbul, got rid of his Russian clothes, grew a Turkish-style mustache, and wore a fez, or Turkish cap.

Izhak Ben-Zvi, a Zionist labor leader and future president of the State of Israel, also learned Turkish and studied law in Istanbul. Ben-Zvi and Ben-Gurion were forced to abandon their studies when war broke out. They returned to Palestine, which was hardly a safe haven. The Turkish army ordered all enemy aliens to leave the country. Accused of belonging to a secret anti-Turkish organization, Ben-Gurion and Ben-Zvi were told to leave Palestine in 1915. They demanded that they be allowed to remain. In a petition to a Turkish leader they swore their loyalty to the Ottoman state. "We believe," they pleaded, "that we have the right to consider ourselves as Ottoman citizens, and because of this we demand from His Excellency but one thing: to treat us as Ottomans, and if you think that we have committed an offense, we demand that we be punished as Ottomans and we are prepared to receive your sentence with all the severity of the law." This passionate appeal had no effect on the Turkish authorities, who sent Ben-Gurion and Ben-Zvi to Alexandria, Egypt.

Some 10,000 Jews were exiled to Egypt during the war. Most of those who remained in Palestine suffered oppression.

In the struggle for control of Palestine, different groups gathered frequently in negotiation. At the surrender of Jerusalem in 1917, a British officer (center) wears a typical British pith helmet, while Turkish leaders wear the traditional Turkish mustache and fez.

The Turks arrested many Zionists for what they claimed were illegal political activities. Forced to do hard labor, and weakened by starvation and widespread disease, the Jews of Palestine declined in number from 85,000 in 1914 to 55,000 in 1918.

The British army captured Palestine in 1917 and held it until the end of the war in 1918. After the war the powers attended a peace conference in Paris, where they redrew the map of Europe and discussed the division of the Ottoman Empire. Chaim Weizmann represented the Zionists at the conference. Faysal, the leader of the Arab revolt and son of Sharif Husayn, met him there and expressed his sympathy for the Zionist movement and his willingness to work together. "With the chiefs of your movement, especially with Dr. Weizmann, we have had, and continue to have the closest relations," wrote Faysal to an American Zionist.

The British and the French did not come to a final decision on the Middle East until another conference, this one held in the small Italian town of San Remo in 1922. Their negotiations produced new Arab states as well as the nation of Turkey. A newly formed international body called the League of Nations, a forerunner of today's United Nations, confirmed British and French control over the newly created nations. Britain got Iraq, Palestine, and Transjordan, a new state formed from the eastern part of Palestine. France got Syria and Lebanon. These states were British and French mandates, which meant that they were temporarily under British and French control but were supposed to be preparing to govern themselves.

The Arabian Hashemite leaders had already rejected this arrangement and demanded that the British keep the pledge they had made to Sharif Husayn. In 1919 Faysal had formed an Arab government in Damascus, and in March 1920 he formally declared Syrian independence. He hoped that the British would fulfill their promise, but they did not, because they did not want to lose the French as allies. Britain did not interfere when France removed Faysal and his followers from Syria. However, the British made Faysal king of Iraq and made his brother Abdullah king of Transjordan.

For the first time, modern Palestine was drawn on the map. Under the mandate, the British passed Palestine's laws, ran its administration, controlled its foreign and religious affairs, and were responsible for its military and taxes. Arabic, Hebrew, and English were the official languages. Both Jews and Arabs could become Palestinian citizens, although the League of Nations agreed that the British mandate should put into effect the Balfour Declaration "in favour of the establishment in Palestine of a national home for the Jewish people." The British recognized the Zionist Organization as the representative of Jewish goals and interests in Palestine.

The Zionists believed that the final outcome of the mandate would be a Jewish state. The British never defined what would follow the mandate and denied that they had a Jewish state in mind. But based on the promise to Sharif Husayn, Britain also had an obligation to the Arabs, although the mandate did not recognize any agency to promote Arab interests or goals. In reality,

David Ben-Gurion poses in 1918 in the uniform of the Jewish Legion, a group of Jewish volunteers who served in the British army. Ben-Gurion later became Israel's first prime minister.

however, Britain's main concern was strategic control of the Middle East, not the welfare or political goals of either the Zionists or the Arabs.

The first British high commissioner in Palestine, Herbert Samuel, was a British Jew. Although he was a Zionist, he tried to satisfy both sides. He even attempted to establish an "Arab Agency" that would represent the Arabs, much like the Zionist Organization represented the Jews as their "Jewish Agency" in Palestine. But because the Arabs did not even consider the British mandate legal, they refused to cooperate with Samuel. The Arabs claimed that the British should establish an Arab state that included Palestine. From Palestine's very beginning the British, the Zionists, and the Arabs had quite different plans for it.

The Arabs outnumbered the Jews in Palestine but were less successful at building the foundations of statehood. Before the war the Zionists of the First and Second Aliyahs had established institutions of self-government and created the beginnings of a national culture. In contrast, the Arab nationalist movement had barely begun. Arab nationalists in Palestine had not called for an independent Palestinian state and could not decide whether they should work toward a single Arab state, unifying the whole Arabic-speaking world, or toward many individual Arab nations. After the war, of course, they lost the chance to try for a single unified state when Britain and France carved up the Middle East into new countries.

In 1919 Palestinian Arabs had held a congress in Jerusalem. There they had decided that Palestine should be united with

Syria, pinning their hopes for Arab independence on Faysal and his Arab government in Damascus. But after the French drove Faysal out of Syria, the Palestinian Arabs began to concentrate on achieving independence within Palestine.

At the Third Palestinian Arab Congress the nationalists formed an Arab Executive Committee. The British did not recognize this committee's authority, but they needed to retain some ties with the Arab community in order to govern. They gave power to wealthy Arab notables, rewarding them with positions of authority in exchange for cooperation. The most influential notable in Palestine during the mandate was al-Hajj Amin al-Husayni from Jerusalem. He was born in 1895 in Jerusalem and belonged to one of the most prominent Muslim families in Palestine: the Husaynis, who considered themselves to be descended from the Prophet Muhammad. Members of the family held positions in the Ottoman administration of Jerusalem. Amin al-Husayni went on pilgrimage to Mecca in 1913, which is how he acquired the title of *hajj*. In his late teens and early twenties, Amin al-Husayni became an active opponent of Zionism and a supporter of Arab independence.

The British appointed Amin's half-brother Kamil al-Husayni to the position of Grand Mufti. A *mufti* was an important Muslim legal expert who issued opinions (*fatwa*s) on a variety of issues. When Kamil al-Husayni died in 1921, the British appointed Amin al-Husayni Mufti, although they dropped the title of Grand Mufti because Amin had taken part in demonstrations for Arab independence that had led to

The British appointed al-Hajj Amin al-Husayni as Mufti (Muslim legal expert) of Jerusalem in 1921, and in the following year, he became president of the Supreme Muslim Council. As the highest Muslim authority in Palestine, he led the Arab cause against Zionism and for Arab independence.

Vladimir Jabotinsky transformed the Zion Mule Corps, a Jewish munitions transport unit under the control of the British army, into the Jewish Legion, a military force that contributed about 5,000 fighters to the British campaign to take Palestine from the Turks. He was the leader of the Revisionists, a Zionist party opposed to the labor movement.

violence in the streets of Jerusalem. Despite al-Husayni's protests against British aims in Palestine, the British wished to demonstrate their fairness to the Arab population by making him Mufti. They also made him president of a newly created Supreme Muslim Council to control Muslim affairs.

The Mufti now had considerable powers over all of Palestine. He was in charge of *waqf* properties—properties that people had left for pious purposes which were permanently protected by Islamic law. He controlled the Muslim courts, religious schools, and orphanages. Ironically, al-Husayni used the power that the British had given him to make his office a center of opposition to British rule in Palestine. He became the leading opponent of Zionism and the most important figure in the Palestinian Arab independence movement.

But the Arab community was constantly divided. Rivals of the al-Husaynis, such as members of the al-Nashashibi family, cooperated with the British and gained seats on city councils. Other groups of Palestinian Arabs challenged the power of the notables. Christian Arabs were concerned about the domination of the Supreme Muslim Council. The mandate also brought major changes in Arab society. A young generation of militant nationalists, impatient with the older Arab leaders, called for violence against the British and the Zionists. Like the Arabs, the Jews in Palestine were a divided community, and Jews too came into conflict with the British. Yet unlike the Arabs the Jews had political organizations that the British recognized, such as the World Zionist Organization. The Jews also had a longer history of

military experience. During the First World War Palestinian Jews—inspired by a militant Russian Zionist named Vladimir (Ze'ev) Jabotinsky—had formed the Zion Mule Corps, a unit of munitions transporters under the control of the British army. After the Balfour Declaration, Jabotinsky turned the Mule Corps into the Jewish Legion, a military force that contributed about 5,000 fighters to the British campaign to wrest Palestine from the Turks. In 1920, worried about increasing clashes with the Arabs, a group of Zionist settlers secretly formed an underground army called the Haganah (Defense).

After the war Chaim Weizmann headed the World Zionist Organization from its headquarters in London. The organization gathered support for Jewish settlement in Palestine and raised money from Jews in many countries. A separate institution called the Jewish Agency was established in Jerusalem in 1929 to work on behalf of the Zionist movement in Palestine itself. It cooperated with the World Zionist Organization, the international body of the movement.

With the help of these institutions and growing international support, the Jews were in a better position than the Arabs to establish a state. But it was to be a long and difficult struggle. More than once it seemed that the Zionists would be defeated.

The Third Aliyah, the wave of immigration following the war, brought about 35,000 Jewish settlers to Palestine between 1919 and 1923. During this time the labor institutions that dominated Jewish Palestine and later the state of Israel developed. The immigrants of the Third Aliyah were

inspired by revolutionary ideals; many of them had just witnessed the Russian Revolution. They gave birth to the Hehalutz (Pioneer) movement, with agricultural labor as its highest ideal. The number of kibbutzim began to multiply. Another movement born during this period was the Hashomer Hatzair (Young Guard), founded in Galicia in 1915. Hashomer Hatzair was a radical movement that proclaimed a rebellion against the Jewish middle classes. It pushed for collective settlements and founded new kibbutzim.

But only a small percentage of Jews lived on kibbutzim, so the Jewish labor movement expanded its influence in the growing towns and cities of Palestine. Out of the Poalei Zion came a broader-based party combined with the labor union. It was called Ahdut Ha'avodah (Unity of Labor). In 1920 members of the Jewish labor movement founded the Histadrut (General Confederation of Labor), with Ben-Gurion as secretary-general. The Histadrut

considered itself above all political parties, with the responsibility of taking care of all the Jewish workers in the country. It established many social institutions, including socialized health care, schools, and youth groups. As many women as men joined the Histadrut, although they did not find equal opportunities; most of the married women became housewives and were given the title "worker's wife." Some women complained that being recognized as a member of the Histadrut simply as homemaker-mother was not enough. Wrote one, "Our demand is that homemaking be recognized as one of the industries of the labor market, and women who work in this field be recognized as workers and as productive members."

The Fourth Aliyah (1924–28) brought a large number of Jews from Poland, mainly from middle-class backgrounds. During this period of worldwide economic crisis and unemployment, the Jewish labor movement in Palestine faced the challenge of

These Third Aliyah Zionist pioneers journeyed to Palestine on board the S.S. Ruslam *in 1919. They proudly display a banner bearing the Star of David.*

מיט א פריש באנייסטערט הארץ
מיט א פרייען שטאלצן בליק
אײלען ײדען זיך צום צוג,
אין אײגען לאנד, צום אײגען גליק...

לשנה טובה תכתבו

נאך ארץ־ישראל.

Jews on their way to Israel are celebrated in this New Year's greeting card from 1920s Warsaw, Poland.

meeting the needs of these newcomers, most of whom settled in the cities. New institutions developed, including various cooperative ventures, Bank Hapoalim (Workers' Bank), and low-cost housing. In 1930, Ahdut Ha'avodah and Hapoal Hatzair merged to form the Mapai or Labor political party, which would dominate political life for nearly 50 years. The labor movement also increased its influence in world Zionism. Ben-Gurion was especially successful in attracting money from foreign sources to support the settlements in Palestine.

The Fifth Aliyah, during the 1930s, greatly increased the Jewish population, which numbered about one-half million by the mid-1940s. Immigrants arrived from Germany, Poland, and Romania. Unlike earlier immigrants, many of them had had only brief connections with Zionism. These prosperous, well-educated German Jews came to Palestine to escape the rising tide of anti-Semitism in Germany after Adolf Hitler's Nazi party seized control of the German government in 1933. Orthodox Jews also arrived during this time, settling in the cities. The Fifth Aliyah led to rapid growth of the cities, especially Tel Aviv and Haifa. German was heard everywhere in

Haifa, while Yiddish was increasingly spoken in Tel Aviv. The Jewish population was becoming more diverse—and greater diversity led to increased political, philosophical, and social divisions.

Herzl had foreseen that different political parties would emerge within the Zionist movement. Until the 1930s, all of the Zionist political movements in Palestine were represented in the World Zionist Organization. Although the labor movement was dominant, the General Zionists had some following, especially outside of Palestine. They were nonsocialist liberals who supported private enterprise. The Orthodox Mizrahi movement, which believed that a Jewish state should be ruled by Jewish law, was also an important part of Zionism. A bridge between nonreligious and religious Zionists existed in the person of Rabbi Abraham Isaac Kook (1865–1935), who settled in Palestine in 1904. Rabbi Kook supported the nonreligious settlers, believing that by settling the land of Israel they were following God's will. Kook thought that the nonreligious settlers, without realizing it, were actually helping to bring about a spiritual rebirth, the aim of religious Zionism.

The loudest opponents of the Labor Zionists were the Revisionists, members of a movement founded in 1925 by Vladimir (Ze'ev) Jabotinsky, who had established the Zion Mule Corps. Jabotinsky strongly opposed the socialism of the labor movement and was very impatient with the slow progress being made toward building a Jewish state. He wanted immediate statehood and was prepared to use force to get it. He emphasized discipline and militarism, characteristics shared by some extreme nationalist movements in Europe in the 1920s. Jabotinsky believed that no agreement with the Arabs was possible until the Jews outnumbered them.

The Revisionists' youth movement was named after the last stronghold of the Bar Kokhba revolt, Betar, which was also a symbol of the Yosef Trumpeldor Association. Trumpeldor was a Russian Jew who lost an arm fighting in the czar's army, immigrated to Palestine, and became a close colleague of Jabotinsky in the Zion Mule Corps. In 1920 he and seven other settlers were killed defending the settlement of Tel Hai in the Upper Galilee against local Arab attackers. Shortly before he died, he supposedly said to a doctor, "Never mind, it is worth dying for the country." Trumpeldor became the first national military hero, and his final words, slightly modified to "it is good to die for our country," became a national slogan. His last stand at Tel Hai is marked today by a statue of a lion, a monument visited by both Israelis and foreign tourists.

The Revisionists soon clashed with the Labor Zionists, doing everything they could to undermine the Histadrut. Violent skirmishes sometimes took place when Revisionists arrived to break up strikes during labor disputes. Tension reached a peak in 1933 when a rising 34-year-old Labor leader named Chaim Arlosoroff was assassinated while strolling with his wife on a Tel Aviv Beach. A Betar activist named Avraham Stavsky was arrested, convicted, and sentenced to be hanged for the murder. However, the conviction was overturned and he was released, although Labor Zionists continued to believe that he and other Revisionists had taken part in a conspiracy to murder Arlosoroff.

In 1935 the Revisionists left the World Zionist Organization to form the New Zionist Organization, led by Jabotinsky. From that time on the Revisionists operated independently of the World Zionist Organization. They gained a sizable following but could not defeat the Labor party. By dealing directly with the practical, day-to-day economic issues that confronted new immigrants, the Labor party built a larger base of grassroots support than the Revisionists, who focused mainly on politics and militarism.

Few Labor leaders recognized the strength of Palestinian Arab nationalism or admitted that the idea of a Palestinian Arab nation might have merit. Jews were still a minority in Palestine. They believed that if the Arabs were allowed to govern themselves they would make it impossible for Jews to create their own state. Almost all Zionists therefore believed that if the Arabs wanted a nation they should look for it in the neighboring Arab states, not in Palestine.

Although the borders of Palestine were somewhat artificial, drawn by European powers at a treaty table, the Palestinian Arabs felt that they had their own identity, separate from the other Arab nations. Yet those other Arab countries were gradually achieving greater independence from Britain and France, while the Arabs of Palestine saw the Jewish population growing and their own hopes of statehood diminishing. Increasingly desperate, the Palestinian Arabs began to rebel against both the Zionist settlers and the British rulers.

Chapter 7

Struggle for the Land and Nation

O n April 4, 1920, Muslim pilgrims from all over Palestine gathered at the entrance to the Old City of Jerusalem. It was the date of an annual Muslim festival, and the British had authorized the gathering as a religious celebration. Instead, the crowd heard inflammatory political speeches by 'Arif al-'Arif, a leading Arab nationalist editor; Musa Kazim al-Husayni, the mayor of Jerusalem; Hajj Amin al-Husayni, the future Mufti of Jerusalem; and other Muslim leaders who declared their support for King Faysal and denounced the Zionists' aims in Palestine. Portraits displayed around the rally hailed Faysal as "King of Syria and Palestine."

Instead of passing through the Muslim quarter of the Old City to their destination at the shrine of al-Haram al-Sharif, the highly excited pilgrims entered the Jewish quarter. Aroused to violence by the heated speeches at the rally, they threw stones at and then rioted against the Jews.

Even before the rioting, the Jews had been afraid of the Arab nationalists' growing hostility. Feeling that the British did not offer them enough protection, Vladimir Jabotinsky and Pinhas Rutenberg had organized a defense organization. At least 500 volunteers began training in Jerusalem, although British authorities forbade Jabotinsky and Rutenberg to use their troops to defend the Jewish quarter. During the rioting some of their members tried to defend the Jewish quarter anyway, and the British arrested these vigilantes—including Jabotinsky, who was arrested for illegal possession of firearms. (A military court later convicted him of subversion, and he went to prison in Acre.)

As the rioting continued, Arab civil police who were supposed to restore order took the side of the Arab rioters. British troops then disarmed the police and ordered them out of the area. Rather than entering the narrow streets and alleyways of the Old City, the British encircled it to prevent more rioters from entering. The rioting lasted for six days. Five Jews and four Arabs died. Nearly 250 people, mainly Jews, were wounded. Ironically, many of the Jewish victims belonged to the Orthodox community that staunchly opposed Zionism.

This 1920 riot in Jerusalem was the first massive incident of violence between Arab

Clashes between Jews and Arabs led to rioting throughout Palestine in 1929. Some of the worst violence was in Hebron, where Arabs massacred about 60 Jews. This photograph shows a room in Hebron destroyed in the riots; Theodor Herzl's portrait hangs on the wall.

and Jewish communities. It was the prelude to a pattern of violence that continued throughout the century.

After the riot, Zionist leaders bitterly accused the British of failing to protect the Jews. On April 5, 1920, Izhak Ben-Zvi, a Labor leader and a future president of the state of Israel, wrote:

> All Jerusalem is in a state of siege. From 6:00 p.m. it is impossible to go out. I am writing in our house in the Arab quarter, where we have no contact with the other quarters. We have lived to be eyewitnesses to an actual pogrom in Jerusalem, a pogrom the like of which we did not have during hundreds of years of Turkish rule. Worst of all is the attitude of the local authorities to the whole matter. All our doubts have become certainties. The local English administration *knew of all the preparations for the slaughter,* and not only did not try to prevent it but even did everything in its power to encourage the thieves and murderers, and on the other hand used every means to impede the Jewish self-defense and arrest its members.

Other Zionist leaders echoed Ben-Zvi's bitterness. "All of us felt," said Chaim Weizmann, "that this pogrom might have been averted had proper steps been taken in time to check the agitation." By using the Russian word "pogrom," the Zionists accused not only the rioters but also the British authorities. The government of Russia, they believed, had been responsible for the anti-Jewish violence there, and now they felt that the same thing was happening in Palestine.

The British denied the charges that they had mishandled the riots and were hostile toward the Zionists. They took steps to prevent further violence, dismissing the mayor of Jerusalem and replacing him with the leader of a rival family. 'Arif al-'Arif and Hajj Amin al-Husayni, who had fled to Syria, were each sentenced to 10 years imprisonment for encouraging people to riot. In the case of 'Arif al-'Arif, however, the charge was false. He had urged nonviolence.

Little did Herbert Samuel know when he took office as the first high commissioner of Palestine that the British were caught in a hopeless trap and would swing back and forth like a pendulum between Arab pressures and Jewish demands. Samuel believed that his task was to enact the Balfour Declaration, so he appointed officials who sympathized with Zionism. But while Samuel also understood the strength of Arab nationalism, he failed to draw Jews and Arabs into a shared political framework. Instead, he dealt with them separately, and the men who followed him in office did the same, doing nothing to heal the widening divide between the two peoples.

Samuel tried to be fair in the wake of the rioting. He released Jabotinsky and other Jewish defenders from prison, and he also released Arabs who had been arrested for their role in the rioting. He pardoned 'Arif al-'Arif and Hajj Amin al-Husayni, gave al-'Arif a position in the government, and made Hajj Amin al-Husayni Mufti of Jerusalem. Samuel's first few months were calm. He wrote to Weizmann that "the country is so quiet that you could hear a pin drop," although he added with some foreboding, "how long that may last no one can say."

When violence erupted in Jaffa on May Day, 1921, the British were taken by surprise. The violence spread to other coastal towns and by May 7, when it ended, 48 Arabs and 47 Jews were dead. Believing that the arrival of new Jewish immigrants was one cause of the tension, Samuel announced that for the time being no Jews would be allowed to enter the country.

In June 1922, just before the League of Nations approved the British mandate over Palestine, British authorities released a document called the Churchill White Paper. Its author was Winston Churchill, Britain's colonial secretary—and future prime minister. Offering a new interpretation of the Balfour Declaration and the Husayn-McMahon correspondence, the White Paper was an attempt to reassure the Palestinian Arabs that their country was not going to become a Jewish land. It stated:

Unauthorized statements have been made to the effect that the purpose in view is to create a wholly Jewish Palestine. Phrases have been used such as that Palestine is to become 'as Jewish as England is English.' His Majesty's Government regard any such expectation as impracticable and have no such aim in view. Nor have they at any time contemplated as appears to be feared by the Arab Delegation, the disappearance or the subordination of the Arabic population, language, or culture in Palestine.

Churchill admitted that the British planned to help develop the Jewish "national home" in Palestine, but the White Paper did not say that the outcome of the mandate would be a Jewish state. The White Paper also stated that immigration would be controlled "to ensure that the immigrants should not be a burden upon the people of Palestine as a whole." The Zionists were unhappy

Winston Churchill (hatless, at center), then Britain's colonial secretary, visits Jerusalem in 1921. Churchill's interpretation of the Balfour Declaration in his 1922 White Paper caused Zionists to be unhappy because it did not state anywhere that the outcome of the mandate would be a Jewish state.

British troops (with steel helmets) block a major intersection with a barbed-wire barrier in 1936. Severe clashes between Arab civilians and British soldiers resulted in a declaration of martial law.

with any limits on immigration. They felt that the Churchill White Paper was, as Weizmann later wrote in his autobiography, "a serious whittling down of the Balfour Declaration." Nevertheless, Zionist leaders signed a letter accepting the White paper, while the Arabs, who objected strongly to the Balfour Declaration, refused to sign. Jewish immigration grew rapidly in the 1920s, despite many disputes between the Zionists and the British, and Palestinian Arabs became increasingly bitter.

Violence erupted again in 1929, this time sparked by competition for religious space in the Old City of Jerusalem. The rioting in Jerusalem soon spread to Haifa, Jaffa, and Tel Aviv. In Hebron, Arabs massacred about 60 men, women, and children of a community of about 700 Jews, most of whom were non-Zionist Orthodox.

The following year the British sent a commission to Palestine to investigate the violence. Its report placed the blame on the Arabs and Arab nationalist leaders. To

remedy Arab discontent, the report suggested that the British should pay more attention to the non-Jewish communities and should limit Jewish immigration. In a new document called the Passfield White Paper, British authorities proposed a suspension of immigration and of land sales to Jews. Later, however, Prime Minister Ramsay MacDonald wrote to Weizmann, assuring the Zionist leader that the British would eventually establish a Jewish national home. Trying to please both sides, the British were swinging back and forth. The result was that both Arabs and Zionists were dissatisfied.

The heart of the growing conflict between these two groups was control of the land. Two-thirds of the Arab population worked in agriculture or livestock herding, but by 1948 Jews had bought nearly a quarter of all the cultivatable land, most of it from absentee landowners who did not live or work on the land. Landowners who needed money—even Arab landowners— were willing to sell their land to Jews.

As in the early days of Zionist settlement, Jews and Arabs continued to have very different ideas about who was entitled to live on the land. The Jews believed that once they had bought the land, it was theirs to farm. They often forced Arab tenant farmers to leave. The Arabs objected to this because in the past land sales had not affected them. Property might change hands, but the owners always let the tenants stay and work the land. The British passed some laws to protect the Arab tenants and keep them on the land, but a growing number of rural Arabs left the countryside for the cities, becoming poor workers or joining the unemployed.

Their situation became much more desperate in the 1930s, a time of economic hardship around the world. To add to the tension, persecution drove many European Jews to emigrate, and some came to Palestine. Land sales to Jews increased. So did the number of Arab peasants leaving the land.

Palestine's Arabs began making louder and more insistent political demands. They saw that the British were giving up political power elsewhere in the Arab world—in Transjordan, Iraq, and Egypt. In these countries Arabs were moving toward self-government. But nowhere on the horizon was the prospect of an independent Arab state in Palestine.

The Arab Istiqlal (Independence) party, founded in 1932, began calling for armed resistance. Arabs also drew on religion to help them resist the British and the Zionists. Some Muslims wanted an Islamic revival and a *jihad* (holy war) to free the country.

In April 1936, Palestinian Arabs rose in a revolt that began with attacks against Jews. Arab nationalists formed a committee that united various factions within the Arab community, called for a general strike and a boycott of Jewish goods, and demanded an end to Jewish immigration and land sales and the establishment of an Arab national government. Urban nationalists and rural villagers joined the revolt. British troops tried to suppress the resistance, and the Haganah, the Jewish underground defense force, stepped up its own military activities.

'Izz al-Din al-Qassam

'Izz al-Din al-Qassam was born in Jebla, Syria, in 1882 to a family of prominent religious leaders. In the first decade of the 20th century, like many aspiring Muslim teachers, he went to Cairo to study. There he met Rashid Rida, one of his generation's most important supporters of Islamic revival. Al-Qassam became convinced that an Islamic revival would free Muslim lands of foreign occupation.

In 1909, al-Qassam returned to Jebla and began his religious teaching. After World War I he fought against the French takeover in Syria but ended up in exile in Palestine. He became a teacher in the Islamic school of Haifa, where he preached the need for holy war against the British and the Zionists. Al-Qassam appealed especially to young nationalists and to the poor, dispossessed peasants living in shantytowns. As president of the Young Men's Muslim Association he visited Arab villages around Haifa, gathering followers.

In the late 1920s al-Qassam began organizing secret cells of *mujahidin,* Islamic fighters. He began organizing attacks against Jewish settlements in the early 1930s. In 1935 al-Qassam and 12 others, fearing arrest, fled to the mountains. Branded as a "bandit," al-Qassam was surrounded by a force of British police and soldiers. He refused to surrender, ordering his men to die as martyrs for the cause of Muslim liberation. All perished in the gun battle that followed. The shootout in the mountains caused a sensation among the Arabs and helped inspire the 1936 rebellion.

Palestinians regarded 'Izz al-Din al-Qassam as a martyr and the founder of the Palestinian armed resistance movement. His influence remains strong—he was an inspiration for the Islamic Jihad organization that was involved in the *Intifadah* (uprising) that began in Israel in 1987. The Hamas organization, founded at the beginning of the *Intifadah,* also admired al-Qassam as the symbol of Palestinian resistance. Its military wing,

the 'Izz al-Din al-Qassam brigades, carried out numerous acts of violence against Israelis, including suicide bombings in 1997 that killed more than 20 civilians.

The revolt continued for months. Hoping to satisfy both sides, Britain sent a group called the Peel Commission to investigate the crisis. The Zionists told the commission that immigration should not be limited. Jewish settlement, they claimed, would bring economic improvement to the country as a whole and this would help reconcile Jews and Arabs. The Arabs called for an independent Palestine with a majority of Arabs in its population.

The commission produced the Peel Plan, which introduced the notion of partitioning, or dividing, Palestine. Under the Peel Plan, the Zionists would get about 30 percent of the territory. Arab Palestine would be united with Transjordan. David Ben-Gurion, now head of the Jewish Agency, accepted the plan, as did many Zionists in other countries. But a number of Zionist leaders in Palestine opposed it, as did the leading Arab nationalists. And although King Abdullah of Transjordan was interested in the plan because it would enlarge his country, other Arab states opposed it to show support for the Palestinian Arab goal of making Palestine an independent Arab country.

With the failure of the Peel Plan, the Arab revolt entered a second phase that lasted until 1939. Political disorder and violence became more widespread as the rebels attacked both the Jews and the British. The authorities arrested many Arab leaders, including Hajj Amin al-Husayni, whom they exiled. The Arabs responded with greater violence. Bands of *mujahidin*— Muslim fighters of the holy war—seized control of the countryside.

By the summer of 1938 the British seemed to be losing control of Palestine. Captain Orde Wingate of the British forces decided to use the Haganah against the Arabs, and allowed the Zionists to take up arms. British soldiers and Zionists formed special field squads. The Revisionist underground military organization, the Irgun, also participated, especially by attacking Arab civilians. At this time the British adopted harsh countermeasures to suppress the revolt. They hanged convicted rebels and dynamited the homes of Arabs who were accused of being involved. By the time the revolt subsided in 1939, thousands of people had been killed, the majority Arabs.

The revolt had brought Palestine's Arabs greater unity than they had known before. Yet it had also highlighted the gulfs between Muslim and Christian Arabs and between rich and poor. The revolt also convinced the Jews of Palestine that the struggle would only get worse. They determined to arm and protect themselves. A final effect of the revolt was that the British realized that the mandate was not working.

Worried about the coming war with Germany, Britain was anxious to settle the question of Palestine. If fighting began in Europe, the British could not afford to have troops tied up in the Middle East. In 1939 they produced yet another White Paper containing yet another plan for Palestine. This White Paper became notorious among Zionists because it reinterpreted the Balfour Declaration. It called for the establishment of a Palestinian state with a Jewish national home within it. Jewish immigration would be limited to 75,000 over five years, after which time the Arabs would have the right to approve immigration.

This White Paper outraged Zionists. How could the British limit immigration to Palestine when Hitler was persecuting Jews in Europe and country after country was turning away desperate Jewish refugees?

The onset of World War II produced a major dilemma for the Jews of Palestine. The Nazis occupied most of Europe, and Great Britain led the fight against them. Jews resented the British because of the White Paper yet supported them in the war against the Nazis. Ben-Gurion said that Jews "must support the [British] army as though there were no White Paper, and fight the White Paper as though there was no war."

Some Jews joined the British fight against the Nazis in the hope that this might cause Britain to cancel the White Paper. The British did not allow the Jews to form a fighting division in Palestine, however, enrolled them in Palestinian units that went to the western front, as the scene of fighting in Europe was called.

At first the war went badly for the British. In 1940 the German army marched into France and the country was defeated. In the town of Vichy in the unoccupied southeastern part of France, a French government under the leadership of Marshall Philippe Pétain was established. The Vichy government, which supported the Nazis, now ruled the French protectorates of Syria and Lebanon. Egypt and Iraq were still partly under British control, but support for Germany was on the rise among

Arab nationalists in those countries—in Baghdad, Iraq, for example, pro-Nazi nationalists tried to seize power in a coup that the British managed to crush. By 1941 the British feared that their position in the Middle East was doomed. Needing allies, they entered a new stage of military cooperation with the Jews of Palestine, allowing veterans of Wingate's field squads from the period of the Arab revolt to form an independent battle reserve called the Palmah. Some of its leaders—Yitzhak Sadeh, Moshe Dayan, and Yigal Allon—came from the Labor movement.

The Palmah's courageous actions during the Second World War became important symbols in the Israeli tradition of national courage. Twenty-three Palmah members went on a daring mission to blow up oil refineries in Tripoli, Lebanon, but the mission failed and the men disappeared; some were probably captured and executed by Vichy troops. The Palmah also helped the British invade Vichy-controlled Syria in June 1941. Arabic-speaking Palmah men sneaked into Syria to prepare for the invasion by sabotaging roads and bridges.

Nazi officers in a German town lead a group of Jews to a railroad station, where they will board trains to concentration camps. Jews were forced to identify themselves with the Star of David, which they carry here.

Slave laborers in the German Buchenwald concentration camp were crowded into wooden bunks, lacking food and sanitation. Few survived these horrible conditions, and many were tortured and executed by sadistic Nazi guards. Thousands had died by the time U.S. troops entered Buchenwald in 1945.

When the Allied invasion began, they guided the troops. Moshe Dayan lost an eye during this operation; in future years his eyepatch would be recognized as a distinctive feature of this Israeli hero.

Cooperation between the British and the Palmah increased in 1942, as the Nazi advance across North Africa threatened the British position in Egypt. Yet the British worried about their inability to control the Palmah. When the British position in the Middle East improved, the British stopped cooperating with the Palmah, which became an underground organization.

In 1942 Palestinian Jews confronted a new dilemma. News of Hitler's concentration camps, in which thousands of Jews were being imprisoned and killed, reached the outside world. The horror that has come to be called the Holocaust was under way. Yet the British were still enforcing their White Paper policy and suppressing the Jewish military underground. Jews in Palestine found it harder than ever to support Great Britain.

Still, Jews were helping the British battle Hitler. In 1942 Jews from Palestine formed a special unit to parachute behind enemy lines. A young poet and parachutist named Hannah Senesh was captured in Hungary and executed in 1944. She became the symbol of Palestinian Jewry's militant resistance to the Nazis. Palestinian Jews also formed a 3,400-strong brigade that landed in Italy and joined Allied forces fighting the Germans. This brigade had little military effect but immense symbolic importance. When the Allies defeated the Nazis and liberated those in the concentration camps, the sight of Jewish soldiers gave hope to survivors of the Holocaust, many of whom desperately wanted to go to Palestine.

While the Jews helped with the war effort, they also defied British policies through underground activities. As early as 1938 the Haganah started bringing illegal Jewish immigrants to Palestine. British officials arrested many Jewish refugees trying to sneak into Palestine; they sent some to detention camps on the island of Mauritius in the Indian Ocean. Around this time the Haganah split into two groups, a "legal" and an "illegal" section. Its illegal or underground activities were called Aliyah Bet (Immigration B). By the end of 1939 the Haganah had brought some 6,100 illegal immigrants to Palestine.

The Irgun, the Revisionist military group that had split from the Haganah in 1931, also brought illegal immigrants to Palestine. After the 1939 White Paper the Irgun began attacking British installations. When the war began, however, some members of the Irgun stopped their underground activities and tried to cooperate with the British war effort. The faction of Irgun that cooperated with the British was called Etzel (National Military Organization).

"The Germans destroyed our families and homes; don't you destroy our hopes!" begs a banner on this old, overcrowded ship bringing desperate refugees from Europe to Palestine.

The Irgun members who wanted to continue their resistance against the British formed a group called Lehi (Fighters for the Freedom of Israel), also known as the Stern Gang after its militant leader, Avraham Stern. In 1940 the deeply anti-British Stern tried to make a deal with the Nazis to ensure that if Germany defeated Great Britain, Hitler would let the Jews have a state in Palestine. Stern stole money from the Haganah to pay for his underground movement. Informers from the Haganah and Etzel turned him in to the British, who killed him in a raid in 1942.

Great Britain maintained its White Paper policy of limiting Jewish immigration throughout the war. Nevertheless, Jews fleeing war and persecution in Europe tried to sneak into Palestine, often in old, unseaworthy ships. The British intercepted many of these illegal immigrants and in 1940 loaded 1,900 of them onto a ship called the *Patria,* which was supposed to take them to Mauritius. To prevent the *Patria* from sailing, the Haganah planted a bomb on the ship. The explosion rapidly sank the ship, killing 240 Jews and 12 British policemen. Another disaster occurred in 1942 when an aging vessel, the *Struma,* sank off the Turkish coast after the British refused to let its 769 Jewish refugees enter Palestine. There was only one survivor.

These sad events, together with the horrible news of the Nazi concentration camps, increased the militancy of Palestinian Jews. They knew that when the world war ended they would face another war—the war for Palestine. The Haganah began stockpiling arms, buying them illegally in Europe and manufacturing them at home.

The Zionists now thought of statehood not as a goal in itself but as an opportunity to give millions of homeless or relocated Jews a new home after the war. They sought American support and hoped that the United States would help them achieve their aims.

Ben-Gurion and Weizmann led a meeting of mostly American and some European Zionist leaders at the Biltmore Hotel in New York City. Some 600 delegates attended. These delegates passed resolutions demanding that the settlement after the war include the establishment of a Jewish commonwealth and that the Jewish Agency control immigration to Palestine. This plan, called the Biltmore Program, increased American awareness of the Jewish plight in Palestine and rallied American Jewish support for the establishment of a Jewish state. After the war this support would prove to be vitally important.

By 1944 Jews in Palestine, seeing that the Allies were unwilling to take resources away from their overall war effort to save Jews from the Holocaust, renewed their attacks against the British. Now the two branches of the Irgun worked together. Two future prime ministers were active at this time, Menachem Begin as the leader of Etzel and Yitzhak Shamir in Lehi. Etzel tended to attack British installations, while the Stern Gang carried out assassinations.

In November 1944 two young Stern Gang members assassinated Lord Moyne,

These young boys have just arrived illegally in Palestine. British soldiers like these stopped 58 of the 63 immigrant ships that secretly sailed for Palestine between April 1945 and January 1948, and many would-be immigrants were turned back.

Britain's deputy minister of state for Middle Eastern affairs, in Cairo. Not only was Moyne the highest British official in the Middle East, but Jews blamed him for the *Struma* disaster. However, Jewish leaders in Palestine feared that the assassination threatened their political future, so the Haganah moved against the Irgun, turning in some of its members to the British. Despite a spate of arrests, the Irgun grew stronger. It organized its underground forces and won sympathy for the way it had been betrayed to the detested British.

World War II ended in 1945, but still the White Paper policy remained in effect—and still the British government left Palestine's future unclear. Britain's foreign secretary, Ernest Bevin, was interested in protecting British interests in the Middle East and was known for outbursts that approached anti-Semitism. In his mind, Britain's interests were more closely linked to those of the Arab nationalists than to those of the Zionists. Furthermore, Great Britain had been gradually giving up control over Egypt, and the British may have wanted to keep their hold on Palestine as a base in the region.

But the British mandate on Palestine was under enormous pressure in Britain and around the world. The British government that had come to power after the war was ready to grant independence to all remaining British colonies, and on the larger scene world opinion had shifted toward Zionism, as the news emerged that 6 million Jews had been killed in the Nazi concentration and death camps. People in many countries had been shaken by images of overcrowded illegal immigrant ships being intercepted by the British navy and of Holocaust survivors waiting miserably in Displaced Persons (DP) camps. A quarter of a million Jewish refugees were clamoring to go to Palestine. American president Harry Truman confronted the British on the issue of the DPs, and his opinion carried weight because of the United States' strong economic position and role in rebuilding postwar Europe.

Circumstances in Palestine also pushed the British toward ending the mandate. The anti-British campaign had intensified at the end of the war. The Haganah was sabotaging railroads and communications, even joining forces with its hated rival, the Irgun. Weizmann, still the head of the World Zionist Organization in England, denounced this violence but at the same time suggested that it was caused by Britain's failure to express a clear policy for Palestine's future. In a sense, Weizmann and the Haganah were working together, for it was the combination of militancy in Palestine and diplomacy in Europe that finally drove the British to action.

Their first action was disastrous for the Zionists. On June 29, 1946, later known to Jews as "Black Saturday," the British authorities rounded up leaders of the Jewish Agency and the Haganah. They hoped that new, more moderate, less militant leaders would replace them, but this did not happen. By now the mandate was becoming costly for the British, who had to keep 100,000 soldiers in Palestine. These soldiers were vulnerable to terrorism, as Britain discovered in July 1946 when the Irgun blew up the King David Hotel, which housed the British military headquarters in Jerusalem. Ninety-one British, Arab, and Jewish officials died in the blast. The Jewish Agency, which had not supported the bombing, made a total break with the Irgun, but Irgun terrorism continued. In May 1947, Irgun fighters burst into the prison at Acre and freed about 250 people—including 41 terrorists—whom the British had imprisoned. When British authorities hanged Irgun members, the radical Zionists responded by capturing and hanging British soldiers. Soon the British troops in Palestine lived in guarded compounds protected by barbed wire, and back in Britain the mandate was becoming very unpopular.

Great Britain decided to turn the whole mess over to the United Nations, a new

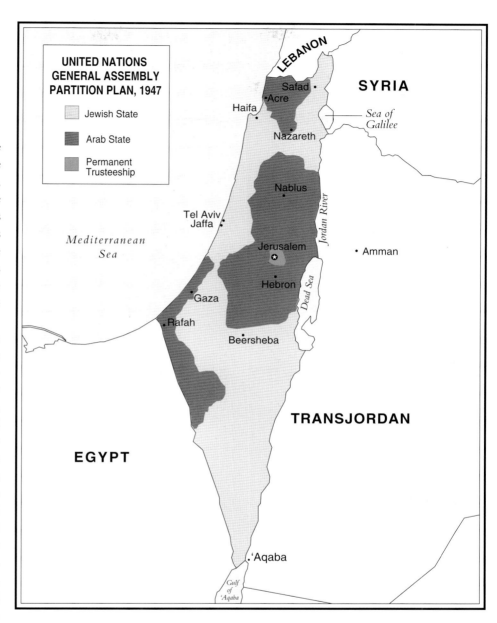

international organization that had been created after the war. The UN formed a Special Committee on Palestine, which recommended an end to Britain's mandate and the partition of Palestine into Jewish and Arab sections.

In November 1947 a majority of the UN member states voted in favor of partition. Their plan called for the Jewish and Arab parts of Palestine to become separate states, with Jerusalem an international city. This plan never went into effect.

In an attempt to restore peace to the region in 1947 the United Nations recommended partitioning Palestine into separate states for Jews and Arabs and internationalizing Jerusalem.

Chapter 8

Independence: Immigrants and Refugees

Golda Meyerson—later to be known as Golda Meir, a prime minister of Israel—was head of the political department of the Jewish Agency when the United Nations voted to end the British mandate and partition Palestine. She long remembered the excitement of that day:

> Like everyone else in the *yishuv,* I was glued to the radio, with pencil and paper, writing out the votes as they came through. Finally, at about midnight our time, the results were announced: Thirty-three nations (including the United States and the Soviet Union) were in favor of the partition plan; thirteen, including all the Arab states, opposed it; ten, including Great Britain, abstained. I immediately went to the compound of the Jewish Agency building, which was already jammed with people. It was an incredible sight: hundreds of people, British soldiers among them, holding hands, singing and dancing, with truckloads of more people arriving at the compound all the time.

"In Palestine and in the Diaspora," wrote David Ben-Gurion, "the resolution was greeted with wild enthusiasm, by Zionists and non-Zionists alike, by the pious and the non-observant, by the right and by the left. While rejoicing seized the whole House of Israel, there were deep anxieties in my own heart."

Ben-Gurion and Meir were worried about the resolution. The British had announced that they would be out of Palestine in six months, and this pleased many Zionists. But the UN plan called for dividing Palestine into Jewish and Arab states. Jewish leaders had accepted the plan, but with some misgivings because the UN partition was not a very neat division. The Jews, who made up 31 percent of the total population of Palestine, would get 55 percent of the territory—but nearly half of the people in that territory would be Arabs. The Arabs rejected the partition altogether, feeling that the UN had ignored their proposals and given in to Zionist pressure.

Soon after the UN vote, renewed fighting broke out. Golda Meir wrote, "Arab riots broke out all over Palestine the next day (seven Jews were killed in an Arab ambush on a bus) and on December 2 an Arab mob set the Jewish commercial center in Jerusalem on fire, while British police stood by interfering only when the Haganah tried to

These young men board a boat in Marseilles, France, in 1945. Carrying the Israeli flag, they leave war-torn Europe for new lives in Israel.

take action." Arab soldiers from neighboring states joined the fighting, which escalated quickly.

The Arab view of these events differed from Meir's. A statement from the Palestinian Arab Higher Committee to the UN said, "On November 30 the Arabs of Palestine rose in self-defense against partition which deprived them of the greater and better part of their country. The Jews, on the other hand, committed the most atrocious crimes."

During the remaining months of British rule, everyone realized that the partition was not going to work. Jewish leaders prepared to proclaim Palestine's independence as the state of Israel, and both Jews and Arabs saw that a battle was coming. On April 6 Ben-Gurion dramatically described the perils that the Jews faced as the mandate drew to an end:

> On May 15, when the Mandatory regime is formally ended, the country will be open to full-scale attack by Arab forces. The ratio between the Jews in this country and the Arabs here and in the neighboring states is about 1 to 40. Moreover, the Arabs have the tools of government at their disposal. Six Arab States are members of the UN, while a seventh, Trans-Jordan, is an ally of England, and is receiving a large proportion of its weapons from the departing British forces. The Jews under attack lack

both a government and international recognition, at a time when they are faced by seven independent Arab states: Lebanon, Syria, Trans-Jordan, Iraq, Egypt, Saudi Arabia, and Yemen. The Arab states have more or less trained armies. Some have air forces. Egypt also has a navy. This is, in brief, the situation—one that confronts us with a more fateful problem than any we have faced in over 1800 years.

Ben-Gurion later spoke of 700,000 Jews pitted against 27 million Arabs. But neither the Arab states nor the Palestinian Arabs were united by common goals. Among the Arab countries, Transjordan was the most unwilling to see the Palestinian Arabs form their own state—King Abdullah wanted to add their territory to his own country. He held secret meetings with Zionist leaders, hoping to make a deal. Meir described one such meeting that took place on the Jordan River shortly before the UN partition vote:

> We drank the usual ceremonial cups of coffee, and then we began to talk. Abdullah was a small, very poised man with great charm. He soon made the matter clear: He would not join in any Arab attack on us. He would always remain our friend, he said, and like us, he wanted peace more than anything else.

Abdullah suggested creating a Hebrew republic within a greater Transjordan. Meir proposed that the Zionists and Transjordan

divide the territory between them. The British, now that they were about to leave Palestine, may have favored an alliance between the Zionists and Transjordan because it would help them maintain their influence in the region by working closely with King Abdullah.

In the months before the British withdrawal, Arab and Zionist forces plunged Palestine into a fierce struggle. The Jewish defense groups enlisted and trained new soldiers, while the British tried to keep both sides from getting their hands on more weapons and to block Jewish immigration. By March 1948 the Zionist position was shaky. Jerusalem was under siege. Convoys of armored trucks tried to get desperately needed supplies to Jews in the city. Today the road to Jerusalem is still marked by old rusty trucks, monuments to those convoys.

The tide turned for the Zionists when they received an illegal shipment of arms from Czechoslovakia. The Haganah broke the siege of Jerusalem, while the Irgun led its own operations. The most notorious of these was an attack on Deir Yasin, an Arab village overlooking the road to Jerusalem. About 120 people were massacred, although the Arabs claimed 250 dead.

Leaders from Iraq, Syria, Lebanon, Egypt, Transjordan, and Saudi Arabia met to make plans for a United Arab force. At the same time, however, Transjordan was still talking with the Zionists. For a final secret meeting with Abdullah, Meir disguised herself as an Arab woman and drove unnoticed past a number of Arab checkpoints before meeting the king. Abdullah told her that Transjordan was now part of a unified force of Arab states and could not act alone.

He hoped that the Zionists would delay declaring Israel's statehood. Wrote Meir:

> "Why are your in such a hurry to proclaim your state?" he asked me. "What is the rush? You are so impatient!" I told him that I didn't think that a people who had waited 2,000 years should be described as being "in a hurry" and he seemed to accept that.

Still, the talks broke down, and Transjordan and the Zionists never made a deal. In the months ahead, some of the fiercest fighting would be between Transjordan's British-trained Arab Legion and the new Israeli army.

The British mandate ended, and on May 14, 1948, Israel declared its independence. Ben-Gurion read the declaration under a portrait of Theodor Herzl—and later wrote in his diary, "The country went wild with joy. But, as on November 29, I refrained from rejoicing. The State was established. Our fate now rests in the hands of the defense forces."

The next day Israel confronted the biggest test of its survival. The Arab invasion began. While the Egyptians advanced along the southern coast, Transjordan's forces besieged Jerusalem. Israel lost control of the Old City, including the Jewish Quarter and the Wailing Wall, at the end of May.

The Israelis did better in their fight against Egyptian and Syrian forces. They captured a large part of the territory that the partition had set aside for Arabs in the Galilee region. However, the largest area given to the Arabs in the partition plan, the West Bank of the Jordan River, was occupied by Transjordan's forces.

Under international pressure to end the war, the United Nations sent a representative, Count Bernadotte, to make peace between the Arabs and Jews. Both sides rejected his proposals. A colleague described what happened as Bernadotte traveled in a car convoy through Jerusalem: "In the Qatamon Quarter we were held up by a Jewish army-type jeep, placed in a roadblock, and filled up with men in Jewish army uniforms. At the same moment I saw a man running from this jeep. I took little notice of this because I merely thought that it was another check-point. However, he put a tommy gun through the open window on my side of the car and fired point-blank at Count Bernadotte and Colonel Sérot." The two men died. Bernadotte's assassins never went to trial, but there is little doubt that they were members of the Stern

Parts of Palestine were destroyed during Israel's War for Independence. When this photograph was taken in Jerusalem in 1948, the newly independent State of Israel was faced with massive rebuilding.

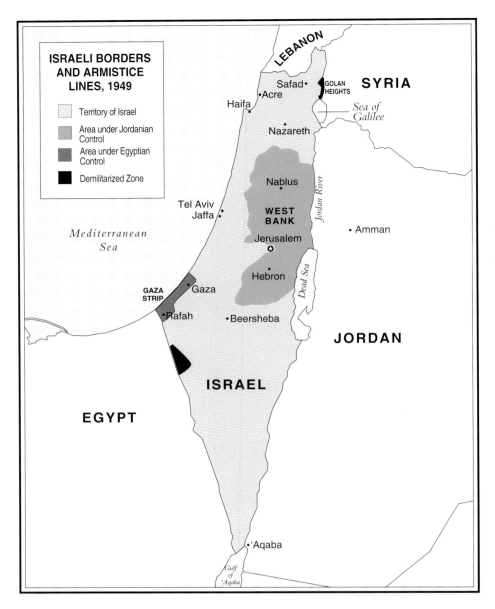

ISRAELI BORDERS AND ARMISTICE LINES, 1949

- Territory of Israel
- Area under Jordanian Control
- Area under Egyptian Control
- Demilitarized Zone

When Israeli borders and armistice lines were drawn in 1949, the Palestinian Arabs had lost all of the territory that the UN voted to give them.

Gang. The Israeli government was quick to condemn the assassination.

That government was provisional—that is, formed to deal with the immediate crisis until elections could take place. The members of the government faced internal struggles in addition to the war. The Irgun, under Menachem Begin's leadership, had maintained its own military units within the army. Now Ben-Gurion and the Labor leaders decided that the Irgun had to be brought under control. In June the Palmah brigades of the Haganah swooped down on the *Altalena*, a ship bringing arms for the Irgun. "Suddenly," wrote Menachem Begin, "we were attacked from all sides, without warning. With machine-guns and

mortars." Ben-Gurion then had some Irgun leaders arrested and abolished the Irgun units that remained in the army.

The final battles were fought in the south with the Egyptians. When Israeli forces pushed into the Sinai Peninsula, the British—who had signed a defense treaty with Egypt—began to threaten Israel. Ben-Gurion pulled Israel's forces out of the Sinai.

By the summer of 1949 Israel and the neighboring Arab states had agreed to an armistice. It was not a peace treaty, merely the end of fighting. Each country kept the territory it had occupied, but no comprehensive treaty existed to define permanent borders. The lack of such a treaty would lead to new wars in the decades to come.

When the fighting stopped, the Palestinian Arabs were the big losers. They controlled none of the territory that the UN had voted to give them. Egypt occupied the Gaza Strip, a coastal area near the Sinai Peninsula that had been designated for Arab Palestine. Israel and Transjordan controlled the rest of Arab Palestine. In 1950 the West Bank formally became part of Transjordan, now renamed Jordan. The Palestinians felt that King Abdullah of Jordan, the only Arab leader who had tried to collaborate with the Zionists and Israel, had betrayed them. In 1951 Abdullah was assassinated when he went to Friday prayers at al-Aqsa Mosque in Jerusalem. Before long Abdullah's grandson Hussein was king of Jordan.

The border between Israel and Jordan was messy and difficult to police. In some places it cut through villages, and it divided Jerusalem. Neither Jordan nor Israel really wanted the city internationalized, as the

UN had proposed. West Jerusalem became Israel's capital. East Jerusalem remained in Jordan's hands.

About 133,000 Arabs living within the new boundaries of the state of Israel became Israeli citizens. No one will ever know exactly how many Palestinian Arabs left their homes and became refugees, although they probably numbered between 600,000 and 760,000. Stateless and homeless, they were scattered in camps in Jordan, the Gaza Strip, Lebanon, and Syria, supported by the United Nations Refugee Works Agency (UNRWA).

For years the Arabs and Israelis argued about the refugees. The Arabs claimed that the Israelis had forced them out of Palestine. The Israelis claimed that they had urged the Palestinians to stay, but that Arab leaders had encouraged them to flee. The real answer is probably that a combination of factors propelled the refugees into flight. Only a few were physically forced out; most fled to escape the fighting, hoping to return when the war ended.

The refugees became an additional source of tension between Israel and the Arab nations that surrounded it. Israel claimed that the refugees were part of an "exchange" of population. Many Jews from Arab countries were immigrating to Israel, and Israel was absorbing them. The Arab states should therefore absorb the Palestinian refugees into their populations. The Arab nations disagreed, claiming that the Palestinians were entitled to a country of their own and that it was not the responsibility of the Arab states to take them in.

Caught between these opposing positions, the crowded refugee camps became permanent slums. Fawaz Turki, a Palestinian refugee and writer, describes the growing despair felt by those in the camps:

> Gradually, Palestinians, finding themselves unwelcome guests in host countries with depressed economies reluctant to absorb or aid them, capitulated and started to line up each month at the newly set up UNRWA food depots. A great many refugees discovered themselves, in the very early stages of homelessness, if not already living in camps, surely gravitating toward them. Hunger, as only those who have felt the ache of hunger know, is a much more potent emotion than pride. The latter is violently smothered when one's sensibilities and intellect are engulfed by nothing other than a daily search for food, warm clothing, and satisfying the needs of a newly arrived baby. Destitution, unwarranted and inexplicable, had then started to leave its shattering effects on the very fabric of our beings.

Whether or not they would have driven the Arabs out by force, many Israelis were glad to see them leave. Their departure meant that Jews would remain a large majority of their new state's population. It also made more land available for Jewish settlers. Long before the war ended Ben-Gurion wrote in his diary, "We must make immediate preparations for settlement of abandoned villages with the assistance of the Jewish National Fund." As masses of Jewish immigrants poured into Israel, they took control of Arab land and settled in empty Arab houses.

For Israelis, independence was a miracle after a desperate and heroic war of national liberation in which about 6,000 Jews had been killed. After 2,000 years the Jewish

Chaim Weizmann, elected Israel's first president, presented a Torah to U.S. President Harry S. Truman on Weizmann's visit to the United States.

Weizmann as its first president. The Mapai or Labor party received the most votes in the first election, so David Ben-Gurion, its leader, became the first prime minister.

In the years since Israel achieved independence, the structure of its government has shaped its political life and culture. No single political party has ever had an absolute majority. All Israeli governments have been coalitions—partnerships between one of the major parties and some of the lesser parties. The leading parties may have come from the secular or nonreligious Zionist tradition, but from the very first government the coalition has always included religious parties, particularly the National Religious party, which formed in 1956. This meant that Orthodox Jews, who envisioned Israel as a religious state, achieved a degree of power and control in Israel beyond their actual numbers. Many secular Israelis have been unhappy with the role of Orthodox Jews in government and public policy.

But the secular socialists themselves were not united. In 1948 a new party, Mapam, split off from the Labor party and became the second-largest party in the first Knesset. Supported by the kibbutz movement, Mapam promoted Marxism and Arab rights.

Although Mapai and Mapam both considered themselves socialists, they became bitter rivals. Mapam followed socialist ideals more strictly and wanted the state to own industries and to give special treatment to the kibbutzim. Mapai wanted Israel's economy to grow by attracting private investments and money from abroad. One result of the Mapai-Mapam rivalry was a crisis in the kibbutz movement. Some kib-

state was reborn—and right after the Holocaust, the worst catastrophe the Jews had known in their long history of persecution.

True to Herzl's vision, the new state was to be a liberal democracy. Its parliament, known as the Knesset, was a one-chamber body with 120 representatives from many different parties. Each political party presented a list of candidates; the number of candidates who would become members of parliament depended on the number of votes each party received. Each party was nationally based, which meant that Knesset members were elected by the entire nation, not by local districts.

Chosen by the Knesset as an important ceremonial figure and public spokesperson for the state of Israel, the president would invite the head of the leading political party to become prime minister and form the government. The Knesset selected Chaim

butzim—and some families—split over differences in ideas.

Under Menachem Begin the Revisionists formed the Herut (freedom) party. In the first election it won only 14 seats, but its power grew. Herut was an antisocialist party that appealed to the Eastern European middle class and to poor Jews arriving from Middle Eastern and North African countries. When the Israeli government accepted money from Germany as repayment to the victims of the Holocaust, Herut staged demonstrations against the payment, calling it "blood money."

The diversity of political parties led to lively debates in the Knesset. But under Ben-Gurion's leadership Mapai did more than any other group to shape the development of the new Israeli nation. It did so at a time of rising discontent and immense economic difficulties. Continuing tension along Israel's borders kept military expenses high. Israel was unable to buy food from the neighboring Arab countries, and food shortages worsened. To make matters worse, there were many more mouths to feed. People from the World War II DP camps, as well as thousands of Jewish immigrants from Eastern Europe and from the Arab countries, were flocking to Israel.

The government launched a "belt-tightening" program and began rationing

Faced with food shortages in their newly independent state, Israelis expand their farming efforts.

In "Operation Magic Carpet," the Israeli government flew more than 49,000 Yemenite Jews to Israel from 1948 to 1950. Almost all of Yemen's ancient Jewish community now lived in Israel.

food and services. People stood in long lines to buy goods—and even then they sometimes went home empty-handed. The government hoped to provide minimum necessities to everyone at a price that everyone could afford, but the program was difficult to enforce. Soon people were buying and selling goods illegally on the black market. To control this problem, the government adopted severe methods, such as searching private homes. Israelis grumbled about the heavy-handed government and rising prices. Public discontent led to strikes in the early 1950s. The Herut party claimed that Mapai was trying to undermine the middle class. Mapam argued that Mapai was attacking the poor. At last the government abandoned its unpopular economic program.

In the mid-1950s the economy and standard of living began to improve. Some of the improvement came about through foreign funds, such as the German payments and aid from Jews in the Diaspora, especially those in the United States. The Jewish Agency and the Jewish National Fund continued to funnel this aid into Israel.

Agricultural production, especially of citrus fruit, increased in the 1950s, as did international trade. Industries developed in textiles, diamonds, food processing, metals, and chemicals. The Histadrut built factories on Israel's outskirts, as well as whole new towns to house large numbers of low-paid workers, mostly immigrants from the Middle East and North Africa.

At the same time, Israeli was undergoing some unexpected social adjustments that had to do with the definition of Jewishness itself. A basic feature of the Jewish state was, as Ben-Gurion wrote, the "ingathering of exiles"—the idea that Jews from around the world, long exiled from their ancestral homeland, could now live in Israel. The Law of Return, passed in 1950, declared that every Jew who arrived in Israel could become an Israeli citizen. "This right," wrote Ben-Gurion, "is inherent in his very Jewishness and is his to exercise at his own free will—it is older than the State of Israel; in fact, it is this right that built the State. It derives from the uninterrupted historical link between the Jewish people and their ancestral Homeland, a link which the law of nations has also recognized." All Jews were thought to be one people. Once they arrived in Israel they would share in the same national values. Israel would serve as a great melting pot for the Jews of the world.

Israelis discovered, however, that in reality there were vast differences between Jews from different countries. As Jews from Asian and African countries began arriving in Israel, the nation's leaders realized that they knew little about the cultures of these people. Israelis called these newcomers Orientals, or *mizrahim,* and Jews from East-

· ·

100 · ISRAEL / AN ILLUSTRATED HISTORY

ern communities (*edot hamizrah*), names that Asian and African Jews began to use themselves. Most of the *mizrahim* were also called Sephardi Jews, or Jews of Spanish descent. Some of them *were* descendants of Spanish Jews who had settled in Morocco and other regions of the Ottoman Empire, but in its more general meaning the term Sephardi distinguished Asian, African, and Spanish Jews from European Ashkenazi Jews.

The new immigrants to Israel included many people from the ancient Jewish communities of Iraq and Yemen. Iraq had fought against Israel in 1948, and the Iraqi government took harsh measures against Iraqi Jews, giving them a very short time in which to decide whether to stay in Iraq or leave the country. The Mossad, the Israeli organization for secret emigration from foreign countries, encouraged Iraqi Jews to leave and even made secret deals with Iraqi government officials to hurry the process.

Between 1948 and 1953 about 125,000 Iraqi Jews came to Israel in what Mossad called Operation Ezra and Nehemiah after the Biblical leaders who returned to the land of Israel from Babylonia.

Israel also wanted Yemen's 50,000 Jews. There were already 30,000 Yemenite Jews in Palestine; some had arrived as early as the 1880s. Yemenites were considered hard workers, ideal residents for the new factory towns and frontier regions. Secret Mossad agents went to Yemen to encourage Jews to emigrate. They also paid the ruler of Yemen, who needed cash, to let the Jews leave and organized an airlift that brought about 49,000 of them to Israel.

Jews in other Arab countries found themselves in a precarious position. During the fighting between Israel and Egypt, many Egyptian Jews were imprisoned under martial law. When the Israeli armed forces dropped bombs on the Egyptian cities of Cairo and Alexandria, mob violence against

Thousands of children were brought to Israel from post-war Europe and the Arab countries by a program called Youth Aliyah. Many of them began a new life at kibbutzim like this one.

Tsafon Ma'arav (Northwest): A Moroccan Musical Group

Israeli culture is constantly being created and re-created. Older immigrant groups sometimes think that new arrivals have little to offer. In the past the Moroccan Jews, for example, were often ashamed of their cultural background.

Some Moroccan Jews began to explore their cultural heritage. In 1978 a group founded Tsafon Ma'arav under the direction of Professor Joseph Chetrit of the University of Haifa. The group's purpose was to make the Israeli public aware of some of the Jewish traditions in Moroccan and North African music from the past 500 years. The musicians play traditional instruments and sing in their original languages, Hebrew and Arabic. They perform in traditional Moroccan clothes and often dance and act out roles, such as bride and groom, or guest and host. Tsafon Ma'arav has performed all over Israel and on Israeli television—a reminder that Israeli culture has been formed by the many different Jewish cultures of the world.

This team of Tsafon Ma'arav musicians and singers performs traditional Moroccan Jewish music before large audiences.

Jews erupted. Arabs in Damascus also rioted. By 1951 some 15,000 to 20,000 Egyptian Jews—between a fifth and a quarter of Egypt's Jewish population—had gone to Israel; others went to Europe. A further 4,000 Jews from Syria and Lebanon entered Israel.

Jews in the non-Arab Muslim states of Turkey and Iran were less troubled than those in Arab countries because both Turkey and Iran had open diplomatic relations with Israel. Still, more than 30,000 Jews from Turkey had come to Israel by 1950 and nearly 50,000 from Iran by 1966. Most of the Iranian immigrants were from the poorer ranks of Iranian Jews, and they remained one of the poorest groups in Israel.

The largest group of immigrants came from North African countries that had been under French rule—Tunisia, Algeria, and Morocco. As French rule neared its end, Jews worried about their future in these countries. Most Algerian Jews went to France. Half of Tunisia's 80,000 Jews went to France and half to Israel. Morocco's Jewish community was the largest in Asia or Africa, numbering about 280,000 in 1948. The majority of Moroccan Jews emigrated to Israel in the 1950s and 1960s; others settled in France and Canada.

This mass of new immigrants placed tremendous strains on Israel's limited resources. Many of the newcomers lived in harsh conditions in immigrant camps; others were placed in prefabricated houses in transit camps in industrial zones near cities. These transit camps were supposed to be temporary, but some stood for decades and became slums.

Both new immigrants and veteran Israelis had to deal with considerable culture shock. The Israeli government and the Histadrut, however, paid little attention to the cultural and religious sensibilities of the immigrants. The official solution to the problem of culture clash was to absorb the newcomers into the culture that had been formed by the early immigrants, most of whom came from Eastern Europe. One of the most bitter controversies during this stressful time was the disappearance of sick Yemenite children from the immigrant camps. Dozens were taken from their parents and never seen again: some died and others were adopted by Ashkenazi families.

During the early years of immigration, the Oriental Jews tended to settle in newly founded communities, such as the develop-

ment towns in northern Israel or at the edge of the Negev Desert. These struggling communities had a higher proportion of Oriental than Ashkenazi Jews because the European veteran immigrants who controlled the government preferred to place Oriental Jews on difficult terrain.

In the 1950s Israelis began to wonder whether unlimited immigration was good for the country. Overburdened by the impoverished masses, in the early 1950s the government began an unofficial policy of more selective immigration, ranking potential immigrants by their usefulness. The veteran immigrants in power began to speak of the latest wave of immigrants, especially the North Africans, as primitive. They feared that if immigration from the "eastern" countries continued unchecked, Israeli society would be at risk. The Eastern European veteran immigrants thought that the Oriental Jews came from backward cultures that were associated with Israel's enemies, the Arabs. "Oriental culture," wrote novelist Albert Swissa, "was identi-

fied with the culture of the 'enemy': it was therefore necessary to play it down as much as possible—if not to ignore it completely." Ben-Gurion echoed this attitude: "We do not want Israelis to become Arabs. We are duty bound to fight against the spirit of the Levant [the Middle East], which corrupts individuals and societies, and preserve the authentic values as they crystallized in the Diaspora." What Ben-Gurion meant was that true Jewish values rested with the Ashkenazim and their secular Zionist traditions, not with eastern Sephardim who shared few cultural traits with the European Zionists. Some Israelis were interested in the exotic cultures of the Jews from far-flung communities, but only as traces of the past to be preserved in folklore exhibits and performances.

By the late 1950s it was clear that many of the Oriental immigrants, especially the North Africans, were having a hard time adjusting to Israeli society. When immigrants rioted in a working-class suburb of Haifa, many Israelis were

shocked. People began speaking about discrimination and saying that there were "two Israels." The Oriental Jews—especially the 500,000 of North African descent and the 200,000 of Yemenite descent—tended to have the lowest-paying jobs. People in power, who were mostly of Eastern European descent, gave the Oriental Jews few positions in government or in the Labor party.

Some of these ethnic divisions diminished over time as people mixed through intermarriage and at school, in the army, and on the job. But many Asian and African Jews did not become part of the dominant European culture. Despite pressures to abandon their culture, they began to find new ways to express it. Many maintained a profound attachment to religion, in contrast to the secularism of the state. Accustomed to pilgrimages to the tombs of saints (*tsaddikim* or "righteous ones") in Morocco and the Middle East, they started making mass pilgrimages both to the tombs of ancient rabbis and to those of distinguished North African rabbis who had died in the development towns. These celebrations gave a new sense of identity and belonging to North African Jews who had lost their traditional communities. Over time, as Oriental Jews acquired some political power and status, these cultural expressions gained greater acceptance in the larger society.

Ethnic divisions tended to diminish over time, but the split between the secular majority and the Orthodox minority widened. The Orthodox themselves were deeply divided between Zionists and non-Zionists. The National

Religious party strongly supported Zionism. Other Orthodox parties were non-Zionist and did not believe in a state not governed by Jewish law. For the Orthodox non-Zionists, God alone could restore Jewish sovereignty to Israel. Despite their opposition to the state of Israel, they participated in politics so that they could look after their own interests. The Orthodox persuaded Ben-Gurion to agree to some of their religious demands, for example that rabbinical students and women would not have to serve in the army. Perhaps, as Israeli writer Amos Oz put it, Ben-Gurion's decision came "out of a tacit, perhaps subconscious, fear of 'wiping out the remnants saved from the Holocaust.' Out of a desire not to extinguish 'the last flickering embers.'" Despite their conflicts with the secular state, the Orthodox were generally regarded as bearers of the Jewish tradition.

Even before independence, the Jewish Agency had made an agreement with the Orthodox, promising that in the Jewish state religion would be observed in certain aspects of public life. The Sabbath would be an official day of rest, when even public transportation would stop. Public institutions would follow dietary laws. The Orthodox would control marriage and divorce and could have their own state-funded religious schools. Ben-Gurion understood the importance of forging unity in the new state, so he made compromises in order to bring the Orthodox into the national enterprise. Perhaps the need for compromises explains why Israel has no written constitution. A constitution might have given permanent form to secular civil rights and limited the ability of Orthodox Jews to influence public life.

For all his compromises, Ben-Gurion could not avoid serious conflicts even at the beginning of statehood. In the immigrant camps, religious parties often clashed with Mapai members, accusing them of being hostile to religious traditions. Secular Israelis complained about the rabbinical students' exemption from military service. The biggest and most violent controversies concerned the Sabbath. The government could not enforce a complete day of rest throughout the country, but the Orthodox succeeded in imposing certain Sabbath restrictions. People could not work in industry or government institutions. No flights were allowed on El Al, Israel's national airline. Public transport was banned in many parts of the country, and in Jerusalem, public movie houses could not

operate—a riot broke out when a theater began showing a movie before the end of Sabbath. Roads leading through Orthodox neighborhoods were blocked by barricades during the Sabbath to prevent traffic from offending those who observed the ban against driving. One of the most gruesome episodes in Israeli history was the murder of David Polombo, a famous sculptor who created the iron gates in front of the Knesset. He was decapitated when some Orthodox Jews stretched piano wire across the road near an Orthodox neighborhood where he was riding his motorcycle on the Sabbath in 1966.

The question "Who is a Jew?" continued to perplex Israelis. According to Jewish law, a Jew is simply someone born of a Jewish mother. But what about conversion? The Orthodox declared that people who were converted to Judaism by Reform or Conservative rabbis, especially in the United States, could not settle in Israel under the Law of Return.

The 1962 case of Brother Daniel underlined the complicated relationship between religion and the state, between national and religious definitions of being Jewish. Brother Daniel was a Polish monk, born to Jewish parents. Hidden in a monastery during the Holocaust, he converted to Catholicism. He moved to Israel and wanted to be recognized as Jewish under the Law of Return because his mother was Jewish. In religion he was a Christian, but he believed that he was a Jew nationally. The Supreme Court, after much deliberation, ruled that Brother Daniel's conversion had canceled his claim to Jewish national identity.

The Law of Return did not apply to Arabs, some of whom were Muslim, some

Christian. Arabs, even refugees who had left their homes in Israel, were not eligible to citizenship under the Law of Return. Only those who had remained in Israel in 1948 became citizens of the new nation. The Druze, another minority in Israel, had split from mainstream Islam during the Middle Ages. In 1957 the Israeli government recognized the Druze as a religious community separate from the Muslims. The government hoped that by giving the Druze their own legal identity it would earn the loyalty of a group that had suffered persecution.

As Israeli citizens, the Arabs could vote, but the government suppressed any expression of Arab nationalism. In 1965, an Arab communist party called Rakah split from the main communist party. In the late 1960s and early 1970s, Rakah drew a significant number of Arab votes, winning four seats in the Knesset in 1973.

The Israeli government gave priority to the needs of its Jewish citizens—after all, it was trying to establish a Jewish state. Arab citizens received no benefit from the Jewish Agency and the Jewish National Fund. The government did not completely neglect the Arabs, who received aid for developing their economy and schools. But despite a rising standard of living and a growing literacy rate, Arab Israelis received far less of the state's resources than Jewish Israelis.

Arabs, in turn, seldom identified with the state of Israel. As members of a minority they were discriminated against. They were influenced by politics of the Arab world, and Israeli Jews often associated them with Israel's enemies. Yet neither did most Israeli Arabs completely identify with the Arabs

who had left Palestine and were now refugees. For better or worse, Israeli Arabs had to find their place in the new nation.

From its earliest days Israel has had three problems that have not yet been solved: the division between Ashkenazim and "Oriental" Jews, the division between secular and religious Israelis, and the division between Jews and Arabs. These divisions caused and are still causing great tension. Yet in the 1950s and early 1960s many Israelis did not choose to focus on these important issues. The excitement of statehood, the recent horror of the Holocaust, and the ongoing threat of war with the neighboring Arab states gave Israelis a sense of national unity and purpose.

The Druze, a religious sect that broke away from the main body of Islam centuries ago, were recognized by the Israeli government as a group separate from the Arab minority. This Druze flag shows the Star of David and the Arabic letters spell out the name of one of their famous leaders, Sultan Pasha.

Chapter 9

In the Shadow of the Holocaust

The biggest archaeological excavation in the history of Israel began in 1963 at Masada, the ancient site overlooking the Dead Sea. Yigael Yadin, a former chief of staff of the Israeli army who had become a professor of archeology at the Hebrew University, conducted the excavation with the support of the government and the Israel Defense Forces, who helped prepare the site. Hundreds of volunteers from Israel and around the world helped in the dig, which became a two-year patriotic event that produced a national monument.

Masada symbolized the national fight for freedom. In the 1940s and the early years of statehood, many Israelis contrasted the ancient Jewish defenders of the hilltop fortress with the Jews who had recently perished in the Holocaust. These Israelis believed—not altogether accurately—that the defenders of Masada had died with dignity because they fought to the bitter end, while the victims of the Holocaust went to their death without putting up a fight, like lambs to the slaughter. Masada became part of a new slogan that reflected the Israelis' determination not to fall to their enemies—"Never again shall

Masada fall"— and the army started swearing in new soldiers at Masada. Some people in Israel began to talk about the "Masada complex," which had two meanings: Never again would Jews be in a situation such as had occurred at Masada, which spelled defeat and the beginning of exile; and never would they permit another Holocaust.

Israeli national identity was woven from two threads. The first was the Holocaust, which more than any event in history proved to Zionists that the existence of the Jewish state of Israel was justified. Fear of another Holocaust haunted many Israelis, who liked to take foreign diplomats and visitors to the memorial and museum of the Holocaust, Yad Va-Shem, located on Mount Herzl in Jerusalem next to the military cemetery where Herzl's bones were buried after being flown to Israel in 1949. The second thread running through Israel's short history has been the threat to its survival as a state. These two forces—memory and fear—shape Israelis' interpretations of events and their view of the world.

Soon after the war of independence Israelis decided that they were right to be fearful. Despite the 1949 cease-fire,

Jewish Israelis take to the streets of Jerusalem in May 1951 to celebrate Israel's third year of independence.

The archaeological excavation in the 1960s at Masada, overlooking the Dead Sea, was a patriotic event. Masada became a great national monument, uncovering powerful emotions: never would Israeli Jews allow defeat and exile, or another Holocaust.

Ben-Gurion's chief rival was foreign minister Moshe Sharett, who believed in avoiding force if possible. Sharett became prime minister in 1953.

Palestinians were sneaking across the border into Israel. Often they merely visited family or relatives or reclaimed property, but sometimes they attacked Israelis. In October 1953 Arabs from Jordan threw a grenade into a home in a town east of Tel Aviv, killing a woman and two children as they slept. The British commander of Jordan's army assured Israel that the infiltrators would be captured and tried. But Ben-Gurion and Israel's military leaders decided to retaliate by striking the Jordanian village of Qibya. Paratroopers led by Ariel ("Arik") Sharon swept through the village, blowing up 45 houses and killing 60 people, mostly women and children. The Israeli public saw the Qibya raid as an act of self-defense. Israelis focused not on the massacre of Arabs but on the feeling that when Jews are victims, whether during the Holocaust or in Israel, the world looks the other way. Reports in Israeli newspapers made references to the Holocaust, comparing Arabs to Nazis.

Israel's leaders, however, were divided on the question of how best to deal with the Arab nations. Ben-Gurion's chief rival was foreign minister Moshe Sharett, who believed in avoiding force if possible. Ben-Gurion did not tell Sharett about the

planned attack on Qibya, and Sharett later recalled how shocked he was to learn of all the casualties.

Qibya turned Sharett and most of the cabinet toward a less militaristic policy. Unable to counter this shift, Ben-Gurion left political office and withdrew to his kibbutz in the Negev Desert, leaving Sharett as prime minister. But Ben-Gurion really had no intention of resigning from political life. He expected loyal followers such as Pinhas Lavon, the minister of defense, and Moshe Dayan, head of the Israel Defense Force, to follow his wishes while he waited for Sharett's government to unravel.

Lavon's militarism got him into trouble in 1954. The British were considering taking their troops out of Egypt's Suez Canal Zone, but Israel did not want to see them go, feeling that a British military presence in Egypt helped control Arab aggression. Lavon approved a secret plan to cause trouble between the British and the Egyptians. With or without Lavon's direct order, Israeli agents organized a spy ring that included Egyptian Jews who placed bombs in U.S. and British embassies and in public places. A few of the bombs went off harmlessly, but the operation was a disaster. Egyptian security police arrested the members of the spy ring.

The trial of the spies in Egypt attracted international coverage. The public learned only some years later that it was an Israeli-led operation, but Lavon was forced to resign anyway for his role in the fiasco. Ben-Gurion returned to the government as defense minister, as militaristic as ever. Tension had been mounting on the Egyptian border, with Egypt sponsoring raids of Palestinian *fidayyin* (guerrillas) across the border. Ben-Gurion ordered a raid in Gaza that killed 40 Egyptian soldiers. The attack did not hurt his political career—in 1955 he again became prime minister.

The Arab world was undergoing major political changes. Old regimes in Syria and Egypt fell. The Arab countries were becoming more hostile toward the Western nations. A charismatic colonel named Gamal Abdul Nasser became not just the head of Egypt's government but an important leader in the Arab world who called for Arab unity and opposition to Israel. Nasser bought arms and received economic aid from the Soviet Union. He also appealed to the Palestinians, whose cause he championed. But Nasser's call for Arab unity made some Arab governments fear for their future. In the winter of 1955-56, rioting against King Hussein's pro-Western position occurred in Jordan.

Against this background, tension grew between Israel and Egypt. Skirmishes across the border increased. Then Nasser blockaded the Straits of Tiran, the narrow waterway where the Red Sea enters the Indian Ocean. The blockade interfered with shipping from Israel's southern port of Eilat, and Israel prepared for war. As part of his preparations Ben-Gurion made Golda Meir his foreign minister.

In Egypt, Nasser too was preparing for a conflict. To eradicate the last traces of foreign control, he took control of the Canal Zone from Great Britain and France. At this point Israel, France, and Britain formed a plan of attack against Egypt.

The war began on October 29, 1956. British planes bombed Egyptian airfields, and British and French troops invaded the Canal Zone. Led by Moshe Dayan, Israeli forces invaded Gaza and the Sinai Peninsula. Four days later the fighting ended with Sinai in Israeli hands. Israel had suffered 172 casualties, compared with hundreds on the Egyptian side. The victory reminded Israelis of the role Sinai had played in biblical history. "After 3,300 years," recalled Ben-Gurion, "we were at Mount Sinai again. The peninsula and the Gaza Strip were rid of the plague of the Egyptians—this was one of the finest military campaigns in Jewish history."

The 1956 war was a military victory for Israel, but not a clear political success. The British and French withdrew their forces and gave up control of the Canal Zone. Israel also withdrew, largely because of pressure from the United States. United Nations Emergency Forces were left in charge of the Gaza-Israel border and the Straits of Tiran. Still, their military victory gave Israelis a much greater sense of security. They considered that the Sinai campaign had been an act of self-defense. Some people in other nations criticized Israel for its attack, but Israelis felt that these critics were hypocrites who had done nothing to save Jews during the Holocaust. If nothing else, the 1956 war had shown the world that

A revolutionary since youth, Egyptian President Gamal Abdul Nasser called for Arab unity and opposition to Israel. He resigned after Egypt's disastrous defeat in the Six-Day War, but popular support for this charismatic leader forced him back into office.

The Mossad

David Ben-Gurion founded the Mossad in 1951. It was in charge of all espionage outside Israel. In 1952 Iser Harel, head of the Shin Bet (Israel's internal security service), also became chief of the Mossad.

Harel headed the Mossad for 11 years, during which time Israel's intelligence service established its worldwide reputation for daring and successful missions. The Mossad often cooperated secretly with foreign organizations such as the American Central Intelligence Agency (CIA) or SAVAK, Iran's secret service. Among Mossad's best-known successes was the abduction of Nazi war criminal Adolph Eichmann from Argentina in 1960. Mossad agents also infiltrated enemy Arab countries to gather information for the Israeli government. Sometimes they cultivated secret ties with Arab leaders such as King Hassan II of Morocco and King Hussein of Jordan. In the 1950s and early 1960s, Mossad agents were involved in secret missions and diplomacy to help Jews from Arab countries emigrate to Israel; the most important of these operations was in Morocco. More recently, in the early 1980s, Mossad agents helped bring thousands of Ethiopian Jews to Israel through Sudan.

One of Mossad's most important activities has been its fight against international terrorism. The most sensational Israeli operation abroad was the July 1976 raid at Entebbe Airport in Uganda. A group of Arab and German terrorists hijacked an Air France jet on its way from Paris to Tel Aviv. They took the plane and its 266 passengers and crew members to Entebbe Airport in Uganda, an east African country hostile to Israel. Mossad agents in Africa and Europe moved quickly to obtain precise information about the location of the hijacked plane, the layout of the airport, and the position of Ugandan troops guarding the plane. This information is what enabled the Israeli military to secretly fly from Israel to Entebbe Airport and rescue the hostages. The operation was a spectacular success, although four of the captives died, and one Israeli officer, Lieutenant Colonel Yonatan Netanyahu, brother of the future prime minister, Benjamin Netanyahu, was killed during the rescue.

After its early years, the Mossad had less success in gathering vital intelligence information—for example, it failed to predict the surprise attack on Israel by Egypt and Syria in 1973. In the 1980s and 1990s it placed more emphasis on assassinating terrorists. Mossad agents killed some of their targets and missed others. In October 1997 agents in Jordan tried to assassinate Khaled Meshaal, a leader of the Islamic pro-terrorist group Hamas. They injected Meshaal with poison but it did not kill him, and the agents were caught by the Jordanian authorities. Israel had to release some of its Palestinian prisoners to get the agents back. The failed assassination attempt drew much criticism of the Israeli government and of Mossad and created a diplomatic crisis with Jordan.

Israel would take aggressive action against its enemies.

During these early years of independence, the legacy of the Holocaust and its meaning for the state of Israel were particularly troubling for Israel's government and its citizens. In 1954 the Holocaust was at the heart of the most politically charged trial in Israel's history. Malchiel Gruenwald, a Hungarian Jewish survivor who had lost his family in the Holocaust and who was known for his vicious criticisms of Israeli political leaders, published an accusation against Israel Rudolf Kastner, who had been head of the Jewish Rescue Committee in Budapest, Hungary, during World War II. Gruenwald stated that Kastner had made a deal with the Nazis to save himself, his family, and friends. Kastner, said Gruenwald, had betrayed Hungarian Jews by failing to warn them of the Nazis' plans for extermination, and, as a result, 500,000 of Hungary's 800,000 Jews had been murdered.

At the time of the accusation, Kastner was a high government official in the Mapai party. The state decided to sue Gruenwald for criminal libel. Shmuel Tamir, a brilliant and politically ambitious attorney and former member of the Irgun and Herut, was Gruenwald's defense lawyer. Tamir was already known for his contempt for Ben-Gurion, whom he called "Minister of Treason and Minister of Abomination."

Although the government had probably expected the support of Judge Benyamin Halevy, the judge allowed Tamir to turn the courtroom into a spectacle. Although Gruenwald was on trial, his name rarely came up. Tamir cleverly made it seem that Kastner and Mapai were on trial instead. One of the witnesses he called was Katarina Senesh, mother of the martyred parachutist Hannah Senesh. Tamir suggested that Kastner had failed to prevent the torture and execution of this great heroine. The courtroom also heard from Tamir how Mapai had collaborated with the British rather than saving Jews.

Halevy reviewed the evidence for nine months (Israel's justice system called for the judge, not a jury, to deliver the verdict). In June 1955 he announced his decision in an opinion that was nearly 300 pages long—he read it to the court for an entire day and part of the evening. Halevy found Gruenwald innocent of libel and said that the accusations against Kastner were true. "Masses of ghetto Jews boarded the deportation trains in total obedience, ignorant of the real destination and trusting the false declaration that they were being transferred to work camps in Hungary," he wrote. Kastner, proclaimed

Adolf Eichmann responds to questions from the judges following the end of cross-examination by the prosecution. Eichmann is protected from the trial spectators by bulletproof glass.

Halevy, "sold his soul to the devil"—a phrase that appeared in huge headlines and was branded into the public's mind.

Ben-Gurion kept his distance from the trial, preferring to let the whole mess fall into the lap of Prime Minister Sharett. After the verdict Mapai's opponents submitted a no-confidence motion in the Knesset. In the Israeli parliamentary system, this meant that if the motion came to a vote and the government lost its majority, it would have to resign. The motion failed to pass, but it shook up the government nonetheless. Three years later Israel's supreme court overturned Halevy's verdict and declared that Gruenwald's accusations were unfounded. Vindication came too late for Israel Rudolf Kastner, who had been shot and killed in front of his home by a former member of the outlawed Stern Gang.

The Gruenwald case may have caused a sensation in Israel and thrown the country into political turmoil, but the case of Adolph Eichmann captured the attention of the world. Eichmann, the principal organizer of the mass deportation of Jews to the Nazi concentration camps, had managed to escape justice and was living in Argentina under the name Ricardo Clement. In 1960 agents of Israel's secret service, the Mossad, seized him, drugged him, and flew him to Israel to stand trial.

Like the Gruenwald case, the Eichmann trial brought the Holocaust to the forefront of public consciousness. It was broadcast live on the radio and reported in newspapers around the world. Legal experts in some countries criticized Israel for taking the law into its own hands by kidnapping Eichmann. Some American Jewish leaders also argued that Eichmann should not stand trial in Israel, fearing that this might hurt the country's image. But Ben-Gurion, again at the height of power as prime minister, wanted the trial to prove a point to the world that had allowed the Holocaust to happen. Jews needed their own homeland. Israel, and Israel alone, could assure Jews' safety.

During the trial, Eichmann sat in a bulletproof glass cage. Prosecutor Gideon Hausner opened the trial with an eight-hour speech—a moving oration that chronicled the sufferings of the Jewish people and the achievements of Zionism. Hausner proclaimed that the millions of victims "were those who awaited the Jewish state and were not privileged to see it." Hundreds of people who had suffered atrociously during the Holocaust were called in to testify. Eichmann was sentenced to death and executed by hanging in May 1962, the only person in Israel's history to be sentenced to death by the courts. Israel's Law of Genocide calls for capital punishment for those who caused the Holocaust.

The Eichmann trial was more than a sensational and patriotic public event for Israelis. It was also a unifying and educational event. Ben-Gurion hoped that it would make a powerful impression on the public, especially on younger Jews and Israel's new immigrants from Morocco and other Arab countries, who had had no direct experience of the Holocaust. Eichmann made the Holocaust more a part of Israel's national identity than ever.

It also gave Ben-Gurion and the Mapai party a chance to show their strength. But the Eichmann trial also coincided with the weakening of Ben-Gurion's domination and growing dissatisfaction with his leadership, and the "Lavon Affair," which also took place in 1960, struck a severe blow to his power. Details of the earlier spy ring and trial in Egypt became known to the public when Pinhas Lavon asked for a formal investigation into his own role in those affairs, hoping to clear his name and improve his chances of political success. Ben-Gurion, who had no use for Lavon, appointed a committee of inquiry—but to his fury it announced that Lavon could not be held responsible for the disaster in Egypt. After a series of resignations, returns, and weak reelections, Ben-Gurion retired from office in 1963, largely because of the "Lavon Affair."

Like other political events, the "Lavon Affair" caused much public debate. Through much of Israel's history such debates have centered on the question of how the nation should respond to the Arabs beyond its borders, the powerful new regional leaders who made Israelis fear for their survival—especially Nasser of Egypt. Nasser had risen from the ashes of military defeat in 1956 to become the leading figure of the Arab world. Arabs throughout the Middle East listened to his radio speeches, in which he condemned Israel and supported the Palestinians.

Meanwhile, Great Britain and France had withdrawn from the Middle East and the United States was taking their place, becoming much more involved in the Arab world. For example, when Lebanon's government

Foreign Minister Golda Meir talks with ex-Minister of Defense Pinchas Lavon over coffee. Lavon resigned in 1955 because of an Israeli espionage fiasco in Egypt, which became known as the "Lavon Affair."

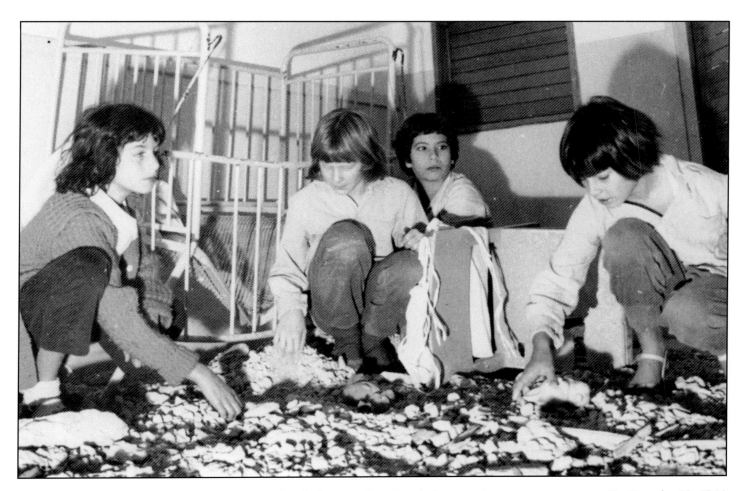

was at risk, American marines landed in Beirut. The United States competed with the Soviet Union to influence Arab leaders. The Soviets made gains in some Arab countries and became the principal arms suppliers to Egypt, Syria, and Iraq.

The 1960s brought growing political awareness and activity among Palestinian Arabs. In 1964 they formed the Palestinian Liberation Organization (PLO), led by Ahmad al-Shuqayri. Nasser backed the PLO, although other Arab states made attempts to control the organization. Syria backed a smaller Palestinian group called al-Fatah. Its leader, Yasir Arafat, wanted to involve the Arab states in a war with Israel.

This background of regional change and rising political tension caused hostilities that in 1967 led to the so-called Six-Day War. With Arab leaders calling for the destruction of Israel, the Syrians began shelling Israeli kibbutzim, possibly as a reaction to Israeli tractors crossing into the demilitarized zone that was supposed to be off-limits between the two countries. Israel responded

to the shellings with tank, airplane, and artillery attacks on Syrians in the Golan Heights region. Arab leaders increased pressure on Jordan to join an Egyptian, Syrian, and Iraqi force against Israel. The Egyptian army mobilized its forces and moved into the Sinai. When Nasser demanded the partial removal of the United Nations Emergency Force (UNEF) from the Sinai, the UN removed the entire force. Once again the Egyptians closed the Straits of Tiran to Israeli shipping, and Jordan joined the defense pact with Nasser.

On the brink of war, many Israelis believed that defeat would bring the utter annihilation of their country. Newspaper articles called Nasser another Hitler. Israel mobilized its forces and called up the reserves.

Did the Egyptians truly want to go to war? Perhaps all Nasser wanted was to bluff Israel into stopping its attacks on Syria or to win territory for Egypt or the Palestinians. The Israelis did not see it that way, however. They feared total

On November 13, 1964, three Israeli farm settlements were shelled by Syrian artillery positions across the border. These children collect pieces of plaster that fell from their bedroom ceiling after their kibbutz was hit.

Israeli paratroopers paid an emotional visit to the Western Wall at the end of the Six-Day War. The Wall, one soldier said, "was what we had been fighting for."

destruction. Nasser's troops were heading toward their borders; the major Israeli cities were within easy range of the Arab armies. The threat of a new Holocaust seemed to loom large. Popular hero Moshe Dayan became minister of defense. He and chief of staff Yitzhak Rabin would lead the country in war.

Israel did not wait to be attacked. On June 5, 1967, it struck first. The Israeli air force bombed Egyptian airfields, demolishing hundreds of Egyptian air-force planes on the ground. By June 9, the army had reached Suez—the Sinai was again under Israeli control. Israeli forces also captured East Jerusalem and the Old City in some of the worst fighting of the war. They took the city by hand-to-hand combat, routing snipers from one house at a time. Their arrival at the Western Wall was a moment of great excitement. One young soldier, after describing the horrific fighting in Jerusalem, exclaimed:

> We got to St. Stephen's Gate and we could see the Western Wall, through an archway. We saw it before, but this time it was right in front of us. It was like new life, as though we had just woken up. We dashed down the steps; we were among the first to get there, but a few had already got there and I could see them, men that were too tired to stand up any more, sitting by the Wall, clutching it, kissing the stones and crying. We all of us cried. That was what we had been fighting for. It goes so deep, this emotion we felt when we reached the wall.

Six days after the start of the war, the fighting stopped. Israel held the West Bank, the Golan Heights, and the Sinai Peninsula. About 800 Israelis, mostly soldiers, had died; the death toll from the combined Arab forces may have reached 30,000. Although Israel mourned its dead, the country was in a jubilant mood. This victory marked a turning point in Israel's history. All of Jerusalem was now in Jewish control. At long last, people felt, the Arab countries would have to accept Israel's existence.

Surely they would agree to exchange the territories they had just lost for peace.

The Arab states, however, ruled that any direct negotiation with Israel was out of the question. Such an act would amount to diplomatic recognition of Israel and would deny the Palestinians their rights. It would also be an acknowledgment of Arab defeat. Furthermore, the Arabs were outraged that Israel, intending to keep all of Jerusalem, had formally made the eastern or Arab part of the city a part of Israel.

As the prospect of making peace with the Arab nations faded, an increasing number of Israelis wanted to keep the territories taken in the war. They did not want to return to the pre-1967 national border that placed Israel's major population centers within artillery range of Arab armies and within a few minutes' flying time of Arab airfields. They did not want their settlements in northern Israel to again become easy targets of the Syrian army perched high on the Golan Heights. Israel argued that the UN Security Council Resolution 242, which called for Israel's withdrawal from territories occupied in the war, did not say "*the* territories"; this meant that Israel only agreed to withdraw from *some* territories. A growing and highly vocal minority of Israelis believed that by occupying Arab territories in the 1967 war, the Israelis were achieving the Zionist dream of restoring *all* of the historic land of Israel.

Israel's continued occupation of the Arab territories had diplomatic consequences. The Soviet Union—as well as most Eastern European nations and many African nations, all of which were strongly influenced by the Soviets—cut diplomatic ties with

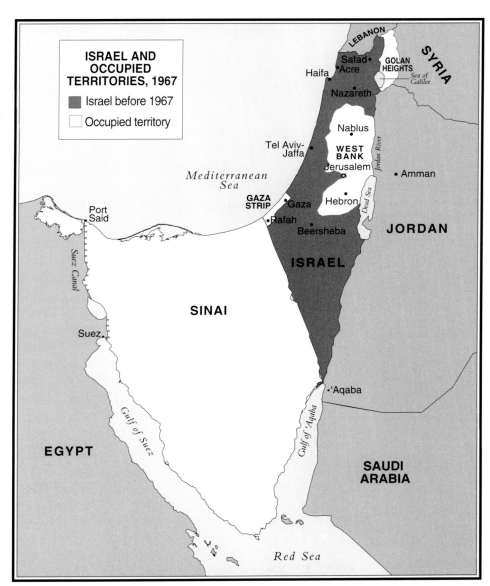

Israel. While Israel was growing stronger militarily and economically, it was becoming isolated in the world community. This isolation only strengthened Israelis' belief that, just as during the Holocaust, they could not rely on the outside world to save the Jews. If need be, like the defenders of Masada of old, Israel would defend itself in any way it could.

This map shows Israel and its occupied territories before and after the Six-Day War.

Chapter 10

The Challenges of a Greater Israel

The Western Wall of the ancient Temple mount in Jerusalem is also known as the "Wailing Wall," because worshipers weep in mourning for the loss of the Temple. Israelis were exuberant when access to this sacred Jewish site was restored following the capture of the Old City of Jerusalem in the Six-Day War.

In April 1968, Orthodox Jews entered the Ibrahimi Mosque in Hebron to pray at the Cave of Machpelah, a site believed to hold the tombs of the biblical patriarchs Abraham, Isaac, and Jacob and their wives, Sarah, Rebecca, and Leah. For centuries the shrine had been controlled by Muslims, who also regarded it as sacred. When the Orthodox Jews claimed their right to pray there, the Israeli government decided to call the Cave of the Machpelah a Jewish shrine and to divide prayer time between Muslims and Jews. This outraged not just the Muslim community of Hebron but Muslims around the world.

The Orthodox Jews' seizure of the site was an act of defiant nationalism. For many of them and their secular supporters, the recent war had not just enlarged Israel's territory—it had returned the historic land of Israel to Jewish sovereignty. When Orthodox Jews began settling around Hebron, the government built the new settlement of Kiryat Arba for them on the outskirts of the town, and later Jews settled in Hebron itself. They recalled the disturbances in 1929, when Arabs had massacred Jews in Hebron. Afterward, British authorities had forced the

surviving Jews to move. Now some Jews were determined to return.

The Labor government was not sure what to do with the territories Israel had occupied in the 1967 war, because it had come to accept the boundaries that had existed from 1948 until the war. After the war, leaders of many nations expected that Israel would not hold the conquered territories—except Jerusalem—for very long. They believed that the Arabs would offer peace to get back their lands. This belief faded when the Arab leaders did not offer to negotiate with Israel. The Labor government considered making permanent adjustments to the national borders.

A new movement called "The Land of Israel" declared that the conquered territories should remain part of Israel and that no Israeli government should ever give back any of these lands. The movement called for immediate Jewish settlement and development of the territories, including areas next to Arab cities in the West Bank.

Moshe Dayan, minister of defense in 1967, played a large part in setting government policy toward the Arabs in the occupied territories. Dayan recollected:

What is properly called the West Bank, but was always known to us by its biblical name, Judea and Samaria, held special boyhood memories for me. The end of summer, between harvest and sowing, was a dead season, of which we took prompt and full advantage. My friends and I would set out on what we called "the long excursion," a walking tour through the country. With a knapsack of food and an army blanket on our backs and a few pennies in our pockets, we would wander around the land, along the Jordan Valley, across Samaria, up to Jerusalem and through Judea.

Now that Israel controlled the West Bank, Dayan was able to revisit Samaria, which, as he recalled:

had become much dearer to me with time. I moved through these ancient territories thrilled by the view and thought of their biblical sites and sounds of their names: Shiloh, where the Israelite tribes assembled before the Ark of the Law; Tekoa, birthplace of the prophet Amos; Beth-El, associated with the Patriarch Abraham, with Jacob's dream, with Samuel's judgment, and with the concentration of Saul's forces when he fought the Philistines; Anathoth, of Jeremiah and two of David's "mighty men."

Although Dayan felt a deep sense of attachment to the land of the biblical past—a land that he himself had known—he did not regard the Arabs as intruders on territory that belonged to the Jews by right of their biblical heritage:

I did not think of them as being interposed between me and the land. Never have I harbored feelings of hostility towards the Arabs. The back-ground of our wars and our conflicts was political and national ambition, not personal enmity. The encounters over *pitta* (flat Arab bread), olives, and dark coffee and the "*Ahalan wasahalan*" [welcome] with which I was greeted whenever I reached the threshold of their homes were broken off from time to time by war, but they were always renewed after the dust of battle had settled.

Israel would maintain military control of the territories, but Dayan's policy was to rule the Arab civilian population indirectly through municipal and village councils. He also created a policy of "open bridges." The Arabs, who would keep their Jordanian nationality, could travel and trade across the Jordanian border. Arab workers from the occupied territories could also cross the former border (called the Green Line) to work during the day in Israel proper. Although they usually received lower pay than Israeli citizens, they still earned more in Israel than they would in their home towns and villages, where there were few job opportunities. Thousands of Arab men from the West Bank and Gaza began traveling daily to work in Israel, especially in the building industry. Some who found it too difficult or expensive to return home every day stayed overnight illegally near their workplaces. Some Israeli employers encouraged this practice.

Not all Israelis were pleased with this situation. For Labor Zionists who clung to the old thinking, the use of Arab workers went against one of the original principles of Zionism: the idea of "Hebrew labor" performed by self-reliant Jews in their own land. But this principle faded after 1967. A native of one of the early Zionist settlements complained sadly to the writer Amos Oz: "I'm seventy-eight years old, and every morning at four or five, I go out to work the land. I want you to know: at five o'clock in the morning this is already an Arab country. To the breadth and length of this country, the Arabs are up and working and the Jews are still fast asleep." But cheap Arab labor helped the country prosper and the construction industry boom.

Jews in the Diaspora—that is, Jews living outside Israel in countries around the world—saw that Israel was more secure than ever after the Six-Day War, which had demonstrated the country's strength. They began to take greater pride in their Jewishness. Jews from Western Europe, the United States, and Argentina moved to Israel in greater numbers than ever before.

The Soviet Union also saw a reawakening of Jewish identity and a growth of Zionism after the Six-Day War. The burst of Jewish feeling was due partly to pride in Israel's victory, and was partly a reaction to the Soviet government's vicious anti-Zionist and anti-Israel campaign. Yakov Kazakov, a Russian Jewish student at the University of Moscow, gave up his citizenship on June 13, 1967. The following year he wrote to the central government, the Supreme Soviet, "I do not wish to be a citizen of a country that arms and supports the remaining fascists and Arab chauvinists who desire to wipe Israel off the face of the earth and to add another two and a half million killed to the six million who have perished. I do not want to be a collaborator of yours in the destruction of the State of Israel because I consider myself to be a citizen of the State of Israel." He was one of the first of many Jews to give up their Soviet citizenship and demand permission to leave the Soviet Union.

The Soviet Union broke off diplomatic relations with Israel following the Six-Day War. After that, the Israeli government actively encouraged Soviet Jews to emigrate to Israel. But the Soviet government refused to allow free emigration and imposed severe restrictions on Jews who wanted to go to Israel. Thousands of Jews did leave, but Soviet authorities refused the requests of many activists, who came to be called *refuseniks*. Those who spoke out and demonstrated for free emigration risked long prison sentences in Soviet labor camps. The most famous of the *refuseniks* was Anatoly Sharansky, who was imprisoned from 1978 to 1986 before he was allowed to emigrate to Israel.

New arrivals in Israel in the late 1960s received tax breaks and other privileges that allowed them to buy apartments and new cars. The newcomers' special privileges and the growing wealth of some veteran Israelis caused much resentment among Israel's poor. The country's newfound prosperity did not reach most Oriental Jews, especially Moroccan Jews who had settled in Israel in the 1950s. The government did little to improve the lives of people in the slums of Jerusalem and Tel Aviv or in the depressed development towns in the north and the Negev Desert. Tensions emerged between the Oriental Jews and the new Soviet immigrants. The old leaders, on the other hand, welcomed the immigration of Soviet Jews—"real" Jews, as some said—because Oriental Jews, insultingly called

Moshe Dayan became foreign minister under Menachem Begin and was largely responsible for successful negotiations that led to the Camp David Accords with Egypt.

"blacks," now outnumbered immigrants from Europe.

External threats often unify a country torn by internal divisions. This is true of Israel, a country whose survival had always seemed at risk. The jubilation over the 1967 victory was short-lived. With no peace between Israel and the Arab states, tensions continued. Egyptian and Israeli forces fired at each other sporadically in 1969 and 1970. This was a "war of attrition," a war in which neither side gained

Anatoly (Natan) Sharansky's Struggle

Anatoly Sharansky is the most famous Russian *refusenik,* or political prisoner, and immigrant to Israel. Born in 1948 in the coal-mining city of Donetsk, he studied mathematics at the Moscow Physical-Technical Institute, hoping for a career in computer technology. His career was cut short, however, when he joined the movement fighting for the right of Jews to emigrate to Israel.

Sharansky applied to leave the Soviet Union in 1973. The authorities refused his request, claiming that he had access to classified materials. Although thousands of Jews received permission to leave, scientists, doctors, lawyers, and teachers were often refused. *Refuseniks* were also getting arrested. In 1974 Sharansky was arrested for the first time. While he was in prison, his fiancée received permission to leave the country. Sharansky was released and they were married the day before she had to leave for Israel.

Sharansky continued to participate in public protests and to pass infor-mation to foreign sup-porters of Soviet Jews. In 1975 his employers fired him. He began giving private lessons in English and mathematics, and he often served as an inter-preter for foreign visitors, including American congresspeople. Sharansky was becoming well known in Europe and the United States as one of the leading *refuseniks.*

In 1975 the Soviet Union, the United States, Canada, and the countries of Europe signed the Helsinki Agreement. They agreed to follow the 1948 International Decla-ration of Human Rights, which states that every person has the right to leave any country, includ-ing his or her own, and to return to it. As a signer of the Helsinki Agreement, the Soviet Union had officially agreed with the principle of free emi-gration—but it did not put that principle into practice. Sharansky was among the founders of the Helsinki Monitoring group, which reported on human rights in the So-viet Union.

Sharansky now be-came perhaps the most well-known leader of the Soviet Jews. Western newspapers, films, and television brought public-ity to his protests against Soviet policy and to his accusations of Soviet vio-lations of human rights. In March 1977 Soviet au-thorities arrested Sharansky and accused him of treason. At once a public campaign on his behalf began in the West.

The authorities im-prisoned Sharansky without trial for 16 months, interrogating him hundreds of times. When it came, his trial lasted only a few days. The verdict: 13 years' deprivation of liberty, 3 in prison, and 10 in a la-bor camp. From Israel his wife led a worldwide campaign to win his release.

Conditions in the la-bor camp were extremely harsh. Sharansky often protested by refusing to work. He also irked the authorities by insisting on the right to practice his religion. As a result Sharansky received an-other prison term of three years. On Yom Kippur in 1982 he started a hunger strike, refusing to eat. Prison authorities force-fed and beat him, and he

In 1977 Anatoly (Natan) Sharansky (right) defended himself against charges of treason in Russian courts. Though he ended his defense with "Next year in Jerusa-lem," it was nine years before he was released from prison and reunited with his wife, Avital (left), in Israel.

came close to death be-fore stopping his strike. In 1986 Soviet authorities released Sharansky as part of an exchange for Soviet spies imprisoned in the West. Stripped of Soviet citizenship, he emigrated to Israel. There he was reunited with his wife, whom he had not seen for 12 years.

Natan (as he called himself in Hebrew) Sharansky became a lead-ing spokesperson for Soviet Jewish immigrants in Israel. By the time of the 1996 elections, Israel had taken in several hun-dred-thousand immi-grants from the former Soviet Union. Many were unable to find work in their professions and felt frustrated because the major parties neglected their needs. In response, Sharansky founded a new political party called Israel Be'aliyah (which means both "Israel on the way up" and "Israel of immi-gration"). The party won seven seats in the Knesset and joined the ruling coa-lition government. Sharansky has continued to be the voice of Russian Jews in Israel.

---

or lost any ground. The United States tried but failed to arrange a peace treaty.

During the fighting, Israelis often man-aged to overlook their country's internal problems, but the end of the war of attrition in August 1970, when Israel and Egypt accepted an American cease-fire plan, brought those problems more sharply into view. Most obvious was the growing rift between Israel's haves and have-nots. In 1971 trouble broke out in Jerusalem when a gang of Moroccan Jews turned their

grievances into a protest movement. To call attention to their cause, they called them-selves the "Black Panthers," after the militant American black group of the 1960s. "We will be like the Black Panthers in the United States, since we are Blacks and screwed," they declared. Following a loud and bois-terous demonstration, Prime Minister Golda Meir agreed to meet with them. Her com-ment on the meeting was, "these are not nice boys." Many people thought that her response showed how far out of touch the

country's leaders were with the problem of "two Israels." The Black Panthers' protest shocked Israelis, who now realized that the social demands of Israel's poor needed to be addressed.

Israel's Arab population was also chang-ing. The 1967 war had been a turning point for the nation's Arab citizens. The conquest of the West Bank and Gaza reestablished contact among Palestinians who had been separated for nearly 20 years. This brought more political awareness to Israeli Arabs, who now began to identify with the political struggle of the Palestinians, harboring deep resentment against the Israeli government. They spoke out against discrimination, protesting that they did not receive their fair share of land and resources. The Arab peasant farmer was becoming a thing of the past. The majority of Arabs now worked as wage earners on Jewish land or in low-paying jobs in Jewish businesses.

In the early 1970s Israel felt militarily secure, armed with weapons bought from the United States. But Anwar Sadat, Egypt's new president, was becoming frustrated. The Soviet Union, Egypt's principal supplier of arms, was not giving him the military aid he wanted. In 1972 Sadat expelled the Russians from Egypt and began trying to win more American support. U.S. president Richard Nixon, however, promised Israel a new shipment of fighter jets.

Sadat decided to attack Israel. Egypt joined forces with Syria, which had been heavily armed by the Soviets. The two nations launched a surprise attack on October 6, 1973. That day was Yom Kippur, the solemn Jewish day of fasting. The Arabs probably assumed that Israel's forces would be at a low level of preparedness since many soldiers would be fasting on that day. But the fact that so many Israelis were either at home or the synagogue made it much easier for the army to call up the reserves, on which Israel's defense depended. It was too late, however, for the soldiers on the front lines. Israel's defenses along the Suez Canal collapsed quickly. The Egyptian army advanced into the Sinai, with Israel in retreat. Syrian soldiers overran the Golan Heights. For several days, Israel's very existence seemed in great peril.

Then, through quick and innovative military strategy, Israel reversed the situation and retook the Sinai and the Golan Heights.

International tension rose. The Soviet Union threatened to get involved, and American forces went on nuclear alert. The Arab nations stopped selling oil to Israel's allies, including the United States. To prevent Israel from utterly defeating and humiliating the Arabs, American secretary of state Henry Kissinger practiced "shuttle diplomacy," traveling between Israel, Egypt, and Syria to make a deal. Israel agreed to a cease-fire after being promised more weapons. In 1974, a United Nations peacekeeping force began patrolling a demilitarized zone along Israel's front lines with Egypt and Syria.

The surprise attack that started the 1973 war made Israel's leaders take a hard look at the country's lack of preparedness. The public blamed especially Moshe Dayan, the minister of defense, for the catastrophe. Dayan wrote in his autobiography, "I had the feeling that the public trust in me was being steadily undermined. On one occasion I passed some demonstrators as I was

Israeli soldiers withdrawing from their position on the Golan Heights. In accordance with the terms of the cease-fire worked out between Syria and Israel in 1974, UN troops served as a buffer on the Golan Heights between the two countries.

Prime Minister Yitzhak Rabin appeared at the National Press Club in Washington, D.C., in 1976. In Israel, Rabin was a hero of the Six-Day War, and known for his firm stance during the intifadah.

leaving a Cabinet meeting, and a young woman, probably a widow of a fallen soldier, cried out, 'Murderer!' It was a dagger in the heart." Dayan decided to serve no longer in the government, and Prime Minister Golda Meir also resigned. Yitzhak Rabin became the new prime minister.

The following years tested Israel's political and economic position. Prosperity gave way to economic woes. Prices rose and the country's currency lost buying power—an economic process called inflation. Israel's rates of inflation and taxation were among the highest in the world. The government adopted austerity measures that slowed inflation but were unpopular because they made life less comfortable. The number of immigrants declined dramatically. For the first time, large numbers of Israelis were moving to other countries. Long lines of people waited outside the American Embassy in Tel Aviv for visas that would allow them to go to the United States. Thousands of them settled in New York, Los Angeles, and other North American cities. The emigration of Israelis sped up in the 1980s, until by 1990 about 400,000 Israelis lived outside the Jewish state.

New dangers developed in Israel's relations with the Arabs. Israel's Arab population became more politically active and allied itself with the Palestinians. When the government made plans to take over Arab land in the Galilee, the Arab communist party Rakah called a general strike, to be held on March 30, 1976. On that day, thousands of Arabs left their jobs and poured into the streets to demonstrate. Six died fighting with the Israeli army. Every year since 1976, Israeli Arabs have demonstrated on the anniversary of "Land Day," often clashing with the military.

The Palestine Liberation Organization (PLO) was gaining strength, political power, and financial support. More Arabs in the occupied territories supported PLO leader Yasir Arafat. In 1974 and 1975 Palestinian terrorists entered Israel and killed innocent civilians. The most shocking attack occurred in May 1974 when three terrorists came from Lebanon to the northern border town of Ma'alot and burst into a school to take 120 children hostage. They demanded that Israel release Palestinian prisoners. The Israeli army stormed the school, with disastrous results. Although the terrorists were killed, 20 schoolchildren and an Israeli soldier also perished. The terrorists belonged to the Popular Front for the Liberation of Palestine, a Palestinian group responsible for a number of other sensational actions during the 1970s.

Israel's government wanted to show a firm, unyielding response to terrorism. It often answered terrorist attacks with air bombardments against Palestinian guerrillas in southern Lebanon, usually in or near refugee camps. Sometimes special Israeli squads went into Lebanon to blow up houses or capture suspected terrorists. As a result, Arabs often suffered a higher number of civilian casualties than the Israelis had suffered in the original terrorist attacks. To many countries in the world, Israel looked like the aggressor.

While Palestinian groups were launching terrorist attacks, the PLO was making gains in the political arena. In 1974 representatives of the Arab countries met for a summit in Morocco. They recognized the

Demonstrators in Tel Aviv protest the "Zionism is Racism" UN Resolution in 1975. The Resolution was reversed in 1991.

PLO under Arafat's leadership as the "sole legitimate representative of the Palestinian people." The following month, to the outrage of Israel and of American Jews, Arafat addressed the General Assembly of the United Nations in New York with a pistol at his side. He had been invited by a majority of member states. The UN gave the PLO official observer status, and a resolution to remove Israel from the UN failed only because the United States vigorously protested. In November 1975, the General Assembly passed a resolution that called Zionism "a form of racism or racial discrimination."

The danger from terrorism and the growing sense of diplomatic isolation did little to make Israel feel peaceful toward its Arab neighbors. This was especially true of groups within Israel who were unwaveringly opposed to compromise, deal-making, or giving anything to the Arabs. In 1974 a group of Orthodox Zionists founded a grassroots organization called Gush Emunim ("Bloc of the Faithful") to push for increased Jewish settlement in the occupied territories. It went ahead and established new settlements, the Labor government doing nothing to stop it.

Prime Minister Yitzhak Rabin resigned in 1977 when the public learned that his wife, Leah, had kept an illegal bank account in the United States. Rabin's chief rival, Shimon Peres, became prime minister. The scandal tarnished Labor's image just before the elections. Its power base decreased, while that of Likud, the principal right-wing opposition party, grew.

Some of Likud's increased support came from the "Oriental Jews." Still underrep-resented in government, Histadrut, and leadership positions, Jews of Asian and African origin felt unwelcome in the Labor party. But the Herut party had long tried to attract Oriental votes, and the Likud party offered positions to Oriental Jews. Menachem Begin and Likud allowed these Jews to feel that they were part of Zionism and of Israel. Likud also appeared to respect their traditional and religious values.

In addition, most Oriental Jews took a hard line on the question of relationships with the Arabs. Like the Likud party, they did not want to return the occupied territories to Arab control. The writer Amos Oz wrote about an encounter with some Oriental Jews at a cafe. They saw Oz as a typical member of the Labor party and besieged him with provocative comments:

If they give back the territories, the Arabs will stop coming to work and then you'll put us back into the dead-end jobs, like before. If for no other reason, we won't let you give back those territories. Look at my daughter: she works in a bank now, and every evening an Arab comes to clean the building. All you want is to dump her from the bank into some textile factory, or have her wash the floors instead of the Arab. The way my mother used to clean for you. That's why we hate you here. As long as Begin's in power, my daughter's secure at the bank. If you guys come back, you'll pull her down first thing.

Shimon Peres served twice as the prime minister of Israel. When he was foreign minister under Prime Minister Yitzhak Rabin, he shared the Nobel Peace Prize with Rabin and Yasir Arafat for his role in reaching the agreement with the Palestinians in 1993.

Egyptian President Anwar Sadat (far left) addresses the Knesset on November 20, 1977. Millions of Israelis watched on television as Sadat appealed for peace between Israel and all its Arab neighbors.

Despite the many signs that Labor's power was weakening, Likud's victory in the 1977 elections shocked many Israelis. After all, Labor had been in power since 1948, and some people still thought of Begin as the dangerous former Irgun terrorist. But Likud succeeded not only because of the scandals and problems within the Labor party, but because Begin had built a broad base of support. His government included some members of the former Labor coalition, and he appointed Moshe Dayan, the Labor veteran, to the post of foreign minister. Begin also promised to introduce a greater spirit of free enterprise. Years of Labor mismanagement and corruption had made people frustrated with government and Histadrut institutions. Likud promised to help the country's poor by creating housing for young couples and improving conditions in the slums. In practice, Likud did no better than Labor at solving these problems, but at election time its promises swayed Oriental voters who were unhappy after years of discrimination and neglect under Labor governments.

Likud planned to develop Jewish settlements until they encircled the Arab population of the West Bank. The Likud government referred to the West Bank territories by their old, biblical names, Judea and Samaria. The government enlarged Jerusalem's boundaries with the idea that the city should become the center of an expanding network of settlements and satellite towns in the West Bank. However, the popular mayor of Jerusalem, Teddy Kollek, called these efforts stupid. "We will end up with a Jerusalem metropolitan area stretching from Ramallah to Bethlehem with an Arab majority, instead of a smaller, stronger Jerusalem with a Jewish majority," he warned.

In 1981 the Israeli government annexed the Golan Heights, formally making that region part of Israel. But although Likud declared that "between the sea and Jordan there will only be Jewish sovereignty," Israel never formally annexed the West Bank. If it had done so, it would have had to decide whether to give the million Arabs who lived there the essential rights required in a democratic state. Likud argued that eventually, when Jewish immigration increased, Jews would outnumber Arabs in Judea-Samaria.

Most Israelis had almost given up hope that any Arab country would seek peace with Israel. They were thunderstruck when Egypt's Sadat announced in 1977 that he would go to the Israeli parliament in Jerusalem to improve relations between the two countries. Sadat's visit to Israel captivated the nation. "Disbelief prevailed and people were practically stunned," wrote Sadat. "The minute I stepped out of the plane, I found myself face to face with Mrs. Golda Meir, who had cut short her U.S. visit in order to see me on arrival. We exchanged greetings. I saw Dayan next—recognizing the man against whom I had fought the 1973 battle." In his speech to the Knesset Sadat appealed for peace while millions of enthusiastic Israelis watched on television.

After Sadat's historic visit to Jerusalem, U.S. president Jimmy Carter hosted meetings between Begin and Sadat, helping the two leaders work out the details of the peace treaty they signed in 1979. Among

other things, the agreement called for Israel to return the Sinai Peninsula to Egypt. Sadat had told the Knesset that he wanted not just to make peace between Egypt and Israel, but to establish peace between Israel and all its Arab neighbors. The final agreement remained unclear about how this might happen after the Israeli-Egyptian peace treaty, but it did say that negotiations to achieve self-rule for the Palestinians would take place. It also declared: "The solution from the negotiations must also recognize the legitimate rights of the Palestinian people and their just requirements." Until then, Labor governments had not even acknowledged the existence of the Palestinians. In the past, most people would have found it hard to believe that Israel would ever sign a document that spoke of Palestinian rights.

In 1978 Begin and Sadat received the prestigious Nobel Prize for Peace in honor of the difficult negotiations they had completed. European countries and the United States praised Sadat for taking a courageous step toward peace. Many Egyptians, however, were uncertain that real peace was possible or even desirable. Other Arab states were either hostile or silent. Many Arabs thought that Sadat had betrayed the Palestinians and the Arab people. For making peace with Israel, Sadat paid with his life. In 1981 Egyptian extremists assassinated him.

Some Israelis also bitterly opposed the peace agreement. They regarded the plan to return the Sinai to Egypt as a betrayal. Several Likud party members broke away and formed their own ultranationalist party, Tehiya, to oppose Israeli withdrawal from the Sinai. Begin had agreed to remove all

Israelis from the Sinai by 1982. Although the government made generous offers to pay the Jewish settlers there for moving, many wanted to stay. In the prospering settlement of Yamit on the northern Sinai coast, settlers took to their rooftops to hurl bricks and burning tires at the soldiers that attempted to remove them. Despite such resistance, the government kept Begin's promise and removed all of the settlers from the Sinai.

Why did Begin sign the peace treaty with Egypt and give up the Sinai? For years, after all, he had staunchly refused to give anything to the Arabs. The Sinai Peninsula did not possess the ancient historical and biblical associations of the West Bank, but it had brought military and economic benefit—especially oil fields—to Israel. Begin thought, however, that it was worth sacrificing the Sinai for peace with Egypt.

Israel's next foreign crisis was across its northern border, in Lebanon. The PLO had been based in Jordan since 1967, but King Hussein had come to feel that the presence of so many Palestinian guerrillas threatened his own power. In 1970 he cracked down on the PLO; more than 3,000 Palestinians died fighting Jordanian forces. The PLO moved its center of operations to Lebanon, and Arafat set up headquarters in Beirut. The PLO launched terrorist operations across the Lebanese border into Israel, and some Pales-

Egyptian President Anwar Sadat (left), U.S. President Jimmy Carter (center), and Israeli Prime Minister Menachem Begin shake hands to celebrate the Camp David Agreement on March 26, 1979.

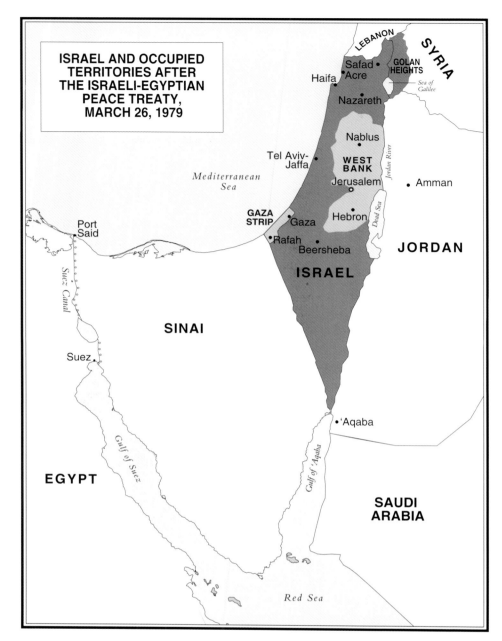

ISRAEL AND OCCUPIED
TERRITORIES AFTER
THE ISRAELI-EGYPTIAN
PEACE TREATY,
MARCH 26, 1979

This map shows Israel and its occupied territories after the Israeli-Egyptian Peace Treaty, March 26, 1979. Some Israelis viewed the return of the Sinai Peninsula, captured in the Six-Day War, to the Egyptians as a betrayal by their leader, Menachem Begin.

When Likud was reelected in 1981, the militaristic Ariel Sharon became defense minister. Israel was ready to try to change Lebanon's political structure.

In London on June 3, 1982, a young Palestinian shot and seriously wounded Israel's ambassador to the United Kingdom. The attempted assassination provided Israel with a pretext for invading Lebanon. Sharon believed that "Operation Peace for the Galilee," as he called the war, would be over in a few days. Israel's aim was to kick out the PLO, install a Christian leader named Bashir Gemayal as president, and get rid of the Syrians. Israel also hoped that if the PLO in Lebanon were destroyed, new Palestinian leaders in the West Bank would be more willing to cooperate with the Israeli government.

But the war was Begin's undoing. For the first time, Israel fought in the vicinity of a major Arab city, endangering civilians. Its aerial bombardments led to an international outcry as nations condemned Israel's actions. Israeli soldiers lost heart as their own casualties mounted. In addition, this was the first war that many Israeli civilians opposed. A number of Israeli soldiers went to prison rather than serve in Lebanon, and a high-ranking officer resigned to protest the war. Some 100,000 supporters of the Peace Now Movement took to Israel's streets to demonstrate against the war. Likud supporters organized a counterdemonstration that may have been even larger. Unrest rocked the country.

With Beirut under siege by the Israeli army, American negotiators helped the two sides make a deal, and Israel allowed the PLO to leave Lebanon. The PLO moved to

tinian refugee camps became centers for paramilitary training.

Lebanon was a deeply divided country, with rifts not only between Christians and Muslims but also between different sects of each faith. Ethnic and religious tensions erupted into all-out civil war in 1975. The Palestinians entered the fray, supporting the predominantly Muslim Lebanese National Movement against a right-wing Christian group known as the Phalangists. In 1976 the Christians led an assault against a refugee camp called Tal al-Zaatar, killing more than 2,000 Palestinians before they were defeated. Syria sent troops to Lebanon to prevent further fighting and they remained

as the "Arab Deterrent Force." Israel got involved, too, creating a militia in south Lebanon to prevent Palestinian terrorists from sneaking over the border.

All of this took place before Begin became prime minister in 1977. Under his leadership, Likud was more willing than Labor had been to consider war as a way to change Israel's relationship with the Arabs and the Palestinians. The peace treaty with Egypt freed Israel's government to turn its attention to its northern border, the West Bank, and the Gaza Strip. After terrorists attacked Israel from a northern beach in 1978, the Israeli army sent thousands of troops into south Lebanon.

Tunisia, an Arab country in North Africa. Bashir Gemayal was elected president of Lebanon, with Israel's approval. As it turned out, Gemayal was not willing to be a puppet of the Israeli government—but that scarcely mattered. A bomb planted by a Lebanese supporter of Syria killed Gemayal and dozens of other people. The assassination ended Israel's hopes of creating a "new Lebanon."

One of the most tragic incidents of the war took place in September 1982, when Phalangists, encouraged by Israel's Ariel Sharon, overran Sabra and Shatilla, two Palestinian refugee camps on the outskirts of Beirut. The Phalangists, many of whom had suffered losses in their conflict with the PLO, massacred innocent Palestinians, including women and children. No one knows how many were killed. The Palestinians claimed the death toll was between 2,000 and 3,000, and it certainly numbered in the hundreds. The slaughter continued for two days, until Sharon finally ordered the Phalangists to leave the camps.

Back in Israel, Peace Now and other peace groups, supported by members of Labor, organized a demonstration in Tel Aviv. About 400,000 people from all over Israel attended the rally, the biggest demonstration in Israeli history. Begin had to do something to deal with the outcry. He called on Yitzhak Kahan, the president of the Supreme Court, to head a commission of inquiry. The Kahan commission declared that Begin was not responsible for letting the Phalangists into the camps, but it criticized Begin and other members of the government for not investigating reports that the Phalangists had entered the camps. The report recommended that Sharon be dismissed from the government. Anti-

government protests mounted. Then someone threw a grenade into a crowd of orderly Peace Now demonstrators in Jerusalem, killing 1 and wounding 10. This event shocked the nation.

Israel withdrew from Lebanon in 1985, leaving behind a force in the south. But Menachem Begin left office before that time. Emotionally shattered by the turmoil that the war had brought to Israel, and depressed by his wife's death, he resigned from office in 1983 and remained in almost total isolation until his death in 1992.

Foreign minister Yitzhak Shamir took over as prime minister. The leader of the Stern Gang before independence, Shamir had been involved in the assassination of British officials. The British Foreign Office had called him "among the most fanatical of terrorist leaders." Although some of Shamir's ideas had softened over time, he still shared many beliefs with the militant nationalists who believed in keeping the occupied territories.

Israel's political atmosphere under Shamir's government may have encouraged Jewish extremists to step up their activities. In 1984 Jewish terrorists were caught wiring bombs in five Arab buses. They planned to blow up the buses to avenge Palestinian attacks on Israeli buses. This group had been responsible for earlier acts of terrorism, such as the 1980 bombings of two Arab mayors who supported the PLO and the 1983 attack on a Muslim college in Hebron—after the killing of a local Yeshiva student—that killed 3 people and wounded 33.

The members of the Jewish Underground, as the group was called, had been

The target of more than a dozen assassination attempts, King Hussein of Jordan has often clashed with other Arab countries and some of his own citizens for his pro-Western policies and moderate stance toward Israel. Here, he addresses the United Nations in 1995.

Yitzak Shamir, foreign minister of Israel, addressed the UN General Assembly on October 2, 1985. He was prime minister from 1986 to 1992.

students in the Jerusalem yeshiva of Rabbi Zvi Yehuda Kook, who had emerged in 1967 as the popular prophet of some new ideas. One was that Jews ought to return to some of their ancient lands that were now in Arab hands. Rabbi Kook's followers regarded the Six-Day War as a miracle that allowed them to do just that, claiming that God wanted the occupied territories to remain part of Israel. When the members of the Jewish Underground went on trial, some government leaders, including Prime Minister Shamir, either remained silent or refused to speak against the acts they had committed.

Shamir could neither get Israel out of Lebanon nor deal with Israel's economic woes. By election time in 1984 Likud's appeal had faded. Neither Labor nor Likud won a decisive majority. Right-wing extremist parties won six seats. One of these parties was Kach, represented by an American rabbi named Meir Kahane who had founded the Jewish Defense League in New York City in 1968. Kahane moved to Israel in 1971. For years Kahane's anti-Arab activities had caused trouble and angered the Israeli government. Despite winning a seat in the Knesset in 1984, his party was later disqualified by Israel's Central Elections Committee for its racist and antidemocratic statements. His assassination in New York City in 1990 ended his disturbing career, although his followers continued to practice what he had preached.

The 1984 elections seemed to favor Israel's hard-line, extreme right. But rather than ally itself with the far right to remain in power, Likud made a new plan with the Labor party. The two parties agreed to rotate the offices of prime minister and foreign minister. Shimon Peres, a longtime veteran of the Labor party, became prime minister and Shamir became foreign minister. The two swapped positions after 25 months. The 1988 elections led to another power-sharing deal between Labor and Likud.

All this time, Arab discontent was festering in the occupied territories of the West Bank and the Gaza Strip. The Arabs' unhappiness had many causes. Some were economic, such as the loss of land and water resources. The chance to work for Jews across the Green Line did little to relieve the sense of hopeless poverty in the refugee camps. Some problems were political, including resentment of the harsh measures taken against protests, the deportation of PLO sympathizers, and the closing of Arab universities. Arabs also resented the growing number of Jewish settlers in the territories and the increasingly militant stance of Gush Emunim, the far-right Jewish group that wanted to keep the territories. Jewish vigilantes often toted guns, breaking up Arab demonstrations and boldly moving through Arab towns to send the message that Jews were in charge. The territories were like a pool of gasoline waiting to explode.

An incident in December 1987 set off an uprising called the *intifadah*. An Israeli truck in Gaza hit a car carrying Arab workers, killing four of them. Riots broke out in Gaza and soon spread to the West Bank. Israeli soldiers used severe means to restore control against a wide variety of opponents, ranging from stone-throwing children to sophisticated terrorists. Groups such as the militant Muslim fundamentalist organization Hamas fought to wrest control of the Palestinians from the PLO. Hundreds of Arabs and more than 100 Israelis died in the fighting. Many Israelis felt an urgent need for a new approach to the Palestinians and the occupied territories.

The *intifadah* also created political momentum within the West Bank. Palestinians in the territories began to consider the possibility of an independent Palestinian state and challenged the PLO to take steps in that direction. In 1988 the Palestinian National Council met in Algeria and issued a declaration of independence. A month later PLO Chairman Yasir Arafat recognized the State of Israel at the United Nations in Geneva. For the Palestinians, who had always denied Israel's right to exist, Arafat's action marked a turning point. For the first time the PLO supported a two-state solution for Israelis and Palestinians. To Israel's dismay, Arafat's declaration also opened the way for the United States to begin talking to the PLO. The very poeple who had been considered outlaws and terrorists were becoming accepted on the international political scene.

The *intifadah* and the question of the occupied territories caused the collapse of the shared government in 1990. Shamir put together a new coalition, this time allying Likud with the far-right parties in order to form a government. Despite being disgraced by his role in the Sabra and Shatilla catastrophe, Ariel Sharon became housing minister. Likud stepped up the pace of Jewish settlement in the West Bank, invest-

In 1988, a young boy participates in the intifadah, *a violent uprising of Palestinian Arabs in the West Bank and Gaza Strip against Israeli occupation.*

ing huge amounts of money to build roads and houses there. The United States, which opposed this policy, threatened to cut off loans to Israel if the expansion of settlements continued.

Changes around the world were having an effect in Israel and the neighboring Arab states. The breakup of the Soviet Union in 1991 ended the Soviets' massive military support to the Arab states. The United States, now the only superpower, had greater influence over events in the Middle East than ever and wished to settle the Palestinian problem.

Another important event was the Gulf War in early 1991. Iraq's leader Saddam Hussein sent a powerful army to seize the tiny, oil-rich country of Kuwait. The United States and its allies—which included Saudi Arabia as well as the European states—launched a large, swift counterattack that drove Iraqi forces out of Kuwait. During the war Iraq shot Russian-made Scud missiles into Israel, causing damage, injuries, and loss of life. Many Israelis were dismayed that Palestinians supported Saddam Hussein, but the Palestinians, after years of bitterness and frustration, were willing to back a strong leader who shook the established order.

In anticipation of chemical attacks, these Israelis wear gas masks in their homes during the Gulf War. The newspaper headline reads "The United States bombards Iraq and Kuwait."

The Gulf War proved that the United States was now the principal foreign power shaping events in the Middle East. After the war the United States wanted to forge peace between Israel and the Palestinians. With the support of Russia and the Arab states, the United States arranged a conference in Madrid, Spain, in November 1991. Delegations from the United States, Lebanon, Syria, Israel, and Jordan attended the Madrid conference. The Jordanian group included some Palestinians—this was the only way that Israel would agree to meet with Palestinians. The negotiations that began at the Madrid conference continued in Washington, D.C.

Far-right members of Israel's government resigned to protest Shamir's negotiations with the Palestinians. But many Israelis had grown unhappy with the Likud government, and in 1992 the Labor coalition won the elections. Yitzhak Rabin became prime minister because he had outmaneuvered his rival, Shimon Peres, to become head of Labor. More popular than Peres, Rabin was a hero of the Six-Day War, and known for his firm stance during the *intifadah*.

Once in power, Labor pursued peace negotiations with the Palestinians. In 1993 the Israelis and Palestinians reached an agreement and issued a statement on Palestinian self-rule. The world could hardly believe it

President of Iraq since 1979, Saddam Hussein sent his army to seize the tiny, oil-rich country of Kuwait in 1991. The United States and its allies retaliated, igniting the Gulf War. Many Palestinians supported Hussein.

when, after a ceremony hosted by U.S. president Bill Clinton at the White House, Yasir Arafat and Yitzhak Rabin shook hands. For many it was a moving event. Others believed it was a dangerous step. A new era in Israeli-Palestinian relations had begun, and Arafat, Rabin, and Peres shared the Nobel Prize for Peace.

The Declaration of Principles that the Israelis and the Palestinians had issued did not resolve all the areas of conflict or provide a precise blueprint for the future. But it did offer a schedule for Israel to withdraw from the West Bank and for the Palestinian Authority to take control. A permanent agreement was supposed to take effect by December 1998. Although Israel fell somewhat behind schedule, Rabin was committed to withdrawing Israeli troops and letting the Palestinians govern themselves. Soon the Palestinian Authority controlled Gaza and Jericho. Other towns in the West Bank were to follow.

Many Israelis were fearful of giving power to the Palestinians. Could Arafat control such groups as Hamas, who were still determined to see Israel destroyed? And a sizable minority of Israelis, especially among the religious Zionists, were bitterly opposed to the agreement. Some regarded Yitzhak Rabin as a traitor. The most extreme of these far-right objectors were members of a movement called Kahane Hai (Kahane lives) that supported anti-Arab vigilante activities.

In 1994 Baruch Goldstein, an American Jewish physician who had settled in Kiryat Arba, burst into the Ibrahimi Mosque in Hebron during Muslim prayer time and opened fire with an automatic rifle. Twenty-

After the singing of the historic peace agreement between Israel and the Palestine Liberation Organization (PLO) on September 13, 1993, Yasir Arafat, chairman of the PLO (center), speaks with Prime Minister Rabin (left), as Shimon Peres, Israel's foreign minister, listens.

nine Arabs were murdered before he was disarmed and then beaten to death. Most Israelis were shocked and outraged by the massacre. But for some ardent supporters of the religious right, Goldstein was a martyr.

Some Zionist rabbis tried to use religion to stop the dismantling of Jewish settlements and the withdrawal of Jewish troops from the West Bank. In effect, they were forbidding soldiers to comply with military orders. The religious Zionists believed that by agreeing to give up the occupied territory to the Palestinians, the secular government was endangering the future of the Jews and their messianic hopes.

On November 4, 1995, Prime Minister Rabin was shot and killed as he left a peace rally in Tel Aviv. His assassin was Yigal Amir, a 25-year-old Orthodox law student who believed that his action was authorized by religious law. Amir and other religious Zionists were inspired by the ideas of Rabbi Kook and by the militant idealism, first pronounced by the founders of Kiryat Arba, that declared that Hebron must remain part of the Jewish state.

Shimon Peres became prime minister. He had been the main author of the agreement with the PLO, and many people regarded him as more of a visionary than Rabin. Although Rabin's assassination brought sympathy to the Labor party, Peres had never been a leader who commanded wide popular support. In the elections of 1996 he lost to a new Likud leader, Benjamin ("Bibi") Netanyahu. The new prime minister appealed to Israelis who feared the peace process with the Palestinians—especially after four suicide bombings by Palestinian terrorists in early 1996. The

1996 elections also marked a change in Israel's electoral law. For the first time, people voted directly for their prime minister, although they still voted separately for the political party of their choice.

After Netanyahu became prime minister, the peace process hit numerous snags and was frequently suspended. A large part of the Israeli population showed its unhappiness with the Netanyahu government in November 1997, when an estimated 200,000 people attended a rally in Rabin Square in Tel Aviv, where Yitzhak Rabin had been assassinated. Leah Rabin, the widow of the late prime minister, spoke before the crowd, saying, "Three gunshots and this terrible loss, but you are always present, present for me, and present for all the nation." Peres said, "We may be sad without him, but we may not despair. We have no other country and we have no other way, except for Yitzhak Rabin's way." But when Natan Sharansky, the only member of the Netanyahu government to attend the rally, stood to speak, the crowd booed.

The 1997 rally was Israel's largest demonstration since the protests against the war in Lebanon in 1982. Many who attended—and many others in Israel—believe that Rabin was killed by the religious right wing. They hold Netanyahu and the Likud party responsible for creating the atmosphere that let the assassination happen. The rally in Tel Aviv revealed a nation profoundly divided about the course it should take to achieve peace and security.

As Israeli deputy foreign minister, Benjamin Netanyahu holds a news conference on the Middle East peace conference in Washington, D.C., in 1991. Netanyahu was elected prime minister in 1996.

Chapter 11

The Israeli People at the End of the 20th Century

American cultural influence in Israel seems to be growing every day, with shopping malls such as this one in Jerusalem appearing on the landscape with greater frequency. But Israeli culture is not simply imitating American culture, and what it means to be an Israeli changes constantly.

Few countries have as diverse a blend of cultures as Israel. Perhaps no other country has had to absorb such a high proportion of new immigrants from so many different countries in such a short time. Israel could not have accomplished this without a national commitment to the principle of the ingathering of exiles.

New waves of immigrants brought Israel's population to about 5,863,000 in 1997. The new arrivals were a great strain on a country with relatively few resources, but overall the Israeli people have remained in agreement that no group of Jews should be kept from settling in Israel.

Herzl and most of the early Zionists had believed that the establishment of a Jewish state would lead to the virtual disappearance of the Diaspora. They thought that all Jews would come to Palestine. In 1997 Israel's prime minister, Benjamin Netanyahu, said that "we must not forget that the realization of the Zionist dream—the ingathering of the Jewish people in the land of Israel—is not yet complete. Our goal for the next decade must be to have a majority of the Jewish people living in Israel." However, the prime minister realizes that not only has the Diaspora not disappeared, but it competes with Israel to shape Jewish culture. Israel's Jewish population is second to that of the United States, the largest in the world.

Most Jews in the Diaspora support Zionism and Israel. They may not always agree with Israel's policies or actions, but they rally behind Israel when others criticize it. Israel is an important part of Jewish identity in the Diaspora, even for the many Jews who have never visited the country. But this solidarity cannot hide the reality that Israel and the Diaspora are growing farther apart.

One reason for the gap between Israeli and American Jews is the refusal of Israel's Orthodox leaders to recognize the Reform and Conservative movements as truly part of Judaism. The Reform and Conservative movements have remained tiny in Israel. And secular Israelis, feeling that Jewishness is a constant part of their lives because they live in the land of their biblical ancestors and study Jewish history and culture in school, consider that they have no need for religious affiliation. They often argue that Jews in the Diaspora risk total assimilation and disappearance through intermarriage, among other factors.

A view of modern Tel Aviv from old Jaffa. The 18th-century mosque in the foreground, Masjid Al Bahr, has been under renovation since 1995.

Zionists believed that once Jews had a nation of their own they would become "normal" like other people, that is, no longer outsiders or minorities. Zionist pioneers in the late 19th and early 20th centuries dreamed of a new type of Jew living on the land. This dream was best expressed in the kibbutz. But the kibbutzim—numbering 270, with a population of about 129,300 in 1991—have never represented more than a small part of the Jewish population, and since the 1980s have faced serious economic problems and a lack of support from the Likud government. At the end of the 20th century, the kibbutz has lost its appeal to the younger generation of Israelis. Many kibbutzim have tried to attract members by altering their original collective principles—for example, by letting children sleep in private apartments with their parents or by charging fees for eating in the dining room. Some kibbutzim now encourage their members to work outside the kibbutz, and observers wonder what future the kibbutz movement will have in the 21st century.

The waning importance of the kibbutz does not mean that Israeli agriculture has failed. Israel's farmers produce many crops for home use and export and excel in developing new agricultural techniques. They have shown that Jews are capable farmers, which was one of Zionism's foremost goals. But the vast majority of Israelis live in the growing cities.

Israel has become a part of the modern, industrialized world. Some older Israelis are sorry to see their original ideals eroding, but most Israelis want the kind of material well-being enjoyed by citizens of prosperous nations and are content to leave menial jobs to foreign workers from Asia and Africa. American cultural influence seems to be growing every day, with shopping malls sprouting up like mushrooms. American fast-food restaurants and chain stores are becoming as much a part of Israel's landscape as its falafel stands.

But Israeli culture is not simply imitating American culture. What it means to be Israeli is constantly being redefined by the country's unique and often argumentative mixture of peoples. Three major divisions in the population can either tear the country apart or provide opportunities for Israelis to forge a creative new future. The first division is between Israeli Arabs and Jews. The second is between secular and religious elements in society. The third is between different Jewish ethnic groups. How have these three major divisions affected Israel in recent years?

Perhaps the rift between Israeli Jews and Arabs will be healed only when there is peace among Israel, the Palestinians, and the Arab states. About one in five Israelis is an Arab. In recent years the majority of Israeli Arabs have defined themselves as Palestinians, but they still struggle to fuse the obligations of Israeli citizenship with their cultural identity as Palestinians. Political and cultural currents in the Arab world influence them—for example, Muslim fundamentalist movements have found a growing number of followers among Israeli Arabs, who have experienced discrimination and injustice and have found it difficult or impossible to fit into the larger Jewish society. At the same time, a generation of Arabs has grown up in Israel. Many young Arabs speak Hebrew as fluently as they do Arabic. In a peaceful Middle East of the future, they may serve as cultural ambassadors between Israel and the surrounding Arab countries.

Fifty years after Israel's birth, the gulf between religious and secular Israelis seems as wide as ever. No one quite knows what percentage of the population is religious. Orthodox Jews, meaning those who conform to traditional Jewish religious practices, make up about 15 to 20 percent of the population. And perhaps as many as 40 percent of Israelis define themselves as *masorati* (traditional). While they do not all observe most requirements of Jewish law, they do follow some aspects of traditional practice, such as keeping kosher, celebrating the Sabbath with their families, or attending synagogue on the major Jewish holidays.

But religious observance is not part of daily life for the majority of Israelis. Most who are entirely nonreligious remain firmly opposed to Orthodox goals and view Israel as a secular society. But few secular Jews would deny that the Orthodox Jews have transformed the cultural landscape. In Jerusalem, for example, new neighborhoods house the growing number of Orthodox Jews who believe in having large families. While secular Israelis flock to the beaches or to the cinema and cafes in Tel Aviv and Haifa on the Sabbath, the streets are quiet in more and more Jerusalem neighborhoods. The erection of traffic barricades on the Sabbath has led to new confrontations and to occasional violence between secular and religious Israelis over control of space in the country's capital. Jerusalem's ultra-Orthodox population is increasing, leading some observers to predict that the ultra-Orthodox will become the majority in the city within a generation.

The Oriental and Sephardi communities have remained attached to their religious traditions. Jewish practices that originated in the Asian and African communities, once discouraged by the Ashkenazi religious establishment, have become more popular in

Top photo: Israelis and
tourists enjoy a summer
night at a café on Ben
Yehuda Street in Jerusalem.

Bottom photo: An aqueduct
from the time of King Herod
is visible to sunbathers on
Caesaria Beach, a popular
tourist spot.

recent decades. This includes worshipping saints and making pilgrimages to the graves of holy men *(tsaddikim)*. During these celebrations the pilgrims light candles, dance, chant liturgical poetry, and often drink quantities of alcohol. They believe that the saints perform miracles such as healing the sick.

Some religious Sephardim have been influenced by the Ashkenazi Orthodox. Because originally there were relatively few Sephardi rabbinical schools, many religious Sephardi youth studied in Ashkenazi schools. This produced a generation of ultra-Orthodox Sephardi Jews. In 1983 they formed a political party called Shas (Sephardi Torah Guardians), which in the 1996 elections won the third-largest number of seats in the Knesset and joined a coalition with the Likud-led government under Prime Minister Benjamin Netanyahu. Many of the Oriental Jews who voted for Shas are not ultra-Orthodox themselves but support the party out of ethnic pride.

New waves of immigrants in the late 1980s and the 1990s are also transforming the country. In the late 1980s, Soviet leader Mikhail Gorbachev began a policy of reform that was to lead to the breakup of the Soviet Union. He released many Jewish political prisoners and eased the restrictions on emigration. Before that time, many of the Jews who managed to leave the Soviet Union went to the United States instead of to Israel, where life was seen as more difficult. Israelis called these emigrants *noshrim* (meaning deciduous, like leaves falling from a tree). Israel's leaders wanted them to come to Israel and made arrangements with the Soviet government to bring them there. New limits on the number of Soviet Jews allowed to enter the United States after 1989 also helped direct the flow of emigrants to Israel. Between 1989 and 1992 about 450,000 of them arrived in the country. By 1998, after several decades of immigration, the total number of Soviet immigrants (or immigrants from the former Soviet Union) approached one million.

Yitzhak Shamir championed the cause of Soviet immigration to Israel, declaring it his government's highest priority. It went together with his goal of keeping all the occupied territories. "We need the space to house all the people. Big immigration requires Israel to be big as well," he told Likud party veterans in a speech in Tel Aviv in 1990. Shamir saw immigration from the Soviet Union as a great opportunity to populate the occupied territories with Jews and undermine Palestinian efforts at self-determination in the West Bank.

Shamir's vision never materialized. The vast majority of the new immigrants chose to settle in the main coastal cities, not the occupied territories. They faced many difficulties adjusting to life in Israel. The country could barely support such a massive increase in population. Unemployment and housing shortages were rampant. Many well-educated, professional immigrants were unable to find work in their professions, often remaining unemployed or taking jobs beneath their capabilities, like the unemployed classical musicians who played on the sidewalks and in town squares.

Although most Israelis supported the immigration and absorption of Soviet and Russian Jews, tensions emerged. Few of the new immigrants had any knowledge of Judaism. Unlike the Soviet immigrants of

the 1970s, they were not committed to Zionist ideals. This offended some religious Israelis, while secular Israelis saw the flow of Soviet and Russian immigrants as a threat to the national identity. Once again Oriental Jews resented the preferences given to the new immigrants, fearing that some of their hard-won political and social gains would be undermined by this growth in the population of Ashkenazim. Feelings of resentment toward the Russians, often based on negative stereotypes, made the new immigrants feel isolated and bitter.

The problems of unemployment and housing improved somewhat over time, but Soviet Jewish immigrants continued to share grievances, feeling ignored by the political establishment. Yet political parties could not entirely ignore their complaints because Soviet immigrants represented a huge number of votes, and in the 1990s the immigrants began to play a greater role in the country's political life. Jews from the former Soviet Union are now Israel's larg-

Women from a committee for Soviet Jewry in Tel Aviv block the road as a visiting Soviet delegation leaves its hotel in 1987. Wearing clothes to imitate prison uniforms and rubber skullcaps, the women demanded the release of Soviet Jews from Soviet prisons.

An Ethiopian Jew's Journey to Israel

Shmuel Yilma was born in a Jewish farming village of about 30 families in northern Ethiopia. At the age of 11 he left for Israel with family members and other families from his village. As an adult Yilma decided to publish his story:

Had the time of redemption really come and was this the Almighty's way of delivering His people? Were two thousand years of exile coming to an end? It really seemed so, for the arrangements for leaving were rapidly gathering pace. They were carried out in secrecy but with great energy—all so as to realize the ancient dream of the return to Zion and Jerusalem.

The land and the houses were not sold. The land (the most valuable part of our property) could not be sold. As for the houses, the idea was that if we were caught by the authorities, we could claim that we were just moving to another area for work and would return sooner or later. Nor could we sell the crops, such as the chickpeas *(atter)* and the *wanzeh* (a sort of barley) that were still unripe. The money from selling the ripe crops paid for three donkeys and two horses—our beasts of burden. Father was careful to hide a sizeable amount of cash amongst the clothes and in the animals' gear. Who could tell what would not happen

along the way and ready cash will always find a use.

It was about eleven o'clock at night and the third day of the week. Most of the village was asleep. No hour could be more fitting for bidding farewell to the village for did not our ancestors also begin their exodus from Egypt at nighttime? Under the light of the full moon, we stepped quietly forward; whatever the donkeys could not carry was slung on our backs or carried in our hands. Mother had lingered behind to kiss the tree behind the house (it bore a special fruit called *owkhi*) and in her hurry to catch up, left behind the umbrella which she had intended to use to protect herself and little Museh on her back from the baking heat. Grandfather, who still could not make up his mind to come with us, remained behind with the flocks and the unsold property. But he came to see us off and pronounce the blessing for a safe journey. We children were very quiet, obedient to our orders not to wake the dogs and so arouse the village.

To keep the secret of the departure, father had not even been able to take farewell of his brother. But at the very edge of the village we passed by his sister Ilf'nesh's house and I remember to this day how he struggled with

himself—to say goodbye to her or to stay in position leading the group away. At last his feeling overcame him and I ran after him. Standing with the gate to the houses between them, they parted with two sentences:

Father: "Keep well, we are leaving tonight."

Aunt Ilf'nesh in tears: "May the rights of our forefathers protect you."

Father: "We shall meet again in Holy Jerusalem."

Aunt Ilf'nesh: "Amen, may it be His will."

With the help of a guide, Yilma's group survived the difficult trek to Sudan. From there they flew to Tel Aviv to begin their life in Israel:

From the airport taxis took us to the absorption center in the little southern town of Ofakim, where we were allotted to long trailer-homes, like buses. At first light, who should be there to greet us but Grandmother and her group! It is so hard to put into words that meeting: brother reunited with sister, mothers with daughters, each and every one found family and friends again—it is so hard to describe the coming to pass of the dream of families reunited on the holy soil of Jerusalem, a dream for which we had sacrificed so much that it is not to be measured. We had abandoned our village and all that we had there, we passed

These two young immigrants arrived in Israel in 1990 from Ethiopia (right) and the U.S.S.R. (left).

through fire and water, jungle and desert, we climbed heights, forded rivers and crossed seas, we outwitted the powers-that-be, deceived neighbors and bandits, overcame wild beasts, conquered disease and affliction. We had traversed foreign states, dry land, sea, and sky, to bring to pass the ancient dream that we held in our hearts. Grandmother raised her arms up high, gazed into the heavens, and declared, "In this moment we make real the small dream of reuniting our families. This small dream was brought about by the great and ancient dream of two thousand years of exile—to go up to the Land of Zion, to Jerusalem. I said to you a few months ago when I set out: 'We shall meet again in Jerusalem. And here by the grace of God we are in Jerusalem!'"

Yilma describes adjusting to life in Israel:

The pangs of absorption in Ofakim hit us children particularly hard. Outside the class, the local children received us with clenched fists. Sneering insults and fists were our welcome if we ever tried to join in the games around the neighborhood. Skin our color they had never seen before and "Little blacks!" was the first and last thing we heard from them.

It took almost two years to win the acceptance of the local children. Yilma was very successful in school. He was the second Ethiopian, following his uncle, to become an officer in the elite paratroopers in the Israel defense forces. After five years, he left the army and began to work on behalf of the Ethiopian community in Israel.

est group of immigrants, outnumbering the North African Jewish immigrants who arrived during the 1950s and 1960s. The Russian language is heard throughout the country. Russian newspapers and publications flourish. The very meaning of what it means to be Israeli is in transition.

Another, much smaller, group of immigrants came from the East African nation of Ethiopia during the 1980s and 1990s. The Jews of Ethiopia call themselves Beta Israel ("of the house of Israel"), but are known in their native language as the Falasha ("the uprooted" or "strangers"). Legend says that they are descended from a union between King Solomon and the Queen of Sheba in the 10th century B.C.E. Little is known about their true origins, although the Beta Israel believe that they were exiled from Israel in ancient times. For many centuries before modern times, they believed that they were the only Jews left in the world.

Isolated from other Jews, the Beta Israel practiced their own, distinctive form of Judaism, which many Orthodox Jews in Israel found unacceptable. Although very strict on matters of ritual purity, observing the Sabbath, and fasting on Yom Kippur, the Beta Israel were totally unfamiliar with the Talmud and its many laws. They did not know about Jewish holidays created after the Babylonian exile, such as Hanukkah and Purim. In the 1950s the Ethiopian Jews learned of the new state of Israel and came to regard it as their homeland. But for years rabbinical experts refused to accept them as legitimate Jews, so the Israeli government would not let them come to Israel under the Law of Return. Critics accused Israel of racism for making no effort to bring the poorly educated, poverty-stricken, black Jews of Ethiopia to Israel.

OPERATION SOLOMON
THE RESCUE OF ETHIOPIAN JEWRY

WORLD ZIONIST PRESS SERVICE

This World Zionist Press Service information folder describes plans for airlifting tens of thousands of Ethiopian Jews into Israel. Very few Jews are left in Ethiopia today.

In 1973 a leading rabbi ruled that the Beta Israel were descended from one of the 10 lost tribes of Israel. The Israeli government made this decision into law and communicated it to the villages where Ethiopian Jews lived. The Beta Israel now saw emigration to Israel as a real possibility—and a welcome escape from a land torn by civil war and famine. In late 1979, with the situation in Ethiopia worsening, thousands of Jews migrated to Sudan in the

The Israel Philharmonic Orchestra

Israel's musical tradition, much like the country itself, draws from many different sources. It was greatly enriched by the immigration of many talented Jewish musicians from Central and Eastern Europe who fled to Palestine after the Nazis came to power. The Palestine Orchestra, founded in 1936 by a celebrated Jewish-Polish violinist, Bronislaw Huberman, performed its inaugural concert in December 1936, led by Arturo Toscanini, the world renowned conductor.

A bilingual poster announces the first subscription series of the Israel Philharmonic Orchestra in 1936–37, to be conducted by Arturo Toscanini.

Dressed in formal attire, the Orchestra plays for Israel Defense Forces at an unknown location in the desert during the Six-Day War in 1967.

The Palestine Orchestra was renamed the Israel Philharmonic Orchestra after the State of Israel was born in 1948. It became one of the great national symbols of the new country, often touring abroad as a major representative of Israel's thriving cultural life. The orchestra has also been closely associated with Israel's struggles. During the War of Independence, the orchestra followed in the wake of the army to perform in Jerusalem and in the Negev Desert as an act of patriotism. The American composer and conductor Leonard Bernstein was long associated with the orchestra. In 1967, he performed Mahler's "Resurrection" Symphony on Mt. Scopus to celebrate Israel's capture of East Jerusalem during the Six-Day War. The distinguished Indian conductor Zubin Mehta was appointed music advisor to the orchestra in 1968 and music director in 1977. This appointment was extended to life in 1981. Under his direction, the orchestra's fame grew throughout the world.

The Israel Philharmonic Orchestra has trained a whole new generation of musicians who were born in Israel. Now, with the massive influx of immigrants from the former Soviet Union, the number of professional musicians highly trained in the classical tradition has grown tremendously in Israel. Some have been integrated in the Israel Philharmonic Orchestra, while others have helped lead to the revival and expansion of smaller orchestras, musical groups, and conservatories in Israel.

hope of entering Israel. Marauding bandits and difficult and parched terrain made the trek terribly perilous. Hundreds died. But airlifts in 1984 and 1991 brought more than 23,000 Ethiopian Jews to Israel. By 1992, few Jews were left in Ethiopia. Israel had about 60,000 Jews of Ethiopian descent in the late 1990s.

The Ethiopian Jews are the most easily recognized minority group in Israel, and they have had a difficult time fitting into society. Not only do they look very different, but they came from rural communities, were poorly educated, and brought few trades or crafts that could be used in Israel. They did not speak Hebrew, and their religious practices differed from those of all other Jews. In schools as well as workplaces, Ethiopian immigrants have experienced abuse and prejudice—sometimes at the hands of other immigrant groups such as Moroccans and Soviets. "These people are from the stone age and don't know anything about modern conveniences. They turn on the faucet, and don't turn it off," complained one Russian immigrant. Many Israelis continue to doubt the Jewishness of the Beta Israel. Ethiopian Jews, who have maintained their religious faith amid tremendous hardship, resent these doubts. Some of them have begun to identify themselves with black Jews in the African Diaspora.

Like the United States, Israel is a land of many cultural and racial differences. It is also a country of religious differences. The dominant religion of Judaism includes a variety of practices and beliefs. Many people believed that immigrants from around the world would blend to form a single type of Israeli, a new kind of Jew. Few people today believe that this has happened, and many Israelis are troubled. They have questioned the very purpose for which modern Israel was founded. At the end of the 20th century, some Israeli scholars and writers have begun to speak of their country as a "post-Zionist" society, a society looking for meaning after the essence of Zionism has faded. Israel may no longer be a necessary refuge for Jews. Today there are few places in the world where Jews are persecuted. Now that the number of new arrivals from the former Soviet Union has dwindled, it is unlikely that there will be any new large-scale immigration to Israel. Some

Israelis have begun to question the wisdom of continuing the Law of Return. This questioning of the very foundation of the nation has led to heated public debate.

Yet it is from these often agonizing questions that a new type of Israel is being created. This Israel looks very different from what Herzl imagined at the First Zionist Congress in Basel and from what Ben-Gurion pictured when he declared Israel's independence. Filled with tremendous cultural diversity and richness, faced with the continuing challenge of ensuring security and making peace with neighboring Arab countries and the Palestinians, Israel is still finding its way at the end of the 20th century.

This billboard in Jerusalem indicates the hope some Israelis have for their future: "Peace" is written in Hebrew, English, and Arabic.

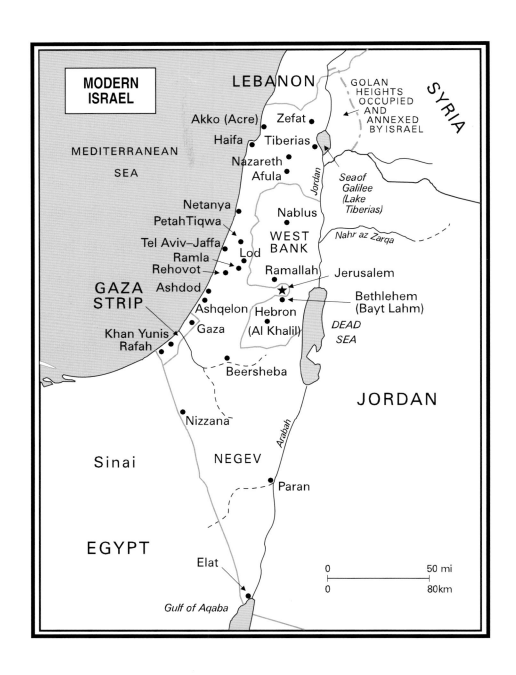

MODERN
ISRAEL

LEBANON

SYRIA

GOLAN
HEIGHTS
OCCUPIED
AND
ANNEXED
BY ISRAEL

Akko (Acre)

Zefat

Haifa

Tiberias

MEDITERRANEAN
SEA

Nazareth

Afula

Sea of
Galilee
(Lake
Tiberias)

Jordan

Netanya

Nablus

Petah Tiqwa

WEST
BANK

Nahr az Zarqa

Tel Aviv–Jaffa

Lod

Ramla

Rehovot

Ramallah

Jerusalem

GAZA
STRIP

Ashdod

Ashqelon

Hebron
(Al Khalil)

Bethlehem
(Bayt Lahm)

DEAD
SEA

Khan Yunis

Gaza

Rafah

Beersheba

JORDAN

Nizzana

Sinai

NEGEV

Arabah

Paran

EGYPT

Elat

0   50 mi

0   80km

Gulf of Aqaba

Chronology

B.C.E.

c. 1020–922
United monarchy of ancient Israel; in 922 the kingdom split into two: Israel and Judah

c. 1000–961
Reign of King David

c. 961–22
Reign of King Solomon; First Temple is built

c. 878–42
Omri dynasty in northern kingdom of Israel

722
Destruction of northern kingdom of Israel by Assyrians

c. 639–09
Reign of King Josiah

587
Destruction of the First Temple by Nebuchadnezzar and the beginning of the Babylonian exile

537
Cyrus, ruler of the Persian Empire, allows the Jews to return to Israel and rebuild the Temple

c. 515
Second Temple is completed

332
Conquest of Palestine by Alexander the Great

301–223
Rule of the Ptolemies in Palestine

167
Antiochus IV Epiphanes bans the practice of Judaism in Jerusalem and other parts of Judea; the Maccabees rebel against Seleucid rule

164
Temple of Jerusalem retaken by Maccabees and rededicated to Judaism

140
Establishment of the Hasmonean dynasty

63
Roman conquest of Palestine; Judea becomes a vassal kingdom of the Roman Empire

37–4
Reign of King Herod

C.E.

66
Beginning of the Jewish revolt against Roman rule

70
Roman destruction of the Second Temple and Jerusalem and the end of the Jewish revolt

73
Fall of Masada, the mountaintop fortress overlooking the Dead Sea, to the Romans

132–35
Jewish rebellion against Roman rule led by Bar Kokhba

c. 200
Completion of Mishnah under Rabbi Judah in Tiberius

312
Christianity legalized by Emperor Constantine

395–638
Byzantine rule

c. 500s
Completion of Babylonian Talmud

622
Year of the Hijra, the "migration" of the Prophet Muhammad from Mecca to Medina, marking the first year in the Islamic calendar

c. 638
Arab conquest of Jerusalem

661
Establishment of Umayyad dynasty, with its capital in Damascus

692
Dome of the Rock in Jerusalem is completed

716
Foundation of Ramle

1099
Crusader conquest in Palestine, and establishment of the Latin Kingdom of Jerusalem

1187
Saladin's conquest of Jerusalem from the Crusaders

1260–1516
Mamluk rule in Palestine

1492
Expulsion of the Jews of Spain; many Jews migrate to the Ottoman Empire

1516
Ottoman conquest of Palestine under Sultan Selim I

1791
Emancipation of the Jews of France

1832–40

Egyptian occupation of Palestine

1878

Foundation of Petah Tikva

1881

Pogroms in Russia and the beginning of Hovevei Zion

1882–1903

First Aliyah

1894

Dreyfus trial

1896

Theodor Herzl publishes *Der Judenstat,* "The Jewish State"

1897

First Zionist Congress in Basel, Switzerland

1903

The Uganda controversy at the Sixth Zionist Congress

1904

Death of Theodor Herzl

1904–14

Second Aliyah

1909

Founding of Tel Aviv

1909

Founding of a small commune that later becomes Deganiah, the first kibbutz

1914–18

World War I

1917

The Balfour Declaration

1919-23

Third Aliyah

1920

Foundation of the Histradrut

1922

Establishment of the British Mandate in Palestine

1924–32

Fourth Aliyah

1929

Arab rioting throughout Palestine and clashes between Arabs and Jews; Arabs massacre Jews in Hebron

1932–39

Fifth Aliyah

1935

Revisionists leave the World Zionist Organization to found the New Zionist Organization

1937

The Peel Commission's plan for the partition of Palestine is issued

1939

The White Paper restricting Jewish immigration to Palestine

1936–39

Arab revolt against the Zionists and the British in Palestine

1939–45

World War II and the Holocaust

1947

United Nations Resolution for the Partition of Palestine

1948

Independence of the State of Israel is proclaimed

1949

Elections to the first Knesset

1949

Beginning of mass immigration of Jews from Europe, Asia, and Africa

1954–55

Kastner affair

1960-62

Capture, trial, and execution of Adolf Eichmann

1956

Suez War

1963

David Ben-Gurion resigns and Levi Eshkol becomes prime minister

1963–65

Excavations at Masada

1966

End of military administration for Israeli Arabs

1967

Six-Day War with Egypt, Syria, and Jordan

1969–70

War of Attrition with Egypt

1973

Yom Kippur War with Egypt and Syria

1976

Israeli Arabs protest land expropriation; leads to clashes with the army; marked each anniversary by "Land Day" demonstrations

1977

Likud government comes to power, with Menachem Begin as prime minister

1978

Egypt and Israel reach a peace agreement at Camp David

1979–91

Mass immigration of Ethiopian Jews to Israel

1982

Israel returns the Sinai to Egypt

1982

War in Lebanon, called "Operation Peace for Galilee" by Israel, and large-scale demonstrations for peace

1983

Resignation of prime minister, Menachem Begin

1984

Government of national unity is formed, with Shimon Peres and Yitzhak Shamir alternating in the positions of prime minister and foreign minister

1987

Beginning of the *intifadah:* the Palestinian uprising in Gaza and the West Bank

1989-92

Mass immigration of Jews from the Soviet Union

1991

Negotiations begin at the Madrid conference between Israel and the Arab states

1993

Oslo agreement between Israel and the Palestinians with a plan for Palestinian self-rule

1995

Assassination of Prime Minister Yitzhak Rabin

1998

Israelis and Jews in the Diaspora celebrate the 50th anniversary of independence of the State of Israel

Prime Ministers & Presidents of the State of Israel

PRIME MINISTERS OF THE STATE OF ISRAEL

1949–53	David Ben-Gurion
1953–55	Moshe Sharett
1955–63	David Ben-Gurion
1963–69	Levi Eshkol
1969–74	Golda Meir
1974–77	Yitzhak Rabin
1977–83	Menachem Begin
1983–84	Yitzhak Shamir
1984–86	Shimon Peres
1986–92	Yitzhak Shamir
1992–95	Yitzhak Rabin
1995–96	Shimon Peres
1996–98	Benjamin Netanyahu

PRESIDENTS OF THE STATE OF ISRAEL

1949–52	Chaim Weizmann
1952–63	Izhak Ben-Zvi
1963–74	Zalman Shazar
1974–78	Ephraim Katzir
1978–83	Yitzhak Navon
1983–94	Chaim Herzog
1994–98	Ezer Weizman

Glossary

Agudat Israel—Federation of Israel. An ultra-Orthodox, non-Zionist political party, founded in Poland in 1912.

Ahdut Ha'Avodah—United Labor party. Socialist Zionist political party founded in Palestine in 1919—merged with Hapoel Hatzair to form Mapai in 1930.

aliyah—Literally "ascent." Immigration of Jews to Palestine and Israel—immigrants are called *olim*.

Arab Higher Committee—Palestinian Arab nationalist leadership established the committee in 1936. It led the movement against Zionism and the British.

Ashkenazi (pl. Ashkenazim)—The branch of Jews originating in German lands, which also came to include the Jews of Eastern or Central European descent.

'ayan—Urban Arab notables.

Beta Israel—Literally "of the house of Israel." The term used by Ethiopian Jews to refer to themselves.

Betar—A Zionist right-wing militant youth movement, associated with the Revisionists.

BILU—A Russian Zionist group established in Russia in 1882. Some members of the group immigrated to Palestine during the First Aliyah with the goal of Jewish self-sufficiency.

Black Panthers—A protest movement of Oriental (mainly Moroccan) Jews founded in 1971 and named after the militant African-American group.

brit—God's "covenant" with the Israelites in the Bible—refers to the Jewish ritual of male circumcision on the eighth day after birth.

Caliph—Successor (from Arabic, *khalifa*) to the Prophet Muhammad as ruler of the Muslim community.

Cohen (pl. *cohenim*)—Priest in charge of religious rituals, especially in the Temple.

Crusaders—Western European Christians who, beginning at the end of the 11th century, set out to conquer and control Palestine, the Holy Land.

dayyan—A Jewish judge in a rabbinical court.

dhimmi—Literally a "protected person." Status given by Islam to Jews, Christians, and other subordinate religions that guaranteed their protection in exchange for legal disabilities.

dunam—A measurement of land area that equaled about one-quarter of an acre.

Diaspora—The "dispersion" of Jews living outside of Israel.

Eretz Yisrael—The Land of Israel.

Essenes—A sect of Jews that removed itself from Jerusalem in antiquity and practiced a strict, messianic type of religion.

Fatah—Palestine National Liberation Movement. Founded in 1959, it launched its first commando raid against Israel in 1965. Led by Yasir Arafat, who took control of the PLO in 1968.

*fellah (pl. *fellahin*)*—Arab peasant.

Green Line—The former 1967 boundaries across which Arabs travel to work in Israel.

Gush Emunim—Block of the Faithful. A movement of religious, right-wing nationalists who advocate Jewish settlement and annexation of the lands occupied by Israel in the 1967 war.

Haganah—Jewish underground defense force during the Mandate—precursor to the Israeli army.

hajj—Muslim pilgrimage to Mecca—al-Hajj is the honorific title of a Muslim who has gone on the pilgrimage.

halakhah—Jewish law and practice—the path by which Jews were to guide their lives.

halukah—Literally "distribution." Funds sent from the Diaspora to support the Jewish communities living in the holy cities in Palestine.

Hamas—Islamic Resistance Movement. Founded in 1987 at the beginning of the *intifadah*. It advocates an Islamic state in all of historic Palestine and the use of terrorism to resist Israeli occupation.

Hapoel Hatzair—The Young Worker. A non-Marxist Zionist political party founded in Palestine in 1905 and inspired by Aaron David Gordon, which supported Jewish labor on the land.

Haram al-Sharif—The Noble Sanctuary. The Arabic name of the Temple Mount in Jerusalem. One of the most sacred sites in Islam.

*haredi (pl. *haredim*)*—Pious, ultra-orthodox Jews.

Hashomer—The Guard. An association of Zionist workers organized to defend Jewish settlements during the Second Aliyah.

Hashomer Hatzair—A socialist Zionist youth movement founded in Galicia in 1915. In 1927 it formed a kibbutz movement (Kibbutz Artsi) that established a number of kibbutzim.

Hasid (pl. hasidim)—A follower of a movement that began in Eastern Europe in the late 18th century, which emphasized mysticism and ecstatic prayer.

Haskalah—The Jewish enlightenment, associated with rationalist thinking within Judaism. The movement in Eastern Europe revived Hebrew for secular purposes.

Hehalutz—The Pioneer. Movement of settlers to Palestine after World War I. It favored agricultural labor as its highest ideal.

Hellenism—Greek culture and language, which greatly influenced the peoples of the Middle East, including the Jews.

Herut—Freedom. The principal right-wing political party that replaced the Revisionists in 1948—it merged into the Likud coalition party in 1973.

Hijra—Literally "emigration" of Muhammad and his followers from Mecca to Medina in 622, it marks the beginning of the Muslim calendar.

hillulah—A pilgrimage to the grave of a holy man on the anniversary of his death. Celebrated especially by Moroccan Jews.

Histadrut—General Federation of Labor in Israel, the central labor union to which many of the workers in Palestine and Israel belonged.

Hovevei Zion—"Lovers of Zion," the first Zionist movement that began in the Russian Empire in 1881. Members of this movement were the first Zionist settlers to come to Palestine during the First Aliyah.

intifadah—The popular Arab uprising against Israeli rule that began in December 1987 in the West Bank and Gaza.

Irgun—Militant nationalist group in pre-state Palestine that advocated the use of force and terrorism to achieve independence. The group split into two branches, Etzel and the more extremist Lehi (also known as the Stern Gang).

Israel Be-'aliyah—Literally "Israel on the way up," or "Israel of Immigration." A political party made up of immigrants from the former Soviet Union, founded by Natan Sharansky in 1996.

Israel Defense Forces (IDF)—The army of the State of Israel (*Tsahal*).

Istiqlal—Independence. A political party of Arabs in Palestine that advocated an independent Arab state in all of Palestine.

Jewish Agency—The organization created during the Mandate period for facilitating the Jewish national home in Palestine. It continues to operate as the main agency for immigration and absorption in Israel.

Jewish Colonization Association (JCA)—A European organization that supported Jewish agricultural communities in Argentina and Palestine.

Jewish National Fund (JNF)—Created by the World Zionist Organization for the purpose of buying and developing land in Palestine. It continues to be active in development projects in Israel.

jihad—Literally "struggle," required by Muslims to improve themselves; the word is also used to describe a holy war against the enemies of Islam.

jizya—Annual poll tax required of adult non-Muslim (*dhimmi*) males in an Islamic state.

Ka'aba—The large black stone in Mecca toward which Muslims pray; it is the holiest spot and center of pilgrimage in Islam.

Kaballah—Jewish mysticism.

Kach—An extremist, right-wing political party that was led by the American rabbi, Meir Kahane.

Karaites—A major branch of Judaism in the Middle Ages. It rejected rabbinical Judaism based on the Talmud, believing only in the authority of the Bible. Few Karaites remain in the modern period.

kashrut—Jewish dietary laws; "keeping kosher."

Keren Hayesod—Foundation Fund. A financial body of the World Zionist Organization, responsible for projects in Israel.

kibbutz **(pl. *kibbutzim*)**—A settlement in Israel where all that is produced in the fields or factories is owned collectively by all members.

Knesset—Assembly. The 120-member parliament of the State of Israel.

kvutzah—A small commune and forerunner to the *kibbutz*.

Labor Alignment—A coalition of labor political parties that came together in 1965.

Law of Return—Passed in 1950, this law declared that every Jew was entitled to Israeli nationality upon arrival in Israel.

Lehi (Stern Gang)—Extremist, terrorist faction of the Irgun.

Levites—Members of the tribe of Levi, who served as Jewish officials in charge of enforcing cultic matters.

Likud—A coalition political party of the right wing founded in 1973. It came to power with Menachem Begin as prime minister in 1977.

Maki—Israeli Communist party.

mandate—The authority given by the League of Nations after World War I to a European power to administrate a country and to prepare it for self-government.

Mapai—The Workers' Party of the Land of Israel. Founded in 1930 by a merger of Ahdut Ha'avodah and Hapoel Hatzair. The dominant Labor party and the main component in the larger Labor Alignment.

Mapam—United Workers' party. Socialist political party that opposed Mapai but has sometimes been part of the Labor coalition government.

Maronite—Follower of the dominant Christian denomination in Lebanon.

maskil **(pl. *maskilim*)**—A follower of the Haskalah, the Jewish enlightenment.

mellah—The Jewish quarter in Morocco.

millet—A Turkish administrative category for minority religious groups in the Ottoman Empire, which accorded them self-governing institutions.

Mizrahi—Orthodox Zionist political party founded in 1902. It merged with Hapoel Hamizrahi to form the National Religious party in 1956.

Mizrahi **(pl. *mizrahim*)**—"Oriental" Jew. Refers to immigrants from Asian and African countries and their descendants.

moshav **(pl. *moshavim*)**—A cooperative settlement of small landholders.

moshavah **(pl. *moshavot*)**—Jewish agricultural village consisting mostly of private landowners.

Mossad—Israel's intelligence services. It was also the name of the government organization responsible for the secret emigration of Jews from foreign countries

mufti—A Muslim legal authority who issues opinions (a *fatwa*) based on Islamic law; became the chief authority for Muslim affairs during the Mandate in Palestine.

mujahid (pl. *Mujahiddin*)—Islamic fighter.

musha'—A system of communal land ownership of Arab villages.

Muslim—Literally "one who submits." A follower of Islam (also sometimes spelled Moslem).

National Religious Party—Orthodox Zionist political party formed from a merger of the Mizrahi and Hapoel Hamizrahi parties in 1956. Known as Mafdal in Hebrew.

Pale of Settlement—The region in the Russian Empire where Jews were allowed to live.

Palestine Liberation Organization (PLO)—Established in 1964, it became the umbrella organization for the Palestinian national movement.

Palmah—Special, elite squadron of the Haganah founded in 1941.

Phalangists—A right-wing, paramilitary organization, consisting mostly of Maronite Christians.

Pharisees *(perushim)*—Literally "separate ones." A group during the Second Temple period known for its piety. The Pharisees' authority was based on their interpretation of the oral Torah.

Poalei Zion—Workers of Zion. Socialist Zionist political party founded in the Russian Empire in 1897 and established in Palestine in 1905. It broadened its base and merged into the Ahdut Ha'avodah in 1919.

pogrom—A wave of anti-Jewish violence in the Russian Empire.

Porte—The Ottoman government. Short for "Sublime Porte."

Quran—The holy book of Islam, written in Arabic and believed to contain God's revelations to the Prophet Muhammad. Forms part of the basis of Islamic law. (Also written *Koran*.)

Rakah—New Israel Communist party. It split from the communist party, Maki, in 1965. Its members are mainly Israeli Arabs.

Reform Judaism—A movement that began in 19th-century Germany, it became the main denomination of Jews in the United States. Reform Jews reject *halakhah* as the basis of Judaism and advocate adapting religion to modern society.

Revisionist—Follower of a right-wing, militant movement led by Vladimir Jabotinsky that broke away from the World Zionist Organization to form the New Zionist Organization in 1935.

refusenik—A Jew who was refused permission to emigrate from the former Soviet Union by the government authorities.

Sadducees—From "Zadokite," the hereditary line of priests starting with Zadok. Portrayed as the priestly upper class associated with the Second Temple.

sanjaq—An administrative district in the Ottoman Empire.

Sanhedrin—The high court and main assembly in Jerusalem during the Second Temple period, in charge of religious and legal matters. It was later reconstituted in the Galilee after the destruction of the Temple.

Sephardi (pl. Sephardim)—Descendants of the Jewish communities of Spain and Portugal; the term is also applied more widely to Jews from the Middle East and North Africa.

shari'a—Islamic law.

sharif—A title for an individual believed to be directly descended from the Prophet Muhammad.

Shas—Sephardi Torah Guardians; an ultra-orthodox political party, supported mainly by North African and Middle Eastern Jews.

Shin Bet—Israel's internal intelligence services.

shtetl—A small town of Jews in Eastern Europe.

Sunni—A Muslim who follows the practice of the Prophet Muhammad; accepts the succession of the caliphs after Muhammad, as opposed to Shi'ites.

Supreme Muslim Council—Created in the British Mandate to control the religious affairs of Muslims of Palestine.

Talmud—A multi-volume rabbinical work containing the "Oral Law," the Mishnah, and commentaries on the Mishnah, the Gemara. Together with the Torah, it is the source of belief and practice in traditional Judaism.

Tehiya—An extreme right-wing political party formed to protest the peace accords with Egypt.

Torah—Jewish religious law believed to have been revealed by God to Moses on Mount Sinai. Also the name of the Five Books of Moses, the first five books of the Bible. It is written on a scroll and read in synagogue.

tsaddik (pl. tsaddikim)—A righteous man. Used by North African and Middle Eastern Jews referring to venerated rabbis, both dead and alive; also refers to the leaders of the Hasidic movement.

United Nations Relief and Works Agency (UNRWA)—Created by the UN in 1950 to provide assistance to Palestinians in refugee camps.

Vichy—The name of a town in a part of unoccupied France during World War II where a French government was formed. The term is used to refer to that French government, which collaborated with the Germans.

Vilayet—Turkish administrative term for a province in the Ottoman Empire.

waqf—Property endowed for pious purposes to Islam; it is permanently protected by Islamic law.

White Paper—A policy paper issued by the British Mandate authorities.

World Zionist Organization (WZO)—The umbrella organization of the Zionist movement, founded by Theodor Herzl in Basel in 1897. Also called the "Zionist Organization."

yeshivah (pl. yeshivot)—A Jewish academy of higher religious study.

YHWH—God's name, never pronounced in the Jewish tradition (corresponds to the Hebrew letters—yod-hé-waw-hé)

Yiddish—A Jewish language spoken by Central and Eastern European Jews.

Yishuv—The Jewish community of Palestine before the establishment of the State of Israel.

Zion Mule Corps—A Jewish unit of munitions' transporters from Palestine under the British army. After the Balfour Declaration a Jewish Legion was formed, recruited first from members of the Zion Mule Corps.

Further Reading

Periodicals

Biblical Archeology Review
Israel Studies
Jerusalem Report
Journal of Palestine Studies
Jerusalem Post
The Journal of Israeli History

General History of the Jews

Baron, Salo Wittmayer. *A Social and Religious History of the Jews.* 18 vols. 2nd ed. New York: Columbia University Press, 1993.

Ben-Sasson, H. H., ed. *A History of the Jewish People.* Cambridge, Mass.: Harvard University Press, 1976.

Eban, Abba Solomon. *Heritage: Civilization and the Jews.* New York: Summit Books, 1989.

Encyclopedia Judaica. 16 volumes. Jerusalem: Keter, 1972.

Johnson, Paul. *A History of the Jews.* New York: Harper Perennial, 1987.

Mendes-Flohr, Paul R., and Jehuda Reinharz, eds. *The Jew in the Modern World: A Documentary History.* 2nd ed. New York: Oxford University Press, 1995.

Pasachoff, Naomi. *Links in the Chain: Shapers of the Jewish Tradition.* New York: Oxford University Press, 1997.

Pasachoff, Naomi, and Robert J. Littman. *Jewish History in 100 Nutshells.* Northvale, N.J.: Jason Aronson, 1995.

Sachar, Howard M. *The Course of Modern Jewish History.* New York: Vintage Books, 1990.

Seltzer, Robert M. *Jewish People, Jewish Thought.* New York: Macmillan, 1980.

Ancient Israel

Alon, Gedalia. *The Jews in Their Land in the Talmudic Age.* Cambridge, Mass.: Harvard University Press, 1989.

Avi-Yonah, Michael. *The Jews of Palestine: A Political History from the Bar Kochba War to the Arab Conquest.* Oxford: Blackwell, 1976.

Bickerman, E.J. *From Ezra to the Last of the Maccabees: Foundations of Postbiblical Judaism.* New York: Schocken Books, 1962.

Bright, John. *A History of Israel.* 3rd ed. Philadelphia: Westminster Press, 1981.

Dever, William G. *Recent Archaeological Discoveries and Biblical Research.* Seattle: University of Washington Press, 1990.

Freedman, David Noel, ed. *The Anchor Bible Dictionary.* New York: Doubleday, 1992.

Goodman, Martin. *State and Society in Roman Galilee, A.D. 132–212.* Totowa, N.J.: Rowman and Allanheld, 1983.

Grabbe, Lester L. *Judaism from Cyrus to Hadrian.* Volume 1: *The Persian and Greek Periods.* Minneapolis: Fortress Press, 1992.

Josephus. *The Jewish War.* Rev. ed. Translated by G. A. Williamson. New York: Penguin Books, 1981.

Mazar, Amihai. *Archaeology of the Land of the Bible: 10,000–586 B.C.E.* New York: Doubleday, 1990.

Neusner, Jacob. *From Politics to Piety: The Emergence of Pharisaic Judaism.* 2nd ed. New York: Ktav, 1979.

Schäfer, Peter. *The History of the Jews in Antiquity.* Harwood Academic Publishers, 1995.

Schiffman, Lawrence H. *From Text to Tradition.* Hoboken, N.J.: Ktav, 1991.

———. *Reclaiming the Dead Sea Scrolls.* Philadelphia: Jewish Publication Society, 1994.

Schürer, Emil. *The History of the Jewish People in the Age of Jesus Christ (175 B.C. – A.D. 135).* Edinburgh: Clark, 1973.

Shanks, Hershel. ed. *Ancient Israel: A Short History from Abraham to the Roman Destruction of the Temple.* Englewood Cliffs, N.J.: Prentice-Hall and Biblical Archaeology Society, 1988.

Smallwood, Elizabeth M. *The Jews under Roman Rule from Pompey to Diocletian.* Leiden: E. J. Brill, 1981.

Smith, Morton. *Palestinian Parties and Politics that Shaped the Old Testament.* New York: Columbia University Press, 1971.

Yadin, Yigael. *Masada: Herod's Fortress and the Zealots' Last Stand.* London: Weidenfeld & Nicholson, 1966.

General History of the Arabs

Antonious, George. *The Arab Awakening.* New York: Capricorn, 1965.

Cleveland, William L. *A History of the Modern Middle East.* Boulder, Colo.: Westview Press, 1994.

Goldschmidt, Arthur. *A Concise History of the Middle East.* 5th ed. Boulder, Colo.: Westview Press, 1996.

Haim, Sylvia G., ed. *Arab Nationalism: An Anthology.* Berkeley: University of California Press, 1964.

Hitti, Philip Khuri. *History of the Arabs from the Earliest Times to the Present.* 10th ed. London: Macmillan, 1970.

Hourani, Albert. *A History of the Arab Peoples.* New York: Warner Books, 1992.

Lewis, Bernard. *The Arabs in History.* New York: Harper, 1966.

Stillman, Norman A. *The Jews of Arab Lands.* Philadelphia: Jewish Publication Society, 1979.

Muslim Palestine

Barnai, Jacob. *The Jews in Palestine in the Eighteenth Century.* Tuscaloosa: University of Alabama Press, 1992.

Batuta, Ibn. *The Travels of Ibn Batuta, A.D. 1325–1354.* London: Hakluyt Society, 1994.

Cohen, Amnon. *Palestine in the Eighteenth Century.* Jerusalem: Magnes Press, 1984.

Edbury, Peter W. *The Conquest of Jerusalem and the Third Crusade.* Brookfield, Vt.: Scolar Press, 1996.

Gil, Moshe. *A History of Palestine, 634–1009.* Cambridge: Cambridge University Press, 1992.

Grabar, Oleg, et al. *The Shape of the Holy: Early Islamic Jerusalem.* Princeton: Princeton University Press, 1996.

Le Strange, Guy. *Palestine under the Moslems.* London: A. P. Watt, 1890.

Parkes, James. *A History of Palestine from 135 A.D. to Modern Times.* New York: Oxford University Press, 1949.

Peters, Francis E. *The Distant Shrine: The Islamic Centuries in Jerusalem.* New York: AMS Press, 1993.

Prawer, Joshua. *The Latin Kingdom of Jerusalem: European Colonialism in the Middle Ages.* London: Weidenfeld and Nicolson, 1972.

General Studies of Zionism, Palestine, and Modern Israel

Arbel, Rachel, ed. *Blue and White in Color: Visual Images of Zionism, 1897–1947.* Tel-Aviv: Beth Hatefutsoth, 1996.

Avineri, Shlomo. *The Making of Modern Zionism: The Intellectual Origins of the Jewish State.* New York: Basic Books, 1981.

Bickerton, Ian J., and Carla L. Klausner. *A Concise History of the Arab-Israeli Conflict.* 3rd ed. Upper Saddle River, N.J.: Prentice-Hall, 1998.

Cohen, Mitchell. *Zion and State: Nation, Class and the Shaping of Modern Israel.* New York: Columbia University Press, 1992.

Eban, Abba Solomon. *Personal Witness: Israel through My Eyes.* New York: G. P. Putnam's Sons, 1992.

Elon, Amos. *The Israelis: Founders and Sons.* New York: Penguin Books, 1983.

Farsoun, Samih K. with Christina E. Zacharia. *Palestine and the Palestinians.* Boulder, Colo.: Westview Press, 1997.

Gerner, Deborah J. *One Land, Two Peoples: The Conflict over Palestine.* 2nd ed. Boulder, Colo.: Westview Press, 1994.

Goldscheider, Calvin. *Israel's Changing Society: Population, Ethnicity, and Development.* Boulder, Colo.: Westview Press, 1996.

Hertzberg, Arthur. *The Zionist Idea.* Philadelphia: Jewish Publication Society, 1997.

Herzl, Theodor. *The Jewish State.* New York: Reprint, Dover, 1988.

Kayyali, Abdul Wahhab. *Palestine: A Modern History.* London: Croom Helm, 1978.

Khalidi, Walid. *Palestine Reborn.* New York: I. B. Tauris & Co., 1992.

Kimmerling, Baruch, and Joel S. Migdal. *Palestinians: The Making of a People.* Cambridge, Mass.: Harvard University Press, 1994.

Laqueur, Walter, and Barry Rubin, eds. *The Israel-Arab Reader: A Documentary History of the Middle East Conflict.* 5th ed. New York: Penguin Books, 1995.

Laqueur, Walter. *A History of Zionism.* New York: Schocken Books, 1976.

Lucas, Noah. *The Modern History of Israel.* London: Weidenfeld and Nicolson, 1974.

Ravitzky, Aviezer. *Messianism, Zionism, and Jewish Religious Radicalism.* Chicago: University of Chicago Press, 1996.

Reich, Bernard, and Gershon Kieval. *Israel: Land of Tradition and Conflict.* 2nd ed. Boulder, Colo.: Westview Press, 1993.

Sachar, Howard M. *A History of Israel from the Rise of Zionism to Our Time.* 2nd ed. New York: Alfred A. Knopf, 1996.

Said, Edward. *The Question of Palestine.* New York: Vintage Books, 1992.

Shapira, Anita. *Land and Power: The Zionist Resort to Force, 1881–1948.* New York: Oxford University Press, 1992.

Smith, Charles D. *Palestine and the Arab-Israeli Conflict.* 3rd ed. New York: St. Martin's Press, 1996.

Tessler, Mark. *A History of the Israeli-Palestinian Conflict.* Bloomington: Indiana University Press, 1994.

Vital, David. *The Origins of Zionism.* Oxford: Oxford University Press, 1975.

———. *Zionism: The Formative Years.* Oxford: Oxford University Press, 1982.

———. *Zionism: The Crucial Years.* Oxford: Oxford University Press, 1987.

Wigoder, Geoffrey, ed. *The New Encyclopedia of Zionism and Israel.* Madison, N.J.: Fairleigh Dickinson University Press; Cranbury, N.J.: Associated University Presses, 1994.

Wolffsohn, Michael. *Israel: Polity, Society and Economy, 1882–1986.* Atlantic Highlands, N.J.: Humanities Press International, 1987.

Zerubavel, Yael. *Recovered Roots: Collective Memory and the Making of Israeli National Tradition.* Chicago: University of Chicago Press, 1995.

Biography, Autobiography, Diaries, and Memoirs

Aburish, Said K. *Children of Bethany: The Story of a Palestinian Family.* Bloomington: Indiana University Press, 1988.

Bar-Zohar, Michael. *Ben Gurion: A Biography.* New York: Weidenfeld and Nicolson, 1978.

Begin, Menachem. *The Revolt: Story of the Irgun.* Los Angeles: Nash, 1972.

Dayan, Moshe. *Moshe Dayan: Story of My Life.* New York: Da Capo Press, 1992.

Eban, Abba. *An Autobiography.* New York: Random House, 1977.

Furlonge, Geoffrey. *Palestine Is My Country: The Story of Musa Alami.* New York: Praeger, 1969.

Gervasi, Frank. *The Life and Times of Menahem Begin.* New York: G. P. Putnam's Sons, 1979.

Gilbert, Martin. *Shcharansky: Hero of Our Time.* London: Macmillan, 1986.

Hart, Alan. *Arafat: A Political Biography.* London: Sidgwick & Jackson, 1994.

Herzl, Theodor. *The Diaries of Theodor Herzl.* Edited and translated by Marvin Lowenthal. New York: Dial Press, 1956.

Jabotinsky, Vladimir. *The Story of the Jewish Legion.* New York: B. Ackerman, 1945.

Katznelson-Shazar, Rachel. *The Plough Women.* New York: Herzl Press, 1975.

Lyons, M.C. and D.E.P. Jackson. *Saladin: The Politics of Holy War.* Cambridge: Cambridge University Press, 1982.

Mattar, Philip. *The Mufti of Jerusalem: Al-Hajj Amin al-Husayni and the Palestinian National Movement.* New York: Columbia University Press, 1988.

Meir, Golda. *My Life.* New York: Dell, 1975.

Pawel, Ernest. *The Labyrinth of Exile: A Life of Theodor Herzl.* New York: Farrar, Straus and Giroux, 1989.

Peres, Shimon. *Battling for Peace: Memoirs.* Ed. David Landau. London: Weidenfeld & Nicolson, 1995.

Rabin, Yitzhak. *The Rabin Memoirs.* Berkeley: University of California Press, 1996.

Reinharz, Jehuda. *Chaim Weizmann: The Making of a Zionist Leader.* New York: Oxford University Press, 1985.

———. *Chaim Weizmann: The Making of a Statesman.* New York: Oxford University Press, 1993.

Ruppin, Arthur. *Memoirs, Diaries, Letters.* London: Weidenfeld and Nicolson, 1979.

Sadat, Anwar el-. *In Search of Identity: An Autobiography.* New York: Harper & Row, 1978.

Schechtman, Joseph. *Rebel and Statesman: The Life and Times of Vladimir Jabotinsky.* Silver Spring, Md.: Eshel Books, 1986.

Sharansky, Natan. *Fear No Evil.* New York: Random House, 1988.

Sheffer, Gabriel. *Moshe Sharett: Biography of a Political Moderate.* Oxford: Clarendon Press, 1996.

Silver, Eric. *Begin: The Haunted Prophet.* New York: Random House, 1984.

Teveth, Shabtai. *Ben-Gurion: The Burning Ground, 1886–1948.* Boston: Houghton Mifflin Company, 1987.

Teveth, Shabtai. *Moshe Dayan: The Soldier, the Man, the Legend.* London: Quartet Books, 1974.

Weizmann, Chaim. *Trial and Error.* New York: Schocken Books, 1966.

Yilma, Shmuel. *From Falasha to Freedom: An Ethiopian Jew's Journey to Jerusalem.* Jerusalem: Gefen Publishing House, 1996.

Zipperstein, Steven J. *Elusive Prophet: Ahad Ha'am and the Origins of Zionism.* Berkeley: University of California Press, 1993.

Late Ottoman Palestine

Ben-Arieh, Yehoshua. *Jerusalem in the 19th Century: Emergence of the New City.* Jerusalem: Yad Izhak Ben Zvi, 1986.

Bernstein, Deborah S., ed. *Pioneers and Homemakers: Jewish Women in Pre-State Israel.* Albany: State University of New York Press, 1992.

Blumberg, Arnold. *Zion before Zionism, 1838–1880.* Syracuse, N.Y.: Syracuse University Press, 1986.

Divine, Donna Robinson. *Politics and Society in Ottoman Palestine.* Boulder, Colo.: Lynne Rienner, 1994.

Doumani, Beshara. *Rediscovering Palestine: Merchants and Peasants in Jabal Nablus, 1700–1900.* Berkeley: University of California Press, 1995.

Halper, Jeffrey. *Between Redemption and Revival: The Jewish Yishuv of Jerusalem in the Nineteenth Century.* Boulder, Colo.: Westview Press, 1991.

Kark, Ruth. *Jaffa: A City in Evolution, 1799–1917.* Jerusalem: Yad Izhak Ben-Zvi Press, 1990.

Khalidi, Rashid. *Palestinian Identity: The Construction of Modern National Consciousness.* New York: Columbia University Press, 1997.

Ma'oz, Moshe. *Ottoman Reform in Syria and Palestine, 1850–1861.* Oxford: Clarendon Press, 1968.

Mandel, Neville J. *The Arabs and Zionism before World War I.* Berkeley: University of California Press, 1976.

Muslih, Muhammad Y. *The Origins of Palestinian Nationalism.* New York: Columbia University Press, 1988.

Penslar, Derek. *Zionism and Technocracy: The Engineering of Jewish Settlement in Palestine, 1870–1918.* Bloomington: Indiana University Press, 1991.

Schama, Simon. *Two Rothschilds and the Land of Israel.* New York: Simon and Schuster, 1978.

Schölch, Alexander. *Palestine in Transformation, 1856–1882.* Washington, D.C.: Institute for Palestine Studies, 1993.

Shafir, Gershon. *Land, Labor and the Origins of the Israeli-Palestinian Conflict, 1882–1914.* Berkeley: University of California Press, 1996.

End of World War I and the British Mandate

Bauer, Yehuda. *From Diplomacy to Resistance: A History of Jewish Palestine, 1939–1945.* New York: Atheneum, 1973.

Bernstein, Deborah. *The Struggle for Equality: Urban Women Workers in Prestate Israeli Society.* New York: Praeger, 1987.

Caplan, Neil. *Palestine Jewry and the Arab Question, 1917–1925.* London: Frank Cass, 1978.

Cohen, Michael J. *The Origins and Evolution of the Arab-Zionist Conflict.* Berkeley: University of California Press, 1987.

Horowitz, Dan, and Moshe Lissak. *Origins of the Israeli Polity in Palestine.* Chicago: University of Chicago Press, 1978.

Johnson, Nels. *Islam and the Politics of Meaning in Palestinian Nationalism.* London: Routledge, 1982.

Khalaf, Issa. *Politics in Palestine: Arab Factionalism and Social Disintegration, 1939–1948.* Albany: State University of New York Press, 1991.

Khalidi, Walid. *Before Their Diaspora: A Photographic History of the Palestinians.* Washington, D.C.: Institute for Palestine Studies, 1984.

Lesch, Ann Mosely. *Arab Politics in Palestine, 1917–1939.* Ithaca: Cornell University Press, 1979.

Lockman, Zachary. *Comrades and Enemies: Arab and Jewish Workers in Palestine, 1906–1948.* Berkeley: University of California Press, 1996.

Miller, Ylana N. *Government and Society in Rural Palestine, 1920–1948.* Austin: University of Texas Press, 1985.

Near, Henry. *The Kibbutz Movement: Origins and Growth, 1909–1939.* Auckland: Oxford University Press, 1992.

Porat, Dina. *The Blue and Yellow Stars of David: The Zionist Leadership in Palestine and the Holocaust, 1939–1945.* Cambridge, Mass.: Harvard University Press, 1990.

Porath, Yehoshua. *The Emergence of the Palestinian-Arab National Movement: 1918–1929.* London: Frank Cass, 1974.

———. *The Palestine Arab National Movement: From Riots to Rebellion.* London: Frank Cass, 1977.

Shavit, Jacob. *Jabotinsky and the Revisionist Movement, 1925–1948.* London: Frank Cass, 1988.

Shlaim, Avi. *Collusion across the Jordan: King Abdullah, the Zionist Movement, and the Partition of Palestine.* Oxford: Oxford University Press, 1988.

Stein, Kenneth. *The Land Question in Palestine, 1917–1939.* Chapel Hill: University of North Carolina Press, 1984.

Sykes, Christopher. *Crossroads to Israel, 1917–1948.* Bloomington: Indiana University Press, 1973.

Wasserstein, Bernard. *The British in Palestine: The Mandatory Government and the Arab-Jewish Conflict, 1917–1929.* 2nd ed. Oxford: Blackwell, 1991.

Israel after Independence

Arendt, Hannah. *Eichmann in Jerusalem: A Report on the Banality of Evil.* New York: Penguin, 1987.

Ben-Rafael, Eliezer. *Crisis and Transformation: The Kibbutz at Century's End.* Albany: State University of New York Press, 1997.

Ben-Rafael, Eliezer, and Stephen Sharot. *Ethnicity, Religion and Class in Israeli Society.* Cambridge: Cambridge University Press, 1991.

Ben-Zvi, Yitzhak. *The Exiled and the Redeemed.* Philadelphia: Jewish Publication Society, 1957.

Black, Ian, and Benny Morris, *Israel's Secret Wars: A History of Israel's Intelligence Services.* New York: Grove Weidenfeld, 1991.

Brecher, Michael. *Decisions in Israel's Foreign Policy.* London: Oxford University Press, 1974.

Cobban, Helena, *The Palestinian Liberation Organisation: People, Power and Politics.* Cambridge: Cambridge University Press, 1984.

Eisenstadt. S.N. *Israeli Society.* New York: Basic Books, 1967.

El-Asmar, Fouzi. *To Be an Arab in Israel.* Beirut: Institute for Palestine Studies, 1978.

Elazar, Daniel J. *Israel: Building a New Society.* Bloomington: Indiana University Press, 1986.

Ezrahi, Yaron. *Rubber Bullets: Power and Conscience in Modern Israel.* New York: Farrar, Straus and Giroux, 1997.

Friedland, Roger, and Richard Hecht. *To Rule Jerusalem.* Cambridge: Cambridge University Press, 1996.

Friedman, Thomas. *From Beirut to Jerusalem.* New York: Farrar, Straus and Giroux, 1989.

Gilbert, Martin. *The Arab-Israeli Conflict: Its History in Maps.* 2nd ed. London: Weidenfeld & Nicolson, 1976.

Gorkin, Michael. *Days of Honey, Days of Onion: The Story of a Palestinian Family in Israel.* Berkeley: University of California Press, 1991.

Hazleton, Lesley. *Israeli Women.* New York: Simon and Schuster, 1977.

Herzog, Chaim. *The Arab-Israeli Wars.* New York: Vintage Books, 1984.

Hunter, Robert F. *The Palestinian Uprising: A War by Other Means.* 2nd ed. Berkeley: University of California Press, 1993.

Jones, Clive. *Soviet Jewish Aliyah, 1989–1992.* London: Frank Cass, 1996.

Liebman, Charles S. and Eliezer Don-Yehiya. *Religion and Politics in Israel.* Bloomington: Indiana University Press, 1984.

Liebman, Charles S. and Steven M. Cohen. *Two Worlds of Judaism: The Israeli and American Experiences.* New Haven: Yale University Press, 1990.

Lockman, Zachary and Joel Beinin, eds. *Intifada: The Palestinian Uprising against Israeli Occupation.* Boston: South End Press, 1989.

Lustick, Ian. *Arabs in the Jewish State.* Austin: University of Texas Press, 1980.

Morris, Benny. *The Birth of the Palestinian Refugee Problem, 1947–1949.* Cambridge: Cambridge University Press, 1987.

Oz, Amos. *In the Land of Israel.* New York: Vintage Books, 1984.

Peleg, Ilan. *Begin's Foreign Policy, 1977–1983: Israel's Move to the Right.* Westport, Conn.: Greenwood Press, 1987.

Peretz, Don. *Intifada: The Palestinian Uprising.* Boulder, Colo.: Westview Press, 1990.

Quandt, William B. *Decade of Decisions: American Policy toward the Arab-Israeli Conflict.* Berkeley: University of California Press, 1977.

Schechtman, Joseph B. *On Wings of Eagles: The Plight, Exodus and Homecoming of Oriental Jewry.* New York: T. Youseloff, 1961.

Schroeter, Leonard. *The Last Exodus.* Seattle: University of Washington Press, 1979.

Segev, Tom. *1949: The First Israelis.* New York: The Free Press, 1986.

———. *The Seventh Million: The Israelis and the Holocaust.* New York: Hill and Wang, 1994.

Shapira, Avraham, ed. *The Seventh Day: Soldiers' Talk about the Six-Day War.* New York: Charles Scribner's Sons, 1970.

Shipler, David. *Arab and Jew: Wounded Spirits in a Promised Land.* New York: Times Books, 1986.

Shokeid, Moshe and Shlomo Deshen. *Distant Relations: Ethnicity and Politics among Arabs and North African Jews in Israel.* New York: Praeger, 1982.

Smooha, Sammy. *Israel: Pluralism and Conflict.* Berkeley: University of California Press, 1978.

Spiegel, Steven L. *The Other Arab-Israeli Conflict: Making America's Middle East Policy from Truman to Reagan.* Chicago: University of Chicago Press, 1985.

Spiro, Melford E. *Kibbutz: Venture in Utopia.* New York: Schocken Books, 1963.

Sprinzak, Ehud. *The Ascendance of Israel's Radical Right.* New York: Oxford University Press, 1991.

Turki, Fawaz. *The Disinherited: Journal of a Palestinian Exile.* New York: Monthly Review Press, 1972.

Index

References to illustrations are indicated by page numbers in *italics*.

Picture Credits